I0729723

DOMENICO GHIRLANDAIO

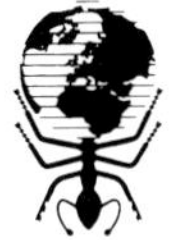

Books in the RENAISSANCE LIVES series explore and illustrate the life histories and achievements of significant artists, rulers, intellectuals and scientists in the early modern world. They delve into literature, philosophy, the history of art, science and natural history and cover narratives of exploration, statecraft and technology.

Series Editor: François Quiviger

Already published

Albrecht Dürer: Art and Autobiography *David Ekserdjian*
Aldus Manutius: The Invention of the Publisher *Oren Margolis*
Andreas Vesalius: Anatomy and the World of Books *Sashiko Kusukawa*
Artemisia Gentileschi and Feminism in Early Modern Europe *Mary D. Garrard*
Benvenuto Cellini and the Embodiment of the Modern Artist *Andreas Beyer*
Bernard Palissy and the Arts of the Earth *François Quivigier*
Blaise Pascal: Miracles and Reason *Mary Ann Caws*
Botticelli: Artist and Designer *Ana Debenedetti*
Caravaggio and the Creation of Modernity *Troy Thomas*
Descartes: The Renewal of Philosophy *Steven Nadler*
Domenico Ghirlandaio: An Elite Artisan and His World *Jean K. Cadogan*
Donatello and the Dawn of Renaissance Art *A. Victor Coonin*
Erasmus of Rotterdam: The Spirit of a Scholar *William Barker*
Filippino Lippi: An Abundance of Invention *Jonathan K. Nelson*
Francis I: The Knight-King *Glenn Richardson*
Giorgione's Ambiguity *Tom Nichols*
Hans Holbein: The Artist in a Changing World *Jeanne Nuechterlein*
Hans Memling and the Merchants *Mitzi Kirkland-Ives*
Hieronymus Bosch: Visions and Nightmares *Nils Büttner*
Isaac Newton and Natural Philosophy *Niccolò Guicciardini*
Jan van Eyck within His Art *Alfred Acres*
John Donne: In the Shadow of Religion *Andrew Hadfield*
John Evelyn: A Life of Domesticity *John Dixon Hunt*
Leon Battista Alberti: The Chameleon's Eye *Caspar Pearson*
Leonardo da Vinci: Self, Art and Nature *François Quiviger*
Lucas Cranach: From German Myth to Reformation *Jennifer Nelson*
Machiavelli: From Radical to Reactionary *Robert Black*
Michelangelo and the Viewer in His Time *Bernadine Barnes*
Paracelsus: An Alchemical Life *Bruce T. Moran*
Petrarch: Everywhere a Wanderer *Christopher S. Celenza*
Piero della Francesca and the Invention of the Artist *Machtelt Brüggen Israëls*
Piero di Cosimo: Eccentricity and Delight *Sarah Blake McHam*
Pieter Bruegel and the Idea of Human Nature *Elizabeth Alice Honig*
Raphael and the Antique *Claudia La Malfa*
Rembrandt's Holland *Larry Silver*
Robert Hooke's Experimental Philosophy *Felicity Henderson*
Rubens's Spirit: From Ingenuity to Genius *Alexander Marr*
Rudolf II: The Life and Legend of the Mad Emperor *Thomas DaCosta Kaufmann*
Salvator Rosa: Paint and Performance *Helen Langdon*
Thomas Nashe and Late Elizabethan Writing *Andrew Hadfield*
Titian's Touch: Art, Magic and Philosophy *Maria H. Loh*
Tycho Brahe and the Measure of the Heavens *John Robert Christianson*
Ulisse Aldrovandi: Naturalist and Collector *Peter Mason*

DOMENICO GHIRLANDAIO

An Elite Artisan and His World

JEAN K. CADOGAN

REAKTION BOOKS

For my sisters, Paula Cadogan and Carol Cadogan

Published by Reaktion Books Ltd
2–4 Sebastian Street
London EC1V 0HE, UK
www.reaktionbooks.co.uk

First published 2025
Copyright © Jean K. Cadogan 2025

EU GPSR Authorised Representative
Logos Europe, 9 rue Nicolas Poussin, 17000, La Rochelle, France
email: contact@logoseurope.eu

Printed and bound in India by Replika Press Pvt. Ltd

A catalogue record for this book is available from the British Library

ISBN 978 1 83639 120 3

COVER: Detail of the artist from Domenico Ghirlandaio,
Adoration of the Magi, 1486–9 (illus. 56). Museo degli Innocenti,
Florence, photo © Raffaello Bencini/Bridgeman Images.

CONTENTS

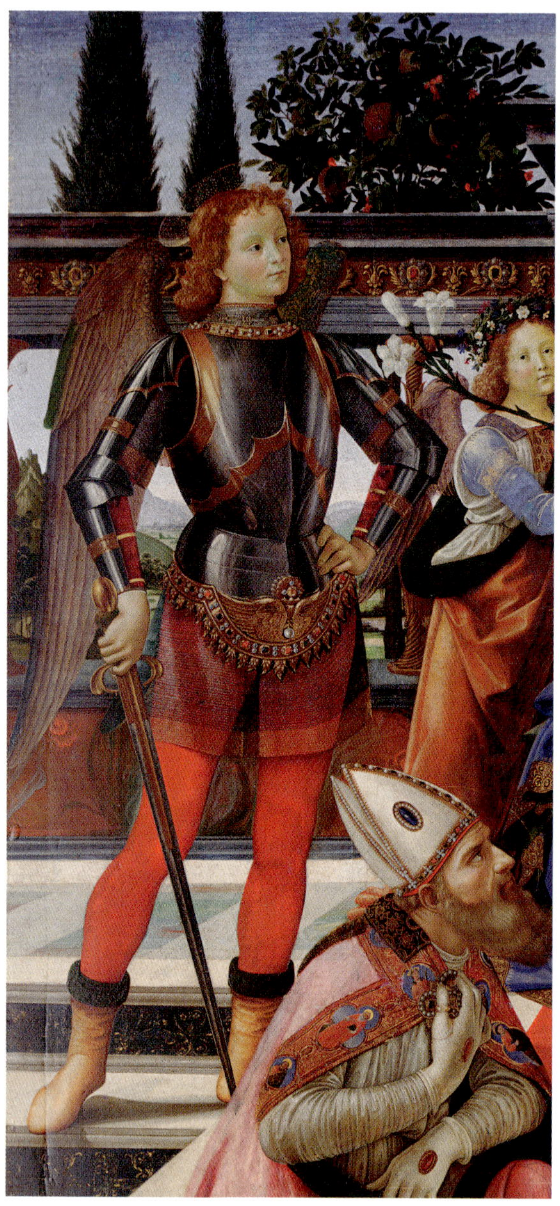

Introduction

From the earliest guidebook in the sixteenth century – Francesco Albertini's *Memorial of Many Statues and Paintings in the Illustrious City of Florence* (1510) – up to now, authors have penned countless books about the fluorescence of visual culture in Renaissance Florence.[1] Most highlight the breathtaking objects and monuments that transformed the city from the thirteenth to the sixteenth century. Many more have been devoted to the astonishingly creative personalities who were the agents of this transformation, from patrons such as Cosimo and Lorenzo de' Medici to artists such as Giotto, Donatello, Leonardo da Vinci and Michelangelo. Domenico Ghirlandaio (1448–1494), a contemporary of Leonardo, acquaintance of Lorenzo de' Medici and master of Michelangelo, is a worthy subject in this series of Renaissance Lives because he exemplifies the elite artisan traditions on which the achievements of the period are based. Unlike the eccentric Leonardo or the irascible Michelangelo, Ghirlandaio left no literary legacy, so we cannot know with precision what he thought about his art or the pressing intellectual, social or political issues of the day. Yet we know a great deal about his life through the many documents that survive in the Florentine archives and elsewhere. Similarly, his surviving murals, panel paintings, drawings, mosaics and stained glass offer a broad view of his skill, artisanship and creativity.

1 Detail of St Michael from Domenico Ghirlandaio, *Virgin and Child …*, *c.* 1480–81 (illus. 28).

From the fifteenth to the nineteenth century, Domenico Ghirlandaio was celebrated by contemporaries, biographers and historians as a 'man to be reckoned with', 'expeditious' and 'rich, yet clear, gay and often great'.[2] The artist and biographer Giorgio Vasari (1511–1574), writing in 1568, begins his account of Ghirlandaio with praise: 'Domenico di Tommaso del Ghirlandaio . . . from his talent and from the greatness and the vast number of his works, may be called one of the most important and most excellent masters of his age.'[3] His reputation as an artist and compatriot, as will be seen, was carefully honed in his lifetime and endured for centuries. Yet the critic Bernard Berenson, writing in 1896, would proclaim: 'Both [Ghirlandaio and Benozzo Gozzoli] were, as artists, little more than mediocrities with almost no genuine feeling for what makes painting a great art. The real attractiveness of both lies outside the sphere of pure art, in the realm of genre illustration.'[4] This precipitous fall in Ghirlandaio's fame led to a sharp decline in scholarly research. No book about the artist and his work appeared between 1943 and 1998, and none in English from 1908 until 2000.[5] In that year, the German scholar Roland Kecks and I each published comprehensive accounts of the artist's biography and artistic output, although with different emphases.[6] As the title of my book – *Domenico Ghirlandaio: Artist and Artisan* – implies, I sought to place Ghirlandaio's works in the context of the craft traditions, guild structure and workshop organization that shaped their form, while clarifying their technical and stylistic characteristics. I analysed Ghirlandaio's drawing practice to reveal his methodical approach to representation and visual storytelling. A *catalogue raisonné* – a systematic treatment of each work, listing its materials, ownership history, bibliography and exhibition history, and discussing each commission's patron, date, imagery and style – was included, as well as an appendix of known documents.

This book is different in its method and its scope, in that I wish to describe more fully the social conditions that shaped Ghirlandaio's career and works. To that end, in Chapter One I have described Ghirlandaio's family history, aided by historians' studies of artisan families and the 2017 publication of a family memoir compiled in the late sixteenth century from now-lost family records.[7] Ghirlandaio's family can be traced in Florence at least as far back as 1354; tax documents into the sixteenth century trace its fluctuating material wealth. By the 1480s, most likely through Ghirlandaio's professional activity, the family achieved a level of wealth and comfort far beyond what they had enjoyed in previous decades. His purchases of land outside Florence and his wife's dowry of a thousand florins – a large sum for a non-aristocratic bride – are indications of improved economic status. At the same time, Ghirlandaio broke from the multigenerational family home to set up his own household, and he secured legal independence from his father, allowing him to manage his own finances and control his wife's dowry.

The family, or *casa* (hearth), comprised not just living members but a spiritual *casa* of ancestors whose memory was preserved through memoirs (*ricordanze*) and family tombs. Ghirlandaio purchased a new family tomb in the Dominican church of Santa Maria Novella at the same time as he established professional independence. The social identity of the family was further defined by the adoption of a family name, Bigordi, widely used by Domenico's father from the mid-1440s and, in the late 1480s, prominently displayed in one of the Santa Maria Novella murals. Family members held offices in guilds and confraternities, further enhancing their social profile. Indeed, Ghirlandaio's own social ambitions, revealed through his marriages, land acquisitions and artistic career, indicate a more fluid social structure in Renaissance Florence than we have previously considered, and it sets the stage for the elevated social status that some artists – including

Ghirlandaio's son Ridolfo but most notably his pupil Michelangelo – achieved in the next century.

In Chapter Two I consider the extra-familial networks that Ghirlandaio constructed through memberships in craft organizations, confraternities and co-parentage groups. As social historians have shown, such webs of relationships are key to understanding events of the past. The recently discovered family memoirs confirm what Vasari had asserted in his life of Ghirlandaio: that he trained as a goldsmith in the 1460s and that his father and uncle had been active in related arts. Ghirlandaio and other family members were products of the guild system that dominated craft activity in the late Middle Ages. Florence's guild system was, however, less rigid than elsewhere, and it encouraged career changes, experimentation and innovation, which were rewarded in the teeming commercial marketplace. Around 1470 Ghirlandaio shifted his professional focus to painting; by 1472 he had matriculated in the guild of doctors and apothecaries (Medici e Speziali) to which painters belonged. Yet the person who taught him to paint is still unknown.

Ghirlandaio's networks extended beyond guild membership to include his participation in several religious sodalities. He was, from 1472, just at the beginning of his career as a painter, inscribed in the Confraternity of St Luke, associated with the Medici e Speziali guild. He also belonged to the flagellant Confraternity of St Paul, to which his father, brothers and son also belonged between the 1440s and the sixteenth century. This sodality expanded Ghirlandaio's links to a wide range of professional and social contacts that included other craftsmen, doctors and notaries and even Lorenzo de' Medici, the de facto ruler of Florence. Ghirlandaio took an active role in both groups, and the relations he forged with potential collaborators and patrons bore fruit in his career. His association with these groups also documents his participation in the civic and religious life of the city.

The next two chapters focus on Ghirlandaio's artistic career: Chapter Three on his work up to about 1480, and Chapter Four on his most productive years – from 1480 until his death in 1494. Early in his career, Ghirlandaio was an itinerant artist, with no fixed workshop, painting altarpieces and murals in Rome, Pisa, San Gimignano and other small towns in Tuscany. Ghirlandaio's embrace of both local traditions and the demands of non-Florentine patrons signalled his adaptability and broadened his professional skills. His reputation among provincial patrons prepared the way for large-scale, highly visible commissions in Florence that would engage him for the rest of his career. Ghirlandaio's training and early work locate him at the centre of an elite group of painters, sculptors and woodworkers, including Alesso Baldovinetti, Andrea del Verrocchio and Giuliano and Benedetto da Maiano, who shaped his career and his approach to image-making. Recent studies of travelling artists, reputation building and the 'business' of art and markets have inflected our understanding of the social and economic forces that shaped Renaissance artists' careers. Adopting these approaches to Ghirlandaio's early career yields telling insights.

The monumental projects of Ghirlandaio's mature years – beginning with his participation in the Sistine Chapel decoration (1481–2) and continuing through murals in the Florentine Palazzo Vecchio (1482–3) and chapel decorations in Santa Trinita (1483–5) and Santa Maria Novella (1485–94) – are also recounted in the fourth chapter. For each commission, in keeping with current views of patronage as a collaborative relationship between principal and client, I have described to the extent allowed by the sources the role of the patron in the genesis of the work and his share in its realization. The intent visage of Francesco Sassetti and the pious mien of Giovanni Tornabuoni in their respective chapel decorations bring forcefully to mind the patrons and spectators for whom the works were created. While we have no letters

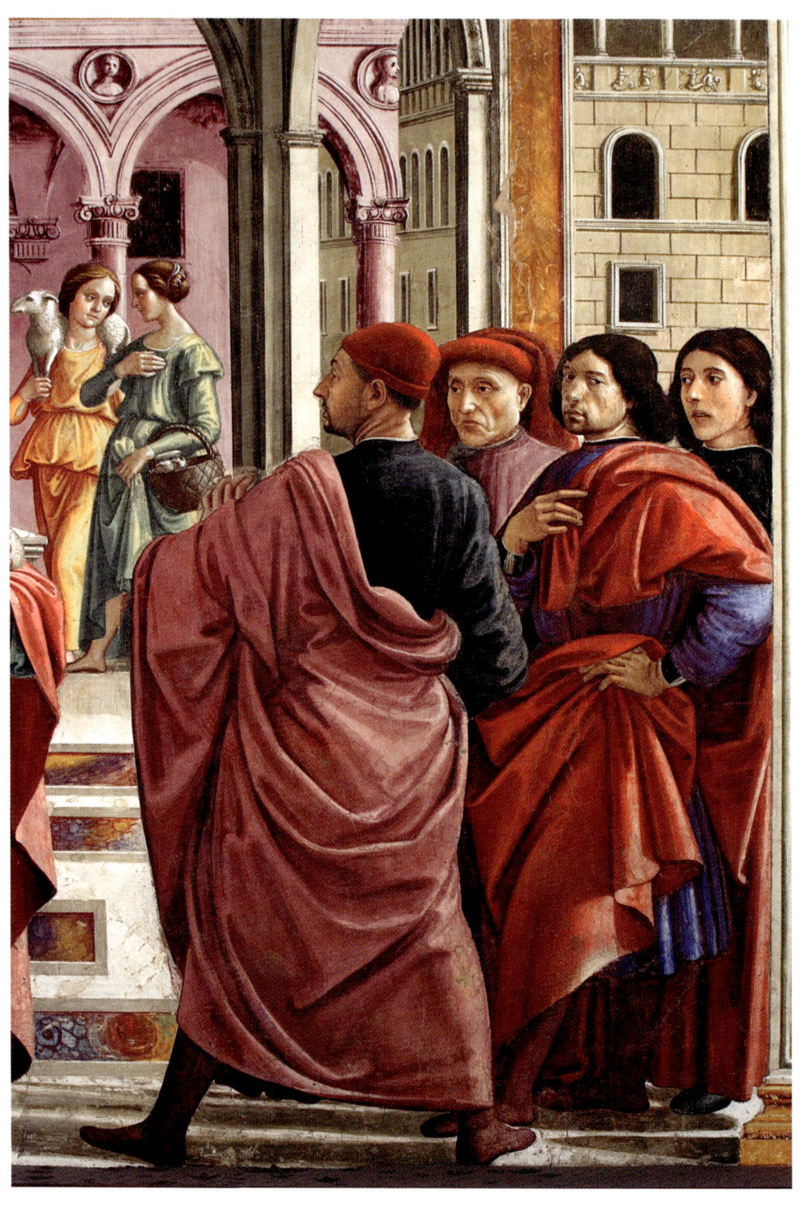

2 Domenico Ghirlandaio, *The Expulsion of Joachim from the Temple*, 1486–90, detail, fresco, Santa Maria Novella, Florence.

or memoirs that can tell us about the personal relationships that Ghirlandaio had with his patrons, we can divine something about them from other sources, which I explore in this chapter. The 1485 contract between Ghirlandaio and Giovanni Tornabuoni for the murals in Santa Maria Novella, one of the most famous contracts of the fifteenth century, is nonetheless ambiguous. We can understand it fruitfully as the product of a back and forth between Ghirlandaio and Tornabuoni, drawn up to establish the parameters of the project as much as to impress the Dominican friars who had ultimate authority over the sacred space. The full-length portraits of Ghirlandaio and his family in the finished murals in both chapels proclaim the artist's skill, honour and piety. Portraits and self-portraits in other panel paintings and murals mirror the audience for which they functioned as aids to devotion, visualizations of sacred stories, simulacra of lived experience and memorial images.

Chapter Five focuses on Ghirlandaio's design process. In keeping with contemporary practice, Ghirlandaio's works were produced collaboratively. Workshop procedures ensured consistency of style – the master's style – and the quality that patrons expected. Documents for several projects identify some of the participants in the workshop and provide clues as to the relative roles of master, pupil and assistants, while visual evidence of style and technique, gleaned from recent restorations, amplifies our understanding of workshop organization. Ghirlandaio's workshop was to some extent a family workshop – a widespread phenomenon in Italy – to which his brothers and brother-in-law belonged. Yet its structure and make-up changed over time to respond to the number and nature of the commissions it had in hand. Domenico's brother Davide, his closest collaborator in his early works, eventually established an independent career. A closer look at their partnership lends insight into the shifting and contingent relationships in the workshop.

Considering the surviving drawings, which number approximately forty, I then propose an account of Ghirlandaio's creative procedure. Starting in the mid-fifteenth century, patrons and critics, stimulated by rediscovered ancient writers on art such as Pliny, demanded varied and life-like representations of familiar subjects. Artists reimagined devotional images of the Madonna and Child as well as narratives like the Adoration of the Magi. Drawings became the primary tool of artists' invention, leading to an explosion of new materials, surfaces and styles of drawing. In their varied techniques and styles, Ghirlandaio's drawings are some of the first to show this new role of preparatory drawings in fifteenth-century workshops. They also reveal that Ghirlandaio's signature style – key to his reputation and professional success – was both a consciously created marker of his uniqueness as an artist and fundamental to his appeal to patrons.

In the conclusion I consider Ghirlandaio's stylistic idiom in the context of his historical persona and late fifteenth-century Florentine painting. Contemporary accounts and historical records confirm the esteem in which patrons and colleagues held him. He incorporated precise observations of nature with figurative and compositional inventions inspired by ancient art. His drawing procedure and his painting techniques highlight the alchemy of craft and creativity that engendered his finished works. His 'good air' as voiced by a contemporary observer captured the skill, imagination and social ease visualized by his painted creations that were appreciated by his compatriots and delight us still today. The following chapters explore Ghirlandaio's world to reveal how his creations emerged from his imagination and experience to assume tangible form.

ONE

Casa Ghirlandaio: Family, Wealth and Social Status

ravelling southwest of Florence, from the Porta Romana through the rolling hills of Tuscany, a traveller comes upon the hamlet of Colle Ramole and the large farmhouse that the painter Domenico Ghirlandaio purchased in 1491 (illus. 4). The tax return filed by his heirs in 1495, the year after his death, describes the small farm (*poderetto*) with a manor house (*casa da signore*), cultivated fields, vines and olive trees, yielding grain, wine, oil, figs, nuts and capons. A small chapel in the *casa da signore* decorated by the painter's son Ridolfo around 1518 has survived subsequent renovations. Above the baroque altar, frescoed images of St Dominic and St Benedict flank the Madonna and Child; personifications of Faith and Hope stand to the left and right, and reclining cherubs lifting circular garlands surmount the arch. Just to the left, Ridolfo's self-portrait engages the visitor, his son Domenico di Ridolfo (b. 1511) kneeling in front (illus. 3). Above, the bust-length figure of Domenico Ghirlandaio, dressed in the red cloak and cap of a prominent Florentine citizen, appears in a painted roundel.[1] Ridolfo wears a blue tunic with voluminous sleeves under a sleeveless red overgown, also signalling his membership in the elite classes.

It is not surprising to find family portraits in this chapel. The inventory of Ridolfo's estate taken after his death in 1561 lists scores of them.[2] Domenico Ghirlandaio, too, inserted his and others' often in his works. The portraits are a visual signature, but they also call attention to the artist's skill. Ghirlandaio's full-length self-portrait in the *Expulsion of Joachim* in Santa Maria Novella shows him with his left arm poised at his waist, his right resting on his breast (illus. 2). He looks out, catching the spectator's gaze. His striking pose calls attention to his right hand, the instrument of his trade and artistic identity, yet it also signifies devotion. Like the other Florentine portraits from this time, Ghirlandaio's figure visualizes his piety, which – according to the contract – was the patron's very impetus for the decoration, which honoured their families and enhanced the church. Santa Maria Novella was the major Dominican church in Florence, the order of which was founded by his name saint. Domenico, as we will relate, purchased a tomb in the church in which family members and he himself would be buried.

In addition, the family portraits at Colle Ramole capture a pivotal moment in the life of the Ghirlandaio family. Ridolfo's self-presentation visualizes the transition from artisan to patrician

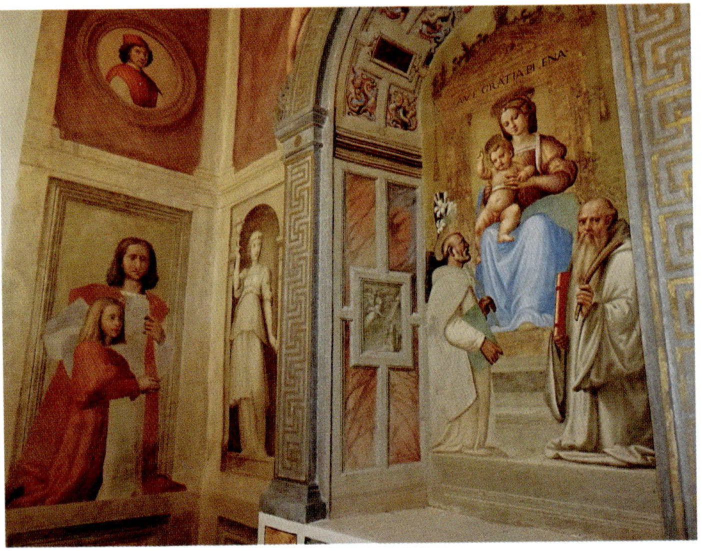

3 Ridolfo Ghirlandaio, *Self-Portrait with His Son, Domenico di Ridolfo, and Father, Domenico, c.* 1518, fresco, Dimora Ghirlandaio, Colle Ramole, Impruneta.

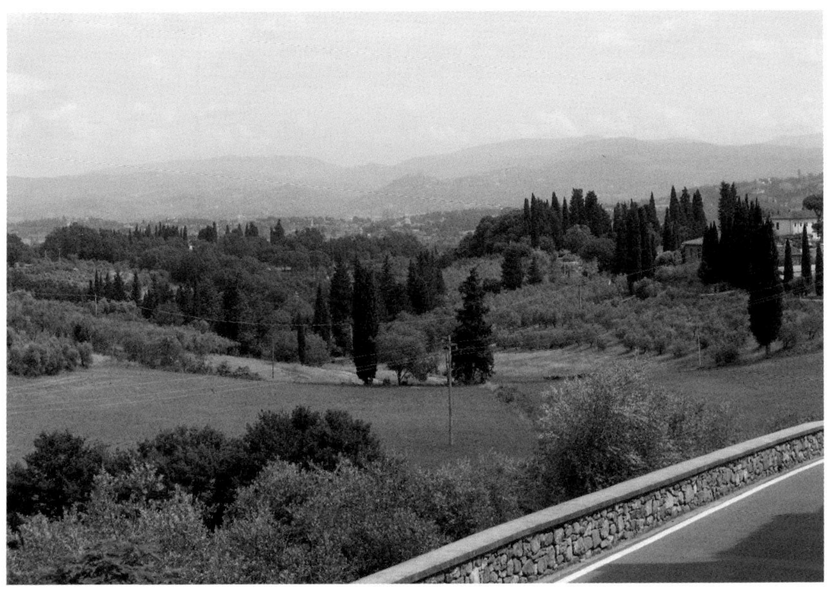

that his family history traces from the fourteenth to the sixteenth century. Domenico Ghirlandaio was born in Florence on 2 June 1448 into a family of craftsmen and shopkeepers. Stimulated by the teeming marketplace of the late medieval city, his father Tommaso pursued economic and social advancement. At just the time his eldest son, Domenico, was born, Tommaso began using a surname – Bigordi – as a marker of family identity and lineage; it signalled a social status that set him apart from the mass of nameless tradesmen. At age fifteen, Domenico was apprenticed to a goldsmith, an elite artisanal profession, but he soon turned to painting; indeed, it is primarily as a painter of murals and panels that he is known to us today. His career is well documented, yet mysteries persist: who was his master in painting? Who were his first patrons? Was it by chance or calculation that he was awarded plum commissions in his youth? These and other questions are treated in Chapter Two. But before we get there, we must first go

4 View of Florence from Colle Ramole.

back: this chapter uncovers the genealogy, material life and social identity of the Ghirlandaio family in the fifteenth century.

The Ghirlandaio family had roots around Colle Ramole. As far back as his 1442 tax return, Domenico's grandfather Currado owned a small farm in the parish of San Martino at Scandicci, just to the north of Colle Ramole, which remained family property until the sixteenth century. Domenico's stepmother, Antonia di Filippo del Puzzola (b. 1434/6), whom his father Tommaso married in 1462, brought in her dowry two plots of land adjacent to the farm called Colle Ramole belonging to Antonia's mother. It was perhaps as neighbours in the countryside that Antonia and Tommaso first came together in their second marriages, conforming to patterns of marriage alliance among neighbours of relatively equal wealth and social status.[3] The Colle Ramole property was valued in 1482 at the considerable sum of 516 florins (the gold coin minted in Florence from 1252), the exact amount Domenico would pay for it in 1491.[4] The estate remained in the possession of Domenico and his descendants until 1562.

According to their 1469 tax return, the Ghirlandaio family also owned land in the countryside north of Florence, bordering on the baptismal church at Cercina. With a small house and vineyard, the property came to the family in the dowry of Tommaso's brother Antonio's wife and yielded small amounts of grain and oil. By the end of the century, the family would also own land to the west, near Prato. Domenico acquired a large farm near the baptismal church of San Giusto for 600 florins in 1484, and his brother Davide also bought a farm in that vicinity in 1492.

Land ownership was widespread among the middle classes – the artisans, shopkeepers, notaries, teachers, doctors and so on, collectively known as the *popolo* – in the fourteenth and fifteenth centuries. Historians have estimated that in 1427 in Florence, land made up more than half the assets of 60 per cent of households.[5] The income produced from rented property, and the yields from cultivation and livestock, supplemented incomes and sustained daily life. Investment in land was also a shrewd financial strategy. For Florentines, we have seen how land figured largely in the financing of dowries, a requirement for marriage and the primary vehicle for women's inheritance. And land in the countryside was often a family's link to past generations who had emigrated to the city, and so it was an important component of family identity.

The very earliest historical evidence for the Ghirlandaio family locates them in the city of Florence, however; and it is as Florentines that the family will be known until the sixteenth century. We learn from the family memoirs that they were living in 1336 in the parish of Santa Maria di Verzaia, a church on the Borgo San Frediano, a street in the Santo Spirito neighbourhood, across the Arno River from the city centre (illus. 5). A family tree accompanying the memoirs shows the oldest member as Doffo, whose son, Currado, would be the painter's great-great grandfather, and whose descendants are the focus of the memoirs (illus. 6). By 1358, other documents identify Currado as resident near the church of San Lorenzo, across the river in the San Giovanni quarter (surrounding the baptistry, near the cathedral complex) in the city centre. This neighbourhood would become the geographical anchor for the family's identity for more than a century. Currado's son, also named Doffo, acquired a house in 1382 on the northeast side of the Via dell'Ariento; the house abutted the tiny street called the Gomitolo dell'Oro. The house, as we know from the surviving legal record of the sale, comprised a loggia and courtyard and cost 220 florins, a not inconsiderable sum. While the property would be enlarged and changed over the years, becoming the centre of family life, it remained in the family's possession until Domenico's brother Davide sold it in 1506, shortly after their father's death in 1503.[6]

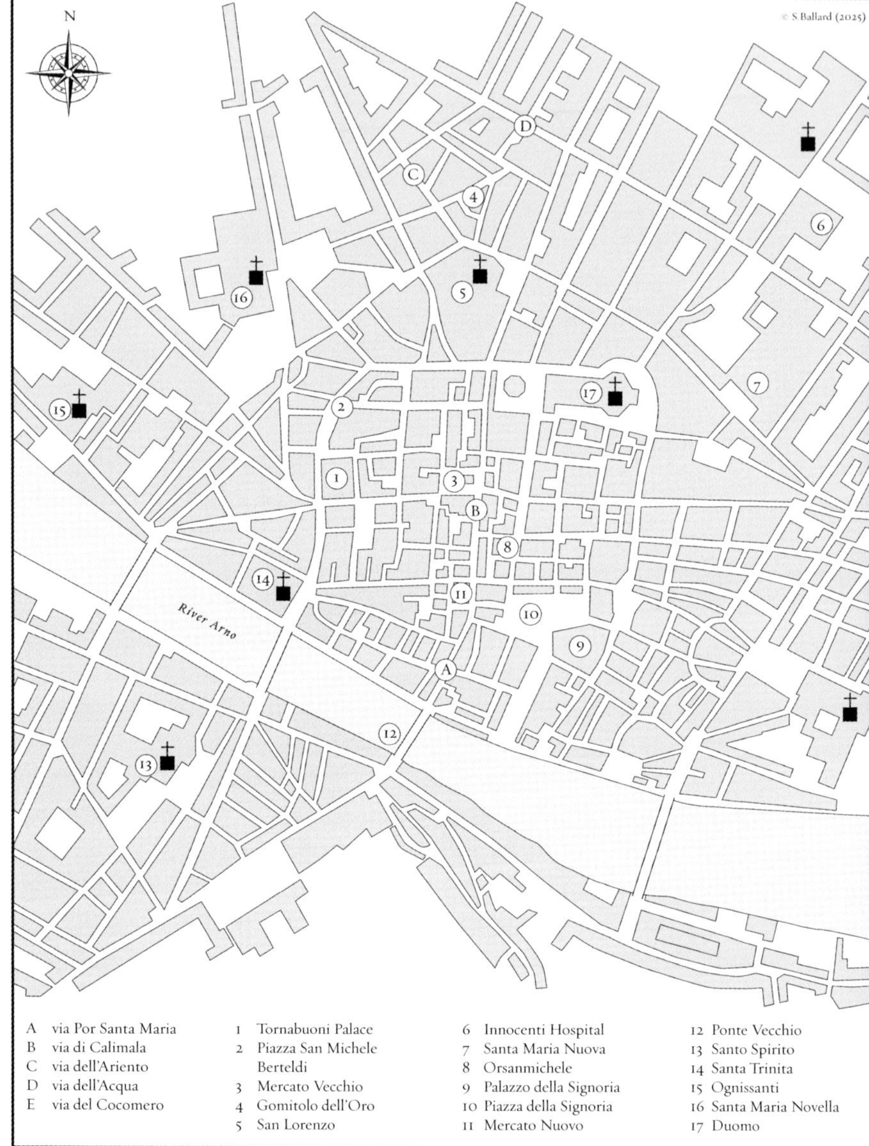

5 Florence in the late 15th century.

Documents from the time interchangeably used the words 'house' and 'family' (*casa* and *famiglia*), for 'family' was defined as those who shared a house. The hearth or household was the basic unit subject to taxation, and indeed tax documents yield a wealth of information about Florentine families, including the Ghirlandaio family. The family benefitted from the exceptionally long lives of two of its heads: Domenico's grandfather Currado di Doffo died in 1471 at age 89 or 90 (born *c.* 1380); and his father Tommaso lived to be 81 or 82 (born *c.* 1421), in an age when men's average lifespan was about 45 years. According to Roman law, the head of the family (*capo di famiglia*) exercised control – called the *patria potestas* – over its members until death. Men who were descended from the head comprised the agnatic lineage: these were the sons, nephews, grandsons and so on of the ancestor recognized as its founder; in the Ghirlandaio family tree, this was the otherwise unknown Doffo. The most important and tangible result of this idea of family was inheritance, which was confined to direct male

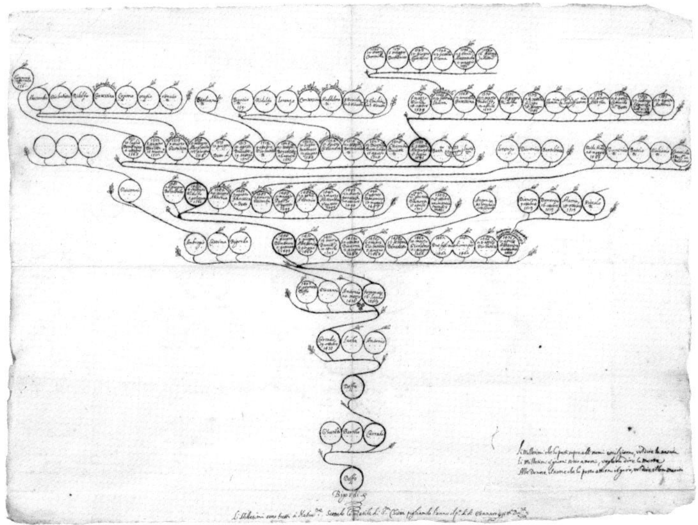

6 Family tree of the Bigordi, *c.* 1578, pen and brown ink on paper.

heirs. Relatives on a mother's side (cognatic kin) and relatives by marriage (affinal kin) were excluded from inheritance. Daughters shared in a family's patrimony through their dowries – essential to marriage for all but the poorest families – and laws ensured that a woman who outlived her husband could reclaim her dowry to marry again if she chose. Nonetheless, difficulties of dowry restitution and pressures against remarriage by in-laws and children limited widows' agency.[7] Another aspect of inheritance law was that all sons inherited equal shares of a father's estate (unlike primogeniture, in which the eldest son inherited the entire estate). Although inheritances varied widely according to family circumstances, the goal of agnatic lineage and partible inheritance was to preserve family resources and promote their collaborative management.[8]

The Ghirlandaio family was also prolific – at least in the generations with which we are concerned. According to the family tree, Tommaso fathered eleven children, Domenico ten and Ridolfo sixteen. Although the survival rate of infants and young children was low, the family was still populous by the standards of their time and class. Tommaso, Domenico and Ridolfo each married several times and, as was customary, their wives were often much younger, thus prolonging family fertility. Domenico was 31 when he married his first wife, who was 19, in 1480. After she died in January 1486 at the age of 25, he married again in April of the same year. His second wife was a widow, whose age is unknown but who bore him six children. The tax returns filed by Domenico's grandfather and father (Domenico never filed his own) reveal a multigenerational household of varying size between 1430, the first year Currado filed a return, and 1480, before the break-up of the extended household. In 1430, Currado's hearth included his mother, his wife and his three sons, which did not change in the next tax declaration in 1442. By the return in 1458, the family had increased to fourteen, including Tommaso's wife

Antonia and his five children, among them Domenico, aged nine, and Davide, aged six. In 1469, Currado was about 89 years old and filed his last return as *capo di famiglia*. At that time thirteen 'mouths' (*bocche*) comprised the household: his three sons, their wives and six grandsons aged three to twenty-three. By 1480, the role of *capo di famiglia* had passed to Domenico's father Tommaso, as we learn from the next tax return (Currado died in 1471). Tommaso's family still occupied the house on the Via dell'Ariento, although their numbers had shrunk to eight, including a daughter, Alessandra, born in 1475, and Domenico's wife Costanza.

The tax returns also give us a view of the family's prosperity. The *catasto*, instituted in 1427, was an inventory of possessions and a census. It included tangible property as well as investments in business ventures and the public debt. Because a household's primary residence was exempt from tax, and deductions were allowed for each family member, the poor and many working-class households paid no tax. This was the case for the Ghirlandaio family in the 1430 and 1442 levies; they were classed as *miserabile*, that is, without significant assets. By 1469, Currado's family's net worth had grown to slightly more than 482 florins, while in 1480 Tommaso's smaller household was valued at almost 285 florins. These figures were average for artisans and shopkeepers in the *catasto* of 1427, and at the median for all Florentine taxpayers in 1480.[9] In addition, as we have seen, the family's assets were primarily in land.

The Ghirlandaio family's fluctuating size and wealth mirrored many artisan and small merchant families in the fifteenth century. As historians of Renaissance Florence have described, small, nuclear families evolved to larger, multigenerational households and then back to smaller groups. Life events, such as the death of the *pater familias*, marriage of sons and births of grandchildren marked the stages of this cycle, as is amply clear in the history of the Ghirlandaio family. As we have seen, the death of Currado in

1471 led to a contraction of the family to two generations and eight members. Domenico's marriage in 1480 and the birth of his first children in 1481, 1483 and 1484 set the stage for the next realignment (Davide would marry for the first time only in 1492, and Benedetto, another younger brother, in 1494). A legal instrument (a *laudum*, or arbitrary sentence) drawn up on 20 October 1484 offers a keyhole view of the Ghirlandaio family dynamic that year.[10] The document provides overall for the preservation of the patrimony, and it is primarily concerned with the ownership of real property. Tommaso, who was said to be aged (for his time: he would have been over sixty years old), wished to prevent any disagreement among his heirs that might arise at his death. Hence, Domenico, the eldest son, was given the house on the Via dell'Ariento, while Tommaso retained use of it during his lifetime (the legal term is *usus et ususfructus*). Davide was given the house and farm at Cercina and Benedetto the farmer's house and land at San Martino at Scandicci. Giovanni Battista, the son from Tommaso's second marriage, had been promised the large farm at Colle Ramole, which had come into the family temporarily through his mother Antonia, in a separate legal document drawn up on 30 September. Through circumstances that are not entirely clear, however, the farm at Colle Ramole, as we have seen, would eventually come into the possession of Giovanni Battista's half-brother Domenico.[11]

In addition, the agreement – citing the sons' health and prosperity as well as their filial duty – obliged the sons to support their father, their stepmother and their unmarried half-sister Alessandra, each contributing according to their means. The amounts specified required Davide to contribute the most, while Benedetto and Giovanni Battista contributed smaller amounts. In this provision, the status of the eldest brother, Domenico, received special consideration. As the only one of the brothers to have married, we learn that his wife brought him a dowry of

1,000 florins, a considerable amount for an alliance between artisan families. Domenico's father-in-law was a linen or flax dealer (*linaiolo*) and a member of the religious sodality of St Paul, to which Ghirlandaio men belonged. We also learn that Domenico had invested 442 florins of this dowry in the family residence on Via dell'Ariento, providing a bed, chests, clothing, linen and woollen cloths, rings and belts.[12] In view of Domenico's family obligations, the agreement allowed Domenico to contribute a smaller amount to his father's and stepmother's upkeep.

About a month before, on 26 September 1484, Domenico and his brothers Davide, Benedetto and Giovanni Battista had been granted legal independence from their father Tommaso. The act of emancipation loosened the bonds of the *patria potestas*, granting the sons the legal right to enter into contracts such as the *laudum*. It also allowed the sons to manage their own incomes and their wives' dowries, draw up their own testaments and buy and sell land. In a family in which the head of the household lived to a great age, as had Currado and as would Tommaso, emancipation unleashed the sons' personal and professional lives. Tommaso himself had been emancipated in 1467, when he was in his mid-forties, and his mercantile activity as a dealer in crafted goods in silk, leather and other materials had reached a level of success. Domenico, meanwhile, was 36 in September 1484, also a significant milestone for him professionally, as we will see.

By terms of this agreement, then, Tommaso effectively retired as *pater familias* and set the stage for the break-up of the multi-generational household. The reasons stated in the document were Tommaso's age and his wish to avoid strife among his heirs at his death (though Tommaso would in fact outlive two of the four sons named in the agreement). But we can perhaps probe more deeply. In 1484, Domenico's career as a painter was well established, as will be related below. The generous dowry he received from his wife's father, an artisan and confrère, reflects his rising status.[13] The expenditure on household furnishings, such as furniture and linens, upon his marriage in 1480 also signals his participation in an upper-class urban culture of physical comfort and virtuous display. Practical needs, such as space for his growing family and perhaps also for greater independence in the management of his assets, must therefore have propelled this break in the family. In any case, the sixteenth-century memoirs note that, shortly after the emancipation but before the agreement of 20 October 1484, Domenico and his brother Davide took out a five-year lease on a house on the Via del Cocomero (present-day Via Ricasoli), in the same neighbourhood as the house on the Via dell'Ariento. As stated in his tax return, Davide was still living in the rented house in 1495, the year after Domenico's death, at which time his brother's children were also living there, with him as their legal guardian. Whether Domenico resided in a different location, independent of his brother, at any time before his death is not known.

Our idea of family as those who share a house can be extended by what historians have called the 'spiritual *casa*' – that is, the family ancestors, whose memory was kept alive through memoirs (*ricordanze*). Compiling family histories was a longstanding habit of Florentine families, and they survive in great numbers from the late thirteenth century to the late sixteenth century.[14] While documents such as tax returns, legal instruments and payment records allow a close view of Domenico and his family's activities over decades, family memoirs offer more intimate echoes of personal relationships, motives and feelings. Giorgio Vasari's biography of Domenico, his brother Davide and son Ridolfo (from *The Lives of the Painters, Sculptors and Architects*, editions of 1550 and 1568) is likewise rich with overtones of interpersonal relations, but it cannot be taken at face value.[15] Vasari was a tireless researcher, especially for the second edition of the *Lives*, and he was personally acquainted with Ridolfo Ghirlandaio. He refers to the Ghirlandaio family records several times, which he says he consulted, probably through Ridolfo, most famously in the account of Michelangelo's apprenticeship.[16] Vasari's biography is remarkably accurate, and it has stood up well to the research of modern scholars. While selective and retrospective, *Ghirlandaria* – the compilation of family records copied in the sixteenth century referred to above and published in 2017 in a fully annotated edition – confirms many facts about the family over generations, and it brings us closer to the lived experience of the Ghirlandaio family in the fifteenth and sixteenth centuries.

The seventeenth-century manuscript of the memoirs in the Archivio Apostolico Vaticano is a partial copy of the original manuscript titled *Ghirlandaria*, which does not survive. The copy, made by Ridolfo di Alessandro (1571–1640), derives from a manuscript compiled by his father Alessandro Ghirlandaio (1531–1595), son of Ridolfo del Ghirlandaio (1483–1561) and grandson of Domenico (1448–1494). Alessandro began the manuscript in 1578, writing:

> For the memory and understanding of who will come after, I resolve to select that which will appear to me to be useful of the memory made by my ancestors and predecessors, taking from their written books that have come to me, old, mistreated and consumed by time, and serving for whatever will come to pass.[17]

Alessandro started the memoir in Pisa, where he resided after a peripatetic career. He married a woman from Pisa and had numerous children, perhaps prompting him to set the facts on paper. His notes contain attestations to his father's character and some personal experiences; he notes, for example, 'I Alessandro di Ridolfo was raised more in the house of the abovenamed Madonna Costanza [his father's sister] than in the house of my father with great affection.'[18] Otherwise, his notes confine themselves to the nitty gritty of family history: births and deaths; marriages; real estate transactions; and inventories of possessions. His son Ridolfo copied the manuscript selectively, while adding some detail pertaining to his own generation.

Florence's mercantile activity, relative social mobility and high levels of literacy fostered a culture of memory-writing to an extent greater than other cities. The earliest Florentine memoirs simply recorded personal wealth, including land and moveable possessions. But over time, compilers began to record life events, such as birth and death dates, to reconstruct the biological history of the family. Eventually, the family book – distinct from private account books and notarial documents – emerged; its purpose was to document patrimonial, economic and political rights, such as eligibility for public office. Authors expressed the need to preserve memories for future generations. Indeed, Alessandro's memoir fits well within the norms of these family books and adds to what we know from the many archival documents that have been published by scholars.

The family tree, probably made at the time of Ridolfo di Alessandro's copy, spreads across two sheets of the manuscript and captures in visual form the lineage as described in the memoirs. It adds precise birth and death dates for selected family members, clearly relying on documents that relate directly to the generations of Tommaso di Currado, Domenico di Tommaso and Ridolfo di Domenico, as the information is most complete for these family members. The patriarchal society of late medieval Florence lent ambiguous status to women, who were rarely considered fully integrated members of their husbands' families. Accordingly, in the family tree, while female children are noted and the names of their spouses sometimes written above, the wives of male family members are omitted.

The spiritual *casa* was also kept alive by tangible memorials such as tombs. From the earliest Christian times, burial has been an important rite, and in Renaissance Florence tomb markers were tangible foci for prayer, commemorative activity and display, perpetuating family memory. Beginning in the 1360s, Florentines' desire to create durable memories of dead family members by erecting tombs and decorating funerary chapels in churches constituted a new 'cult of memory'.[19] A document in the Vatican archives, annotated in Domenico Ghirlandaio's hand, shows that he purchased a tomb on 6 June 1486 in the church of Santa Maria Novella, the major Dominican church in Florence and home to what would be the artist's largest chapel decoration.[20] Just nine months earlier, Domenico, along with his brother Davide, had contracted with the banker Giovanni Tornabuoni to decorate the main chapel of the church, to which Tornabuoni had patronage rights. As discussed below, the project would occupy him in one way or another for the rest of his life. It was perhaps because of this engagement with the Dominican friars there that Domenico sought to establish his tomb in the church. His relationship with Giovanni Tornabuoni, for whom he had worked since at least 1477 and whose family had long been involved at Santa Maria Novella, may have facilitated access.[21] Domenico's first wife, Costanza, who died in January 1486, was buried in a tomb of her father's family in Santa Maria Novella. It was perhaps this event that revealed to Domenico the need to have his own family tomb. In fact, according to Alessandro's *ricordi*, her body was moved to Domenico's tomb shortly afterwards.

The Ghirlandaio family tomb is described as an arched sepulchre and was in the cemetery adjacent to and east of the main body of the church (Santa Maria Novella, unusually, was oriented on a north–south axis). Then as now, the perimeter of the cemetery was lined with arched niches into which sarcophagi were set. These tombs were built between 1297 and 1314 and decorated with distinctive white and green marble revetment in 1349, at the same time as the lower level of the facade. The tomb that Domenico

Ghirlandaio acquired for himself and his family is along the west wall of the cemetery, the third from the south entrance portal (illus. 7).[22]

The tomb is in the form of an *avello*, a wall tomb consisting of the sarcophagus and an engaged stone canopy, in this case with a pointed arch.[23] At Santa Maria Novella, a great number of such *avelli* survive, although in reduced condition. That of the Ghirlandaio family still displays their coat of arms – escutcheons with a rider on a rearing horse that flank a cross, carved in relief on the front of the sarcophagus. A similar crest of a mounted rider inlaid with black and white marble surmounts the apex of the arch. The imagery was described by Alessandro as 'a jouster, or shall I say *il bigordo*, such as is the name of a jouster on horseback', derived from the family name Bigordi.[24] An eighteenth-century writer described a life-sized portrait of Domenico adorning the niche, presumably painted on the back wall under the arch; this sadly does not survive.[25] Alessandro also related that the family's tombs had previously been in the portico of the church of San Lorenzo, near the house on the Via dell'Ariento. The original tomb was probably a floor tomb with inlaid designs; Alessandro states that the crest at the top of the new tomb had been transferred from San Lorenzo.

We can also construct the Ghirlandaio family history by tracing the use of a family name. As mentioned above, the name Bigordi, visualized by the rearing horse, was used by family members, but it was a relatively recent invention. Family names, associated with social rank and civic office-holding, emerged in the thirteenth and fourteenth centuries as newly prominent merchants and bankers consolidated their lineages in the male line and fostered the *casa's* social identity. But the earliest members of the Ghirlandaio family were identified by a sequence of first names, including those of a father and grandfather, and this usage continued into the fifteenth century. Often these names repeated,

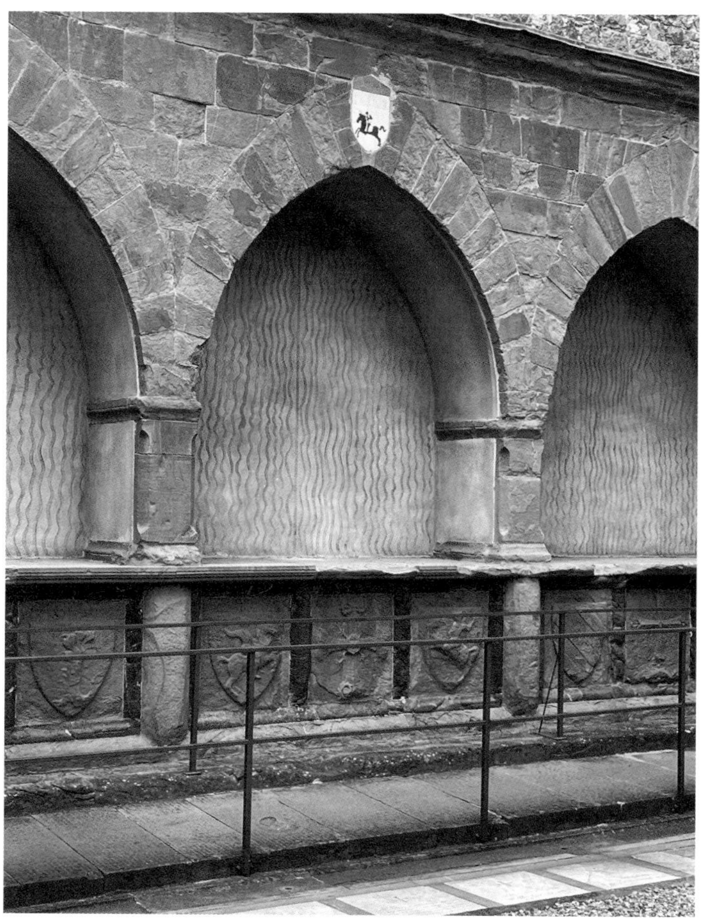

with the names Doffo and Currado (given to firstborn sons) alternating in the first five generations of the family. Tommaso, a younger son, named his sons Domenico, Davide, Benedetto, Giovanni Battista and Girolamo; these names repeated in successive generations of his numerous descendants. Daughters were often named after a deceased first wife or grandparent, again primarily from the male line; Domenico's daughter Costanza,

7 Tomb of Domenico Ghirlandaio, *c.* 1486, Santa Maria Novella, Florence.

born in 1487, was named after his first wife, who had died the year before. Male and female first names were also given to children after the death of a sibling, in effect 'remaking' the family member. Tommaso's daughter Alessandra died in 1464; another daughter born in 1475 by his second wife was named Alessandra after her half-sister; and Domenico named one of his daughters Alessandra as well. The names repeated over generations comprise what has been called aptly a family patrimony of given names that lent cohesion and longevity to the lineage.[26]

The origin of the surname Bigordi or Bighordi is not known.[27] Both Currado di Doffo and Tommaso were referred to as de' Bigordi in records of the religious confraternity of San Paolo starting in 1448; the name also appears in Tommaso's matriculation record into the guild of the Galigai (tanners and leatherworkers) in 1447 and in Currado di Doffo's tax returns of 1458 and 1469. Domenico takes on the name sometime before 1472, in his matriculation into the Company of St Luke, a sodality associated with the guild of Medici e Speziali, and it is used frequently from then on into the sixteenth century.[28] Most prominently, Domenico would inscribe it in classical majuscules on the inlaid, gilded wainscoting of the chamber in the *Birth of the Virgin* scene in Santa Maria Novella, finished around 1488–90.

A further motivation for keeping family memoirs and constructing the social identity of the *casa* was to document qualifications of family members for public office. Florence was governed by three executive bodies – the Signoria, or priorate, and two advisory colleges, the Buonomini (Good Men) and the Gonfalonieri di Compagnia (Standard-bearers of the Company) – collectively called the Tre Maggiori.[29] Male citizens older than thirty years of age and active guild members were eligible for nomination for office in the Tre Maggiori, although the requirements changed over time and were sometimes ignored. Serving in the Tre Maggiori, especially the priorate, was an honour that was duly recorded in family books and passed down to descendants; indeed, even being nominated for office by fellow guildsmen or by neighbours, regardless of whether a citizen assumed office, was prestigious.

Although none of the Ghirlandaio family in Tommaso's or Domenico's generation served in the Tre Maggiori, we do know that Domenico and Davide were candidates for officers of the Medici e Speziali guild, of which they were members from the early 1470s. As Chapter Two will explain, Florence was unique in integrating guilds into the fundamental structure and function of the government from the late thirteenth to the sixteenth century.[30] Domenico's name was drawn by lot for the position of guild consul in 1495, shortly after his death. Davide's name was drawn in 1491 and 1494, although he was disqualified from serving both times because he was in arrears on his taxes.[31] While less prestigious than the Tre Maggiori, guild office-holding was a mark of leadership and esteem, even if the Ghirlandaio brothers seem to have acceded to this distinction only late in their careers. They were, however, extremely active for long periods in the leadership of the several confraternities to which they belonged, as detailed below.

Ridolfo di Domenico was, by contrast with his father and uncle, elected to public office on several occasions. That he would be more politically engaged was perhaps signalled from the beginning; his name was entered into the *Libro di età* of the *Tratte*, a public record of birth dates that established eligibility for public office and was part of the electoral records. Later, in 1516, Ridolfo was nominated to the lists of eligible citizens for public office by the Gonfaloniere di Giustizia (Standard-bearer of Justice), but this nomination was from Duke Lorenzo di Piero de' Medici, not from a civic body, and it reflects the evolution in Florentine government from a republic to a principate after the return of the Medici in 1512. Indeed, Ridolfo's relations with the Medici, like those of his father before him, bore fruit in his professional career as a painter. In 1518, Ridolfo was selected to serve in the council of Good Men, but he was in arrears in his taxes so unable to serve. According to Alessandro's memoirs, Ridolfo was also nominated in 1526 for minor office (this time in the neighbourhood *gonfalone* of the Lion d'oro in the San Giovanni quarter, the ancestral home of the family), and he was also elected to serve on several civic committees and as representative official in countryside towns in the 1550s and '60s.[32] He reportedly served as a consul and *camarlingo* (treasurer) of the Galigai guild on several occasions. Even so, unlike other artisan families – the Gaddi most notably – no Ghirlandaio ever ascended to the priorate; instead, they centred their public activity on guild and confraternity membership.[33]

The Ghirlandaio *casa* was the locus of personal experience for its family members, for in Renaissance Florence the family was the fundamental unit of society. In its tangible form (residences and land) and intangible form (lineage and memory, actively constructed by memoirs, tombs and surnames) the family shaped individual lives. Outside the *casa*, primarily male family members interacted with neighbours, co-workers and friends, and it is to the professional and social life of Domenico Ghirlandaio and his family that we now turn.

TWO

Building Networks:
Guilds and Confraternities

While family was the primary unit of society, centred on the *casa* or hearth, extra-familial relations unfolded in the dense urban fabric of the walled city, in its streets, piazzas, loggias and bridges.[1] As they moved through the streets from the Via dell'Ariento in San Lorenzo to the Duomo, to the Piazza della Signoria and across the Ponte Vecchio to the Oltrarno, Domenico Ghirlandaio and his family members met neighbours, acquaintances, friends of friends, business associates, suppliers and customers. News of employment opportunities, properties for sale, economic and market trends, as well as politics and gossip circulated through such personal encounters. Historians have described these patterns of social relationships as patron–client networks. Patrons provided clients with introductions, recommendations, information and protection. In return, clients offered loyalty and potential favours. The roles were endlessly variable; a patron could be a client and vice versa. Webs of contacts overlapped and intersected, creating a dense skein of relationships that animated social life. Close inspection of the letters of prominent patrons such as Lorenzo de' Medici or Ser Lapo Mazzei reveals the workings of patron–client networks in detail.[2] Sadly, for Ghirlandaio and his family, we have no letters, but we can still gain an insight into his networks of friends, patrons and partners by examining his membership in guilds, craft organizations and lay brotherhoods.

Tommaso di Currado apprenticed his son Domenico to the goldsmiths Bernardo di Guccio and Bartolomeo di Stefano in 1463.[3] Medieval goldsmiths enjoyed high prestige among artisans for their technical skills, costly materials and wealthy patrons. Although no objects produced by Ghirlandaio's masters have survived to enable us to assess the nature or quality of their work, biographical facts emerge from tax and other documents. Bernardo di Guccio (born *c.* 1417), from a Florentine family of goldsmiths and metalworkers, had matriculated in the Arte della Seta (the silk guild, of which the goldsmiths formed part) in 1437 at about the age of twenty. Meanwhile, Bartolomeo di Stefano (born *c.* 1432) matriculated in the Arte della Seta in 1448. The two had partnered sometime between 1457 and 1463, and by 1469 they had rented a workshop in the Via di Calimala, near the commercial centre of the city.[4]

Ghirlandaio's apprenticeship marks his entry into the system of craft production established in the late Middle Ages.[5] In Florence's booming thirteenth-century economy, artisans, merchants, manufacturers, shopkeepers and notaries – mainly persons who were not protected by powerful families – formed associations to safeguard their economic interests and to offer social and spiritual support. The guilds were autonomous, self-governing organizations to which the commune granted legal status. Their statutes set standards for the practice of a craft or trade by protecting the quality of products, controlling access to membership through regulation of apprenticeship and setting limits on competition among members. The guild council, comprised of select members, wrote the statutes and presided over disputes involving contracts, substandard goods or fraud.

Florentine guilds were unique in constituting the basic structure of the mercantile republic. In 1293, the popular government declared the Ordinances of Justice. This excluded elite families from government and instituted the Priorate of the

Guilds. Carefully apportioned guild representatives comprised the councils that made up the government. In the fourteenth century, the guilds were divided into seven major and fourteen minor guilds, totalling twenty-one in all. The major guilds, to which the richer and more powerful men belonged, included the Calimala, the international merchants, bankers and commodity traders; the Cambio, the bankers and moneychangers; the Lana, the manufacturers of woollen cloth; the Guidici e Notai, the judges and notaries; the Seta, the manufacturers and retailers of silk cloth (also called Por Santa Maria, the name of the street in which it had premises); the Vaiai e Pellicciai, furrier manufacturers and dealers; and the Medici, Speziali e Merciai, physicians, apothecaries and mercers or haberdashers. Minor guilds included construction workers (Maestri di Pietra e Legname); butchers (Beccai); shoemakers (Calzolai); and second-hand dealers and linen drapers (Rigattieri e Linaioli), among others. Since the number of guilds was limited, certain guilds embraced a broad range of activities with sometimes competing economic interests. The Medici, Speziali e Merciai, for example, was a 'guild conglomerate' organized into different groups or members: doctors; sellers of drugs, spices and other concoctions; and makers and sellers of a wide range of goods such as hats, purses and gloves.[6] The activities of the *merciai* often overlapped with those of other guilds, such as Por Santa Maria. Interpenetrating jurisdictions and heterogeneous memberships weakened the guilds' ability to regulate economic activity and safeguard members' interests in the market. Their political role became their primary function, and indeed some men sought guild membership only as a qualification for political office.

Nonetheless, guilds structured society in fundamental ways, for they organized groups of workers related by activity, contiguity of workplace and shared values.[7] Hence guilds shaped social identity as well as economic activity. The interpersonal relationships among members of the group were based on trust – *bona fides* – between master and pupil, between master and other masters and between masters and clients. *Bona fides* predicted behaviour and respect for norms and agreements, and acted as a guarantor of security, thereby reducing risk and uncertainty in dealing with members of the group. It thus effectively extended predictable relationships to non-family members. The guild also established a member's good reputation – *buona fama* – as a basis for interaction. Hence guilds offered an institutional and collective form of trust that was essential to the formation of economic, social and personal networks. It also sustained a system of reciprocal guarantees to safeguard the transmission of knowledge and to control quality of production, access to primary materials and basic conditions of work for its members.

At the beginning of his apprenticeship in 1463, Domenico – then aged fourteen or fifteen – would have already learned to read and write in primary school, and he may have attended an abacus school of commercial arithmetic or perhaps assisted in his father's workshop. The family memoirs record that his initial apprenticeship was for two years, for which Domenico was to receive 11 florins; the contract was renewed on 28 June 1465 for two more years for a salary more than doubled at 24 florins, and again on 3 November 1467 for two years, the first year for 20 florins and the second for 24 florins. The last renewal for one year only at an unknown salary was on 15 November 1469 and noted his reduced attendance. Although we do not know the precise terms of Ghirlandaio's apprenticeship contract, general practices are clear.[8] Regulating the transmission of technical knowledge via apprenticeship was a primary function of guilds and the means through which they controlled competition and perpetuated group identity. The student lived or worked in the *bottega*, serving the master and safeguarding tools and materials. He was obliged to avoid fraud and complete the contract. In return, the master taught the student professional skills and may have lodged, clothed and fed him. The 1315 statutes of the Medici e Speziali specified the minimum length of apprenticeship at nine years.[9] Cennino Cennini, author of one of the earliest treatises on painters' practices, famously claimed to have been trained by Agnolo Gaddi for twelve years and Agnolo's father Taddeo by Giotto for twenty-four years; but we know that the lengths of apprenticeships varied widely.[10] Statutes did not prescribe the curriculum or the method of training; this was the prerogative of the master. While some guilds limited the number of apprentices a master could take on at one time, in reality the status of the various members of a workshop was vague, as reflected in the range of terms that described them: *discepoli* (learners), *apprendisti* (apprentices), *fattori* (factors or agents), *garzone* (boys or lackeys), *lavoranti* (labourers), *salariati* (wage earners). Between the period in which the apprentice was learning and the end of the contract, he was providing essentially free or discounted labour to the master, hence it was to the advantage of the master to extend the apprenticeship period.

The careers of Ghirlandaio family members from the fourteenth to the sixteenth century shed light on how Florence's artisan economy worked in practice. They changed professions frequently and joined multiple guilds. Tax records show that, in the mid-fourteenth century, Currado di Doffo was a barber (*barbitonsorus*).[11] In theory the barbers belonged to the Medici e Speziali, since they, like physicians, dealt with personal care and wellness; but we have no record of Currado di Doffo's enrolment in the guild. In 1372, however, Currado di Doffo's son Doffo matriculated in the Medici e Speziali, where he was called a haberdasher (*merciaio*). Ten years later, in the tax record of 1382, however, he was called a silk worker (*setaiuolo*), whose activity was regulated by the guild of Por Santa Maria (Arte della Seta). Like the Medici e Speziali, however, the Por Santa Maria included makers of silk clothing and accessories whose activities over-lapped with the *merciai*. Doffo may have also joined the guild of Por Santa Maria at this time, as his son would later matriculate in the guild with a reduced fee for relatives of members. In the 1390 tax record, however, Doffo was listed as a barber, having reverted to his father's profession.

Currado di Doffo, Domenico's grandfather, matriculated in the Medici e Speziali in 1410, where he was called a *merciaio* and a grocer (*oliandolo*). The grocers had their own, minor guild, the Arte degli Oliandoli e Pizzicagnoli, in which Currado seems not to have matriculated. Documents also suggest that he matric-ulated in the guild of the second-hand dealers, the Arte dei Rigattieri, at an unknown date. His tax returns in 1442 and 1451 declare him to be a tax collector at the city gates, and hence he seems to have abandoned his trade by then. Nonetheless, in 1448, Currado matriculated in the Arte della Seta, qualifying for a reduced matriculation fee because his father had been a member of the guild. At the age of 68, it seems unlikely that Currado in-tended to change occupations; he probably matriculated to secure the same privilege for his son Antonio, who enrolled in the guild the next day.

The next generation, comprising Currado's sons, Giovanni, Antonio and Tommaso, pursued shifting career paths and mul-tiple guild affiliations. Tommaso, Domenico's father, was partic-ularly mobile in his professional pursuits. He began as a tanner or leatherworker (*cuoiaio*), matriculating in the guild of the Galigai in 1447. We know that, in 1451, his older brother Giovanni had a workshop for leather-dying in the neighbourhood of Santo Stefano a Ponte, near the Ponte Vecchio and with access to the water necessary for his industry. Giovanni had matriculated in the Arte dei Galigai in 1443, and hence Tommaso must have been working with him. Tanning leather was primarily undertaken in the late spring and early summer when warm temperatures

accelerated drying and treatment. In summer, activity was halted
by climate and concerns for public health, so leatherworkers
sought alternative work; for example, in trade or money lending.[12]
Tommaso seems to have pursued new directions by 1451, when he
was listed in the records of the religious confraternity of St Paul
as *fu cuoiaio*: formerly a leatherworker. Indeed, his grandfather's
tax declaration of that year states that Tommaso and his brother
Antonio had a shop in the Mercato Nuovo (new market) where
they traded in silk and related goods such as doublets, purses
and hose (*setaiuoli a minuto*). Antonio, as we have seen, had enrolled
in the silk guild in 1448. The family memoirs go on to tell us that
Antonio and Tommaso had formed a partnership in 1451 for
two years to practise the craft of *setaiuoli*, in which Tommaso was
the junior partner. They then signed a five-year lease for a workshop in 1453. So although we have no evidence that he ever matriculated in the silk guild, family connections clearly shaped Tommaso's
early career.

Antonio and Tommaso's business must have thrived during
the 1450s for, as the memoirs claim, they invented a popular
women's hair ornament called garlands (*grillande* or *ghirlande*),
from which Vasari and others trace the name Ghirlandaio.[13] It is
at just this time that records first referred to Tommaso as a garland maker (*grillandaio*). The garlands were circular headdresses
made of semi-precious materials, such as enamelled flowers and
peacock feathers, and were part of a bride's costume.

Tommaso seems to have expanded his activity beyond hair
ornaments for, in 1458, the confraternity records refer to him
as a *merciaio*, that is, a haberdasher or dealer in buttons, ribbons
and other notions. Like other artisans *a minuto* (in small quantities), he seems to have expanded from fabrication into trade.
By 1469 and 1470, he is referred to in confraternity records as
a broker (*sensale*) who received a percentage of the value of goods
traded, and his 1480 tax return again lists his profession as a

sensale. In 1466, the apothecary Luca Landucci noted wedding expenses – including a silk belt with gold and silver ornaments, a jewelled brooch and a pearl necklace and headband, totalling over 421 lira – plus payment to Tommaso di Currado for brokerage, a commission of approximately 3 per cent.[14] The family's 1469 tax return shows a dramatically improved net worth, more than 482 florins, which may reflect Tommaso's and his brothers' professional success.

Tommaso's career reveals the weakness of Florence's guild system, for his activities as a *setaiuolo*, *merciaio*, *grillandaio* and *sensale* should have required membership in one or both of the Arte della Seta and the Arte dei Medici e Speziali. Instead he was trained by his brother, evading formal apprenticeship, and in partnership with him practised as a *setaiuolo* without joining the guild in his own right. At the same time, Tommaso's changes in career show how the loose guild structure and lack of rigid boundaries between crafts allowed workers a wide choice of occupations and the possibility of developing diverse talents. This system encouraged ambition, collaboration, inventiveness and versatility of skill. It appears that Tommaso's career traced an ascending material and social status for him and his family. His first job as a leatherworker was in a low status trade (as was his father's and grandfather's practice as barbers), denigrated because of its work with animals and the impurities and odours associated with its processes.[15] The more complex technical procedures and the elevated value of the materials he worked with as a *setaiuolo a minuto* conferred higher status. The prestige of clients, such as those from socially prominent families who bought Tommaso's *ghirlande*, also increased his social standing.

Domenico's seven-year apprenticeship to Bernardo di Guccio and Bartolomeo di Stefano reflects the intensive training in complex technical processes and proficiency in handling a broad range of materials, including precious metals and gems, demanded of goldsmiths.[16] Goldsmiths produced objects in gold and silver, including jewellery, tableware and cutlery for private clients, ornamental objects such as parade weaponry and horse trappings, belts, buttons and clasps, medals, dies for coins and seals and liturgical objects for religious ceremonies. As we know from technical manuals, notably one by the goldsmith and sculptor Benvenuto Cellini (1500–1571), and surviving works themselves, goldsmiths invented designs, prepared materials and tools, and created objects using a wide range of techniques. Metals had to be refined before use, removing impurities, separating precious metals from base metals and gold from silver using various processes. Exacting manual skills were required to trace elaborate surface designs using burins (a sharp-pointed engraving tool) or punches. These designs were often inlaid with silver or gold (damascening), filled with niello (copper or silver sulphide) or covered in translucent coloured enamel. Precious and semi-precious gems were mounted in varied settings.[17] Opaque enamels applied in various techniques adorned costly gifts. Methods of embossing or repoussé (in which designs were produced by hammering the metal from the back) and chasing (in which the metal was worked from the front) were part of the goldsmith's decorative skills, as was filigree (in which gold or silver wire or beads formed intricate tracery). They also needed drawing skills to transcribe stock patterns from books and to develop and propose new designs to patrons. Cellini touted his prowess in inventing intricate figurative and natural forms, while goldsmiths such as Lorenzo Ghiberti (1378–1455) also supplied designs for large-scale execution in painting, sculpture, stained glass, inlaid wood and tapestry. Goldsmiths forged objects such as bowls or chalices with a hammer, working on an anvil or other surfaces. They also cast gold, silver and baser materials for jewellery and decorative mounts from models fashioned in wood, clay, wax or plaster. The casting process, when used for parts of objects such as handles, was by the lost wax method, in which a wax model was encased in clay and melted away to form the mould. Other moulds could be removed in pieces and reused to cast multiple objects, while metal dies enabled motifs to be reproduced in large quantities. The parts were joined using rivets or solder. Gold leaf, produced by specialist goldbeaters (*battiloro*), was applied to silver and copper alloys and burnished to a high shine.

Illustrations of medieval goldsmiths at work show the tools they used and wares they created. The workspaces had a hearth or furnace, workbenches and display cases, and large windows for light. Chisels, dividers, callipers, hammers, anvils, files and saws, and scales and weights for measuring, cover the tables. Workshops were open to the inspection of passersby, as required by statute for the Florentine guild to ensure honest dealing. Meanwhile, Cellini's treatise vividly describes the materials whose properties, preparation and handling were mastered by gold-smiths.[18] Judgements of quality in craft, design and innovation also pervade his account. For instance, he praises skills in judging the colour, sheen and luminosity of gems and metals. Cellini relates how goldsmiths worked in relief and in the round, as well as on flat and curving surfaces, using a wide variety of tools and techniques to ornament and add texture to surfaces.

Goldsmiths' familiarity with metals and gems meant that they were called upon for appraisals of finished works, and the high value of their materials demanded *buona fama* (good reputation) to reassure prospective clients that their money would be well spent. In the arc of Tommaso's career that we have traced, therefore, the apprenticeship of his son to a goldsmith represented a decided leap in professional status from that of *setaiuolo a minuto* or *sensale*.

The seven years of Domenico Ghirlandaio's apprenticeship also reflect Tommaso's investment in his son's career, for during that time Domenico was not available to work in the family business. For some families, forgoing children's contributions to the household income was a hardship, but Tommaso's tax returns during the 1460s suggest he was able to afford it. Domenico also received a modest salary. The rise in his wages from 11 florins in the first year to 24 towards the end of his apprenticeship is consistent with those of other apprentices and reflects the value of the skills he acquired during this time.[19] Tommaso also apprenticed Domenico's younger brother Davide to the jewellery maker Lorenzo di Giovanni in 1465, then for two years ending in August 1468 with Bartolomeo di Stefano, the same goldsmith training Domenico, for 8 florins a year. Davide then apprenticed to the painter of wool or linen cloth used for curtains and other objects (*sargiaio*) Bartolomeo di Giovanni Masini for two years ending in December 1472, for a salary of 12 florins the first year and 16 the second.[20]

It is surprising that, after Domenico's rigorous training in goldsmithing, he seems never to have matriculated as a goldsmith in the Arte della Seta, or indeed to have practised the craft.[21] His name is missing from the membership lists of the Arte della Seta in the years around 1470 when his apprenticeship ended, even though he would have paid a reduced matriculation fee, since his grandfather and uncle had been inscribed in the guild. His competence in goldsmithing must have been well known, for in 1481 he designed and gilded candlesticks for the Florentine cathedral, and in 1486 he appraised a silver censer (*turibolo*) made for Santa Trinita, but no object survives that can be associated with his hand. Instead, by 1472, two short years after the conclusion of his apprenticeship, he is called a painter in the membership lists of the religious confraternity of St Luke, a sodality associated with painters in the guild of Medici e Speziali.

Domenico's turn to painting from goldsmithing must have been rapid. Perhaps the renewal of his apprenticeship contract in 1467, with a reduced salary, and the final renewal in 1469 for only one year, indicates that he was already learning to paint. The family memoirs tell us that, at the end of his apprenticeship, Domenico turned to drawing and painting and quickly left the craft of goldsmith and jeweller for that of painter.[22] Vasari recounts the same tale: 'Being thus apprenticed to the goldsmith's art, but taking no pleasure therein, he was ever occupied in drawing.'[23] Florence's lack of rigid boundaries between trades, the relatively liberal market environment and the free exchange among professions that valued invention and risk likely encouraged his transition.[24] However, we have no further documentation of his apprenticeship as a painter or who might have taught him. Guild rules effectively prohibited an apprentice from 'serving two masters', so it is likely that Domenico had no formal apprenticeship contract with any painter up to 1470.[25] If, by 1472, he was already a painter, his formal training must have been swift. Certainly, Domenico had learned skills in drawing and design central to the goldsmith's craft that were transferrable to painting. But between 1470 and 1472, he would have had to learn to prepare pigments, emulsions and grounds and to paint on walls and panels.

Domenico's membership in the Company of St Luke suggests that he was by then also matriculated in the Arte dei Medici e Speziali.[26] He could have enrolled with a reduced fee, as his great-grandfather and grandfather were members of the guild, having matriculated in 1372 and 1410, respectively. The practice of favouring family members in guild inscription has been alluded to several times above, and it points to another peculiarity of Florentine guilds.[27] Family solidarity through guild membership is not unknown in Northern Europe, but admission of sons or relatives who did not even practise the craft of their forebears (or indeed of prominent citizens regardless of their profession) is unusual.[28] Neither the Arte della Seta nor the Medici e Speziali required a minimum period of apprenticeship or a demonstration of skill

– perhaps because, as large 'conglomerate' guilds, their members practised a vast range of activities and such regulations would have been unenforceable. In addition, guilds delegated to the master the recognition of competence, generally understood as having served the term of the apprenticeship contract. The guilds reserved a right to examine candidates for their technical capabilities and personal character, but in practice this was rarely done. Production of a masterpiece, as demanded by Northern European guilds, was not required in Florence. Moreover, as part of the artisan culture in the city, people assumed that, to maintain a family patrimony of technical knowledge, elders trained younger family members well.

Why did Domenico become a painter? By the fifteenth century, the goldsmiths' profession was changing. In Florence, large-scale public statuary in gilded and silvered bronze, such as Ghiberti's two sets of bronze doors for the Baptistery and his statues for Orsanmichele, brought widespread renown to the goldsmith-turned-sculptor.[29] Large-scale works in precious metals had been made in the fourteenth century, such as the silver altar for the Baptistery, but the new statues were outdoors and accessible to a broad audience, and they were understood as expressions of civic pride as much as ornament to important religious buildings. Monumental works in public spaces brought greater prestige and visibility to their makers than the small-scale liturgical objects that had been the most admired expressions of the goldsmiths' art. For artists such as Ghiberti, whose professional and intellectual ambitions would profoundly alter the idea of the artisan for fifteenth-century contemporaries, monumental sculpture in bronze was the ticket to reputation and renown. Domenico must have felt that the skills he had learned during his apprenticeship were inadequate in this new market.

Moreover, the gold industry, including gold beaters (*battiloro*), tinsel makers (*orpellaio*), brass makers (*ottonaio*) and buckle makers (*fibbiaio*) as well as goldsmiths, underwent a consolidation in the fifteenth century.[30] The number of gold workers declined as gold-smiths expanded into the production of objects such as belts and brooches normally produced by specialist makers. Silk manufac-turing in Florence also increasingly engaged gold workers, especi-ally the gold beaters, who supplied metallic thread for fashionable luxury textiles. Indeed, Andrea del Verrocchio famously com-plained in his 1457 *catasto* of little work as a goldsmith, prompt-ing his turn to bronze sculpture and painting.[31] (Though it was in precisely this year that Antonio Pollaiuolo was among the artists commissioned to make the silver cross for the Florentine Baptistery altar, a lucrative and prestigious work, so we should take Verrocchio's complaint with a grain of salt.[32])

Goldsmiths who consciously shaped their reputations might also have been mindful of the precarious survival of their work. Objects in precious metals were not infrequently melted down to recapture valuable gold, silver and gems or to remake them in more up-to-date designs.[33] Changes in taste and economic and political fortunes could therefore lead to the loss of goldsmiths' work. Taxes and special levies for wars also led public and pri-vate owners to give up their gold and silver objects. Ghiberti, in his memoir and theoretical tract, the *Commentari*, tells the tale of one goldsmith – Master Gusmin of Cologne – whose skill equalled that of the ancient Greeks. But Louis, Duke of Anjou (1339–1384), was forced to melt down the works that Gusmin had made 'with such love and art', causing the master to retreat to a mountain hermitage and become a penitent.[34] The direct relationship of gold and silver with money – gold leaf, used by goldsmiths and painters, was fashioned from beaten gold coins – encouraged this practice. For these reasons, the prestige of goldsmithing declined, so that, by the creation of the Accademia del Disegno in 1563, painters, sculptors and architects were included but goldsmiths were not.

Ghirlandaio's turn to painting, then, was perhaps spurred by these concerns. He might also have seen an opening for a painter in the contemporary Florentine market. By 1470, the major painters of the mid-century had passed from the scene: Fra Angelico died in 1455; Andrea del Castagno and Francesco Pesellino in 1457; Domenico Veneziano in 1461 and Fra Filippo Lippi in 1469. Of older artists, Benozzo Gozzoli (*fl.* 1421–97) worked throughout the 1460s outside of Florence, in San Gimignano and Pisa, returning to Florence only in 1495. Neri di Bicci (1419–1491) ran a productive workshop, documented by his *Ricordanze* from 1453 until 1475, but he seldom had prestigious clients, especially in his later career. Cosimo Rosselli (1439–1507) produced few works of significance during the 1460s and, by 1470, his major clients were artisan confraternities. Painters Baldovinetti (*fl.* 1425–99) and Antonio (*fl.* 1432–98) and Piero (*fl.* 1441–96) del Pollaiuolo were involved in the most prestigious commission in Florence in the 1460s: the Chapel of the Cardinal of Portugal in San Miniato al Monte. While Piero del Pollaiuolo executed panel paintings during the 1470s, Antonio gradually shifted his focus to sculpture, moving to Rome in 1484 to undertake the monumental tomb of Pope Sixtus IV. Verrocchio (1435–1488) was primarily a sculptor whose workshop produced panel paintings under his direction but to which he seldom put his brush. Neither Verrocchio nor Antonio del Pollaiuolo were mural painters. Of Ghirlandaio's near contemporaries, Botticelli (1444–1510) had just received his first prestigious commission in 1469, while Filippino Lippi (1457–1504) was still an apprentice in Botticelli's workshop. Just then, Domenico may have sensed an opportunity to make a career as a painter.

Though we do not know who taught him, Domenico must have served a focused apprenticeship to learn specialized skills of panel and fresco painting from the late 1460s to the first years of the 1470s. Vasari says Baldovinetti was 'Domenico's master in painting and in mosaic', and written and stylistic evidence supports this view. Baldovinetti was one of the few Florentine painters who made mosaics, and Domenico's work in mosaic is documented from the 1480s. Born into a patrician family, Baldovinetti may have appealed to Tommaso's and Domenico's social ambitions. In addition, as I will argue in Chapter Three, Domenico's early work in the 1470s shows a lingering influence of Baldovinetti's style, and his approach to his career mirrors to some extent that of Baldovinetti.

Domenico's membership in the guild of Medici e Speziali by the early 1470s extended his network of contacts beyond family. In the society of early Renaissance Florence, as we have seen in Chapter One, family provided the basis for personal identity and professional development. Professional corporations such as guilds, by extending reduced matriculation fees to sons and relatives, assured their survival as social institutions over generations. Members relied on the guild for exercise of their professional activities, political rights and social support. In this sense, the guild became an enlarged family. Understanding the social and dynastic role of guilds might explain Domenico's enrolment in 1473 in the Arte dei Galigai, the leatherworkers guild that his uncle and father had joined in the 1440s.[35] Certainly Domenico did not practise the craft, which was low status, and the guild itself was minor: it has been ranked sixteenth of the twenty-one guilds.[36] Domenico's brother Davide and son Ridolfo would also join the Arte dei Galigai, continuing the tradition of family membership and signalling the evolution of guilds from craft organizations to social clubs that occurred during the fifteenth century.

Guilds also exercised their social roles through the religious confraternities associated with them.[37] As we have seen, by 1472, Domenico was a member of the religious confraternity of St Luke. Founded before 1339, the date of its earliest known statutes, the confraternity was distinct from lay religious sodalities in that its members practised related crafts. Drawn from both the Arte dei Medici e Speziali and the Arte dei Maestri di Pietra e Legname (the guild of workers in stone and wood), its membership by the late fifteenth century included a wide range of occupations such as gold beaters, miniaturists, woodworkers, goldsmiths and painters. Like other confraternities, the Company of St Luke paid medical costs, made weekly payments if a member fell ill or encountered financial setbacks, contributed to a daughter's dowry and organized funerals. The membership came from every quarter of the city, and it allowed members to forge relationships beyond family and neighbourhood.

Domenico and his brother Davide were active members in the Company of St Luke, serving from time to time as members of the governing body. Domenico was one of the four captains in 1477 and 1484, while Davide was one of the three councillors in 1482; he was also appointed procurator, an agent or purveyor, in 1509, and surviving attendance lists indicate that his involvement in the confraternity endured throughout his life. Domenico's son Ridolfo and his brother-in-law Sebastiano Mainardi were also members, as were associates and collaborators of Domenico throughout his career, including Verrocchio, Baldovinetti, Antonio and Piero del Pollaiuolo, Botticelli, Cosimo Rosselli, Filippino Lippi, Pietro Perugino and many more. Baldovinetti may have trained him, and he was deeply impacted by the art of Verrocchio and the Pollaiuolo brothers. Indeed, collaborators in the Sistine Chapel – as we will see, a landmark commission for Ghirlandaio – included Botticelli, Rosselli and Perugino. Another member, the miniature painter Francesco di Antonio del Chierico, would provide an estimate for one of Ghirlandaio's altarpieces in the 1480s. Meanwhile, Davide's painting teacher, the cloth painter Bartolomeo di Giovanni Masini, was an officer of the company in 1482. The professional network based in the confraternity of

St Luke thus inflected Domenico's career in terms of both grand, collaborative projects and mundane exchanges of favour.

Ghirlandaio family members were also long-term and active members of another confraternity, the Company of St Paul.[38] While the company of St Luke was primarily a professional and social organization, the company of St Paul was a religious sodality devoted to the spiritual well-being of its members. The confraternity, founded in 1434, was just one of many Florentine lay brotherhoods founded between the fourteenth and sixteenth centuries. Unremitting plague and war from the second half of the fourteenth century into the mid-fifteenth century drove members to seek solace in confraternity activities. Laymen joined confraternities to venerate saints on feast days, maintain altars, sponsor masses and bury dead brothers. Pious behaviour and obligations prescribed in the company statutes – such as the recitation of daily prayers, fasting, confession, attendance at meetings on feast days and at memorial masses – forged the fraternal bond, while the costume and insignia of the confraternity visualized their union. Through such sodalities, laypersons performed acts of devotion, charity and penance, embracing an active piety.

The confraternity of St Paul was one of the especially devout 'companies of the night' (so-called because they met at night) that performed self-flagellation as part of their devotions. Self-flagellation had long been practised in Christianity, and it experienced a popular revival in the late thirteenth century. A flagellant imitated Christ's suffering during the Passion as penance for his sins. On Saturday nights, the confraternity met in their oratory on the Via dell'Acqua, now part of the present-day Via Guelfa, a short distance to the northeast from the Bigordi home on the Via dell'Ariento. The statutes of the company, newly redacted in 1472, described the ritual of these meetings. Upon arriving, members donned a hooded robe – which assured anonymity – open at the back for purposes of flagellation. Seated randomly in the oratory, they performed the rites of confession, prayer and self-flagellation in darkness and silence. Afterwards, they slept on humble cots in a dormitory, departing the next morning. As such, the ceremony suspended the social hierarchy and patterns of behaviour that governed life outside the oratory. Participating in this ritual must have been an intensely emotional event for each brother, their shared experience deepening personal bonds.

Domenico's father Tommaso joined the confraternity of St Paul in 1448, when he was about 26 years old. Domenico joined in 1470 (aged 21), Davide in 1473 (aged 20) and Benedetto in 1480 (aged 21). Since the statute books, membership lists, attendance logs and some financial accounts survive for the company, we know a great deal about its structure and activities, and we can reconstruct with clarity Bigordi family participation over decades. Tommaso remained an active member until 1484, when, as we saw in the previous chapter, he gave up his role as *pater familias*, although he occasionally attended meetings up until 1502. From 1451, he served in every office, including that of *governatore* – the highest official – in 1455. Domenico and Davide attended meetings regularly during their early years of membership although, as their professional careers gained momentum, they were absent for long periods, when they must have been working outside Florence. They occasionally served as officers but not as frequently as their father did, and they were never *governatore*. Domenico's son Ridolfo would also join the confraternity in 1503 and was sporadically active until 1544.[39]

Membership in the confraternity of St Paul, like several of the other flagellant companies in Florence, was younger, more affluent and more geographically diverse than that of the companies devoted to singing hymns (the *laudesi*). The members' mean age was 37 years old, and their median family net worth – as gauged from the tax returns of 1480 – was 605 florins, compared to the city median of 235 (as we saw, the Bigordi family net worth was 284 florins, representing a decline from the 482 florins of 1469). They were bankers, notaries and goldsmiths, as well as peddlers, tanners, purse makers and barbers, residing in every quarter of the city. St Paul membership embraced major guildsmen as well as artisans, shopkeepers and manual labourers. Lorenzo de' Medici, de facto leader of the Florentine state, served as an officer multiple times and as *governatore* for the first time in 1472, when he directed the revision of the statutes. Although he was a member of several confraternities, he was especially devoted to St Paul.[40]

Domenico's connections in the sodality were familial and professional; his father-in-law, the woolworker Bartolomeo di Antonio di Nuccio, and his brother-in-law, Sebastiano Mainardi, were members of St Paul, as was the family notary, Ser Migliore di Manetto di Masino. Among painters, Filippino Lippi and Francesco di Antonio del Chierico were also members. The confraternity linked Domenico to associates of varying wealth, social standing and profession, connections that enriched his personal and professional life.

We can further reconstruct Domenico's web of personal connections through the family memoirs, which recorded the birth of children and the names of their godparents.[41] Naming godparents or 'co-parents' for children at baptism was a long-standing practice. Godparents were responsible for children's religious education; they held them at the baptismal font, promised their acceptance of Christianity and offered gifts to them and their families. Knit together by bonds of regard and mutual obligation, godparents became spiritual kin of the children and their parents. Choosing godparents was an illuminating indicator of social relationships. As in the confraternities examined above, the web of relationships woven by god-parenthood extended friendship beyond blood kin to a wide range of persons.

Canon law officially limited the number of godparents to three but the true number varied widely, and in some cases children of socially elite families had ten or more. Piero de' Medici had as godparents to his firstborn son Lorenzo (b. 1449) twenty members of the signoria in which he was serving; Gregorio Dati (1362–1435), a silk merchant and diarist, named as godparents to his son Niccolò, born in 1411, all but two of his fellow standard-bearers in the militia company of his neighbourhood, thirteen in all. Multiple children meant that parents named many co-parents; Dati, who had 26 children with four successive wives, recorded 52 godparents in his diary. Many godparents were neighbours of a child's family in the city or countryside, while others were parents' professional associates or business partners. Others were suppliers of goods and services, such as notaries, stationers or shoemakers. Socially, godparents ranged from poor widows and wives of artisans to social equals and superiors. Choosing godparents 'for the love of God' was also an act of charity. In these cases, parents made gifts to the godparents. Clergy were among the recipients, being particularly suited to the role as guardians of religious education. These religious godparents were often from outside the parents' parish, thereby establishing ties of spiritual kinship beyond the neighbourhood.

The family memoirs list godparents for several generations of the Bigordi, including Tommaso's and Domenico's children.[42] Domenico, Tommaso's eldest child, born 2 June 1448, had three godparents: one a priest and chaplain at Florence cathedral, one from the parish of San Frediano in the Oltrarno and the other from Tommaso's home parish of San Lorenzo. Alessandra, his next child, born in 1450 (d. 1464) had a *cimatore* (cloth-shearer) from the parish of Santa Felicita, a shoemaker from the parish of San Lorenzo and Madonna Brigida from the parish of San Pancrazio. Davide (b. 13 March 1452) had godparents including a *merciaio* from the parish of San Pier Scheraggio and a shoemaker from the parish of San Lorenzo. A second daughter, Dianora, born in 1454 (d. 1464), had as godparent Francesco di Agnolo di Antonio Tucci from the Santo Spirito quarter and a member of the Arte dei Galigai, who held minor public offices. He would also be a godparent to Giovanni Battista, born in 1456 (d. 1464). Tommaso's third surviving son, Benedetto, was baptized with Francesco di Antonio del Chierico, holding the infant at the baptismal font. In 1466 another son, also named Giovanni Battista, had as godparents Bartolomeo di Stefano *orafo* (goldsmith), to whom both Domenico and Davide were apprenticed at the time, as well as Giuliano di Nardo da Milano *legnaiolo* (woodworker), plausibly identified as the important woodworker, sculptor and architect Giuliano da Maiano. We know that, up until 1465, the da Maiano family had been next-door neighbours of the Bigordi on the Via dell'Ariento, so their association is not surprising.[43] Alessandra, also 'replacing' her deceased older sibling, was born in 1475 and had as godparents the great *maestro del disegno* Verrocchio with two others, including a *guainaio* (scabbard maker) and a *battiloro* (gold beater). Surveying this group of co-parents, about twenty in all including two women, Tommaso seems to have gradually extended his relations outside his neighbourhood artisan associates to encompass fellow guild members and confraternity brothers, as well as artisans who were important to the careers of his older children Domenico and Davide. Of these, as we will see in the next chapter, Giuliano da Maiano and Andrea del Verrocchio would be especially influential.

Domenico's choice of godparents for his children seems by contrast designed to extend his network of associates across a more elite social and professional range. For his first son Bartolomeo, born 26 June 1481, he named as godparent Giorgio Antonio Vespucci (1434–1514), a tutor to the Florentine elite who eventually became a friar at San Marco and a follower of Savonarola. It was possibly for Vespucci that Domenico painted the St Jerome in Ognissanti (see Chapter Three). The second co-parent was Francesco di Roberto Martelli from the Florentine patrician family, residents in the San Giovanni *quartiere* and close adherents of the Medici.[44] Ridolfo, born 4 February 1483, had as godparent Madonna Pippa Barbadori, a member of a family of silk workers who served in the city councils in 1451. The well-known woodworker Francesco d'Angelo detto la Ciecca and the painter Filippino Lippi, Domenico's fellow brothers in the Company of St Paul, were godparents to Antonia, born in 1484. Her younger sister Francesca, who was born in 1485 but died three days after birth, had as godparents Bartolomeo di Giovanni Masini *sargiaio*, the painting master of her uncle Davide, and the painter Biagio d'Antonio, who had worked in the Sistine Chapel and in the Palazzo Vecchio with Domenico. Baldovinetti, the painter and mosaicist and most likely Domenico's master, was co-parent to Costanza, born in 1487, while Antonio, born in 1489, had the miniaturist Attavante degli Attavanti. Alessandra, born in 1492 (d. 1494), had two *scarpellatori* (stone carvers): one, Simone di Tommaso Pollaiuolo, called il Cronaca, would become a well-known architect. Meanwhile a second Francesca, born in 1493 (d. 1494), had painters Vincenzo da Lucca and Jacopo di Alessandro Tedesco, the latter of whom Vasari named as one of Domenico's students. Domenico's last child was born on 1 August 1494 (d. 1495), after his own death the previous January. He was given the name Domenico, and his godparents were again the painter Bartolomeo di Giovanni *sargiaio* and the unknown Biagio di Michele Monti. Domenico thus chose spiritual kin – eighteen in all, with one woman – strategically to enhance his professional and social identity. His son Ridolfo, who would have eighteen children, chose more than thirty co-parents, many of whom were important officials in the Florentine government, signalling a more overtly political strategy in his choices.[45]

The extra-familial networks that Tommaso and Domenico built through memberships in guilds, confraternities and parentage groups extended bonds of trust and obligation beyond the confines of blood family to a large group within the city of Florence. How Domenico deployed those networks in building his career is the subject of the next chapter.

THREE

Making a Career:
The Itinerant Artist

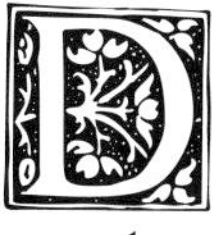omenico Ghirlandaio decided to become a painter in the late 1460s, just as his apprenticeship to the goldsmith Bernardo di Guccio was ending. Vasari's assertion that Alesso Baldovinetti was Ghirlandaio's master has met with scepticism, but there is reason to think that the older master would have been an astute choice for the aspiring painter. During the late 1460s, when Domenico was likely casting his eye on painting as a profession, Baldovinetti was engaged in the most sumptuous and prestigious project in Florence: the decoration of the Chapel of the Cardinal of Portugal in the church of San Miniato al Monte.[1] The chapel was constructed to house the tomb of Cardinal James of Portugal, who died aged 25 in Florence on 27 August 1459. A prince of the Portuguese royal family, his mother Princess Isabella of Portugal and his aunt the Duchess of Burgundy contributed to the chapel's construction, decoration, furnishings and endowment for memorial services. Work began in June 1460 and proceeded rapidly, as can be followed with precision owing to the almost complete survival of the accounts kept with the Cambini bank in Florence by James's estate executors. The chapel was designed by Antonio di Manetto Ciaccheri (1404/5–1460), sometime collaborator of Brunelleschi; by the summer of 1462, stained-glass windows and a glazed terracotta vault by Luca della Robbia (*fl.* 1400–1482) had been installed. The tomb, carved by Antonio Rossellino (1427–1479),

was contracted in December 1461 and finished by 12 September 1466, the day the cardinal's body was translated to his sarcophagus. Rossellino also executed the bishop's throne on the wall opposite the tomb between February and September 1466, while a Roman mason created the inlaid marble floor between July and September.

At the time of the translation, the chapel's lavish furnishings – the gleaming marble and porphyry of the tomb and throne, the brilliant glazed terracotta vault, the rich encrustation of the pavement, and green damask hangings – made for striking effect; but blank surfaces loomed in the lunettes beside the windows, the spandrels of the arches and the tympanum above the throne. The altar, furnished with expensive cloths and a missal, had no painting. This situation was quickly remedied. Baldovinetti, charged with filling 'all the blank spaces' (*tutti e vani*), began painting the Evangelists and Church Fathers in the lunettes that October and had finished them and the frieze with the coats of arms of the Portuguese royal family by November 1467. He filled the spandrels with Old Testament figures in the spring of 1468. He likely painted the panel with the *Annunciation* in his workshop in the winter of 1467–8; it was installed in 1468. Meanwhile, the Pollaiuolo brothers painted the altarpiece, with the panel and frame supplied by the woodworker Giuliano da Maiano (1431–1490), between May 1467 and March 1468. They also painted the angels pulling back fictive curtains on either side of the oculus in the lunette above the altarpiece.

When the apprentice goldsmith Domenico Ghirlandaio stepped into the completed chapel, he would have been struck by its luxury. Baldovinetti's *Annunciation* panel may have drawn his attention for its refined technique, particularly in the rendering of rich surfaces (illus. 8). In sadly reduced condition today, when the picture was new the young artist might have been dazzled by the simulated porphyry and serpentine backdrop and the verdant lawn on which the figures calmly enact the drama of the Annunciation. A closer look at the Angel Gabriel, kneeling in pure profile, would reveal liberal use of gold leaf on his dalmatic and wings. The Virgin's mantle was lined with gold, glazed over with a translucent red pigment, and the cloth of honour behind her was worked in crimson and gold in a pomegranate pattern. The young goldsmith may have studied the coral beads of the angel's diadem, the winged jewel set above his forehead and the pearls lining his bodice and sleeves. He might have been impressed by the figures rendered with precise drawing, rich colours and subtle modelling in light and shade. Mimetic details, such as the reflections of the heads on the gilded haloes, enhanced the impression of visual truth. Domenico's skills in drawing and in coaxing luminous effects from materials such as gold and gems surely heightened his appreciation for Baldovinetti's ability to render them in paint.

Casting his eyes up, Domenico would have taken in the imposing figures of Baldovinetti's Evangelists and Church Fathers in the spandrels beside the windows (illus. 9). Painted in a mixed fresco (on wet plaster) and secco (on dry plaster) technique, they too are poorly preserved, yet hints of brilliant colour and incisive drawing still impress. Floating on clouds, the seated figures grasp books while their cloaks fall in abundant folds, modelled by sharp light and deep shade. Fine details, such as the stubble on St Gregory's chin, hint at the illusionism of their original appearance. The artist of these imposing figures surely had something to teach the young goldsmith about painting on walls in monumental scale. Nor were Baldovinetti's skills confined to painting. He had supplied designs for the stained glass in the chapel, and he had carried out mosaics for the Baptistery in Florence and elsewhere. Domenico's training as a goldsmith – alongside his experience of the dynamic artisan milieu through the professional careers of his family – could well have made him gravitate towards the multifaceted Baldovinetti as his master in painting. Ghirlandaio later made mosaics and designs for stained glass, skills he may have learned from Baldovinetti. Neither the contemporary workshops of the Pollaiuolo brothers nor the virtuoso sculptor Andrea del Verrocchio are known to have taken on these tasks, making it likelier that Ghirlandaio studied with Baldovinetti.

Baldovinetti was also involved, though more peripherally than at San Miniato, in the other great artistic project of the 1460s: the furnishings of the Sacristy of the Masses in Florence cathedral.[2] The north sacristy had been outfitted with panelling and benches between 1435 and 1440/45, but the east (window) and west (entrance) walls remained incomplete. Master woodworkers Giuliano da Maiano and Giovanni da Gaiole were commissioned to complete the decoration in 1463, and it was finished in 1465. In 1464 Baldovinetti noted in his record book that Giuliano owed him 3 lire for having coloured the heads of five figures designed by Maso Finiguerra (1426–1464) for the sacristy: a Virgin, an angel and a St Zenobius plus two deacons.[3] These last three are the exact figures that Giuliano executed in intarsia (wood inlay) in the panels of the east wall (illus. 10). The rather small payment indicates that Finiguerra, a well-known goldsmith and Giuliano's brother-in-law, must have already supplied a drawing for the figures.[4] Baldovinetti's task would have been to specify the modelling of the heads for translation into intarsia.

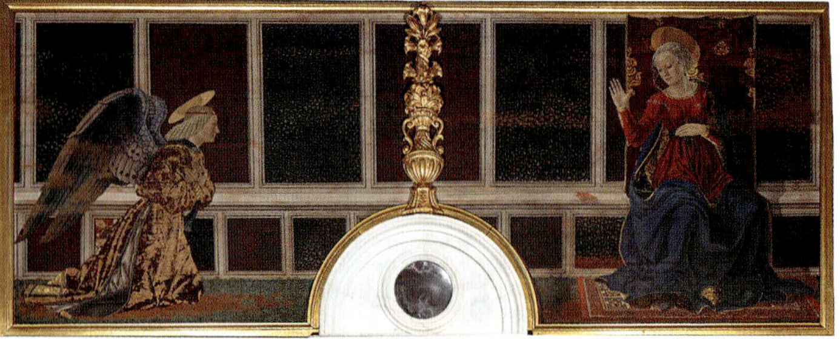

8 Alesso Baldovinetti, *Annunciation*, 1468, tempera on panel, Chapel of the Cardinal of Portugal, San Miniato al Monte, Florence.

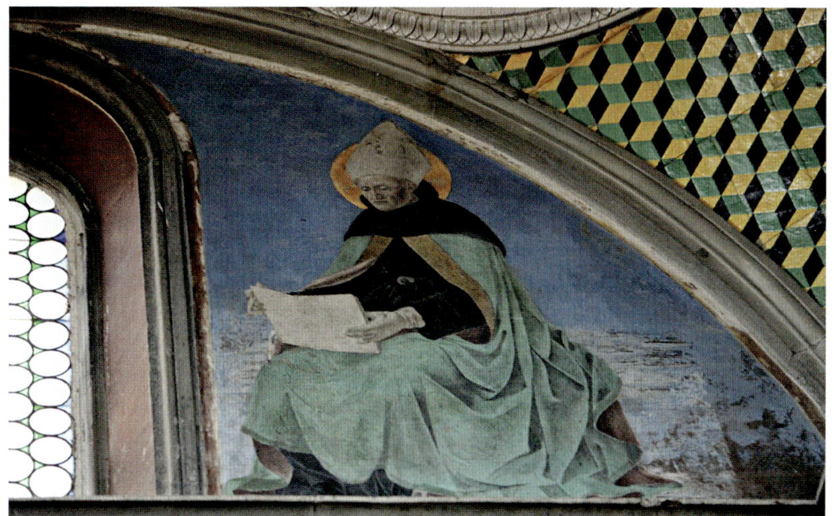

Since the intarsias depended for their verisimilitude on the assembling of differently shaped pieces of wood chosen for their varying colour and texture, the outline drawings supplied by Finiguerra and the chiaroscuro patterns elaborated by Baldovinetti were essential to successfully realized figures. It is also possible that Baldovinetti's designs guided how the woods were to be dyed or glazed to enhance the figures' facial expressions, such as adding red for the lips and cheeks.[5] The division of labour suggests that Giuliano da Maiano designed the architectural setting of the window wall, with its rich architectural detail and dramatic perspective design, but for figures he relied on Finiguerra, with elaboration by the painter Baldovinetti.

Ghirlandaio was probably aware of the cathedral sacristy project not only because of its high-profile location but because he was well acquainted with the da Maiano family. We recall that Giuliano da Maiano had been a godfather to his younger brother Giovanni Battista, born in 1466, and that the family had lived next door to the Bigordi family on the Via dell'Ariento until 1465.

9 Alesso Baldovinetti, *St Augustine*, 1468, fresco and tempera, Chapel of the Cardinal of Portugal, San Miniato al Monte, Florence.

It has even been proposed that the young artist may have designed the figures of St Peter and St Paul for the intrados of the entrance arch in the sacristy, but this idea is difficult to reconcile with the chronology of Ghirlandaio's training as we know it today.[6] These figures were among the last to be set in place in the sacristy, probably by 1468, but Ghirlandaio was still serving his apprenticeship as a goldsmith at that time. Although the figures bear some resemblance to those of Ghirlandaio's early works, for now the question of their authorship must remain open. A professional link with Giuliano da Maiano and his younger brother Benedetto (1442–1497), who was likely also involved in the sacristy project, may have been established at this time and would set the stage for their fruitful collaboration throughout Ghirlandaio's career.

Even if we have no documentary evidence for Ghirlandaio's training as a painter, visual evidence provides clues. The end of his apprenticeship with Bernardo di Guccio and Bartolomeo di Stefano by November 1470 establishes a starting date, confirmed by his inscription in the Company of St Paul in March 1470 where it is noted he was 'with a goldsmith' (*sta all'orafo*). Yet when he was listed as a member of the Company of St Luke in 1472, he was called a painter: *dipintore*. This brief, two-year period when Ghirlandaio became a painter argues for his training to have begun before 1470. One undocumented work that may be the product of his hand at this time is the painting on the left wall of the church of Sant'Andrea a Brozzi in the village of San Donnino, just to the west of Florence.[7] The mural shows the seated Madonna and Child flanked by St Sebastian at the left and St Julian at the right (illus. 11). The figures stand on a narrow terrace with balustrade; beyond is a panorama of hills and a river. The scene is framed by fluted piers with composite capitals supporting an entablature, flanked by panels of simulated green serpentine and red porphyry. The setting refers to the altarpiece of the Pollaiuolo brothers in the newly completed Chapel of the Cardinal of Portugal, where three saints stand on a balcony with distant views.[8] At Brozzi, the side piers and panels and the pavement of porphyry and serpentine slabs reference the classicizing architecture and rich revetment of the Florentine chapel. Certain details reveal the cathedral sacristy as another source of inspiration. The shell niche the Madonna occupies recalls Giuliano da Maiano's panel of *St Zenobius and Two Deacons* on the east wall of the sacristy, and the strong lighting from the left – indicated by cast shadows from the piers, standing figures and the niche – replicate the strong chiaroscuro effect there. Ghirlandaio's design shows that these models were fresh in his mind as he began his painting career.

Above the *Virgin and Child*, Ghirlandaio painted the *Baptism of Christ* in a pointed-arch lunette (illus. 12). Here the scene takes place in a lush landscape, with gentle hills flanking a meandering Jordan River. Christ stands ankle-deep in the flowing stream, while the Baptist leans towards him with his baptismal cup. Pairs of angels, holding garments on the left and poised in adoration at the right, flank the standing figures. The painted moulding

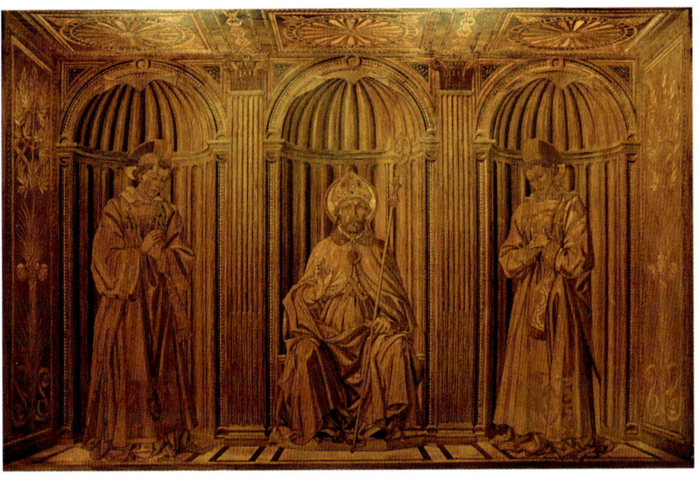

10 Giuliano da Maiano, after design by Maso Finiguerra and Alesso Baldovinetti, *St Zenobious Enthroned with Sts Crescentius and Eugenius*, 1463–5, intarsia, Sacresty of the Masses, Santa Maria del Fiore, Florence.

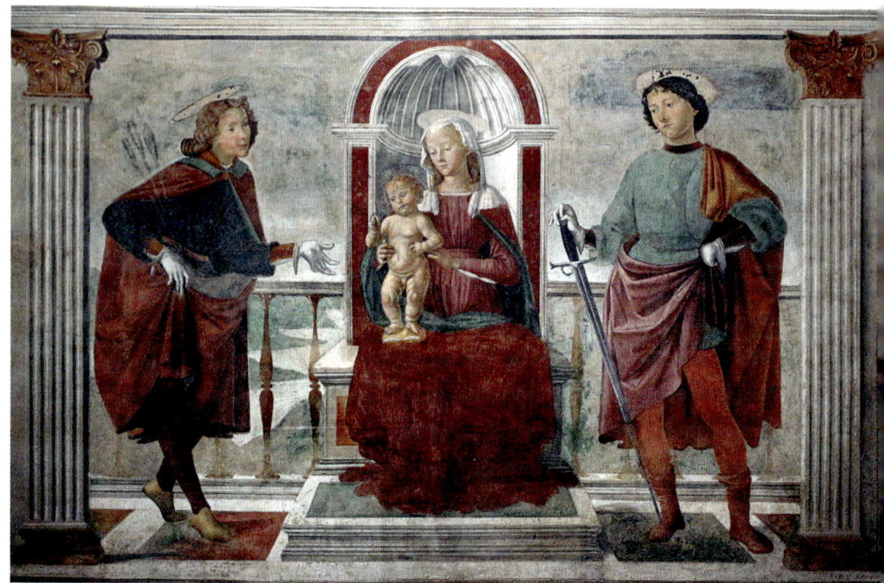

places the figures just behind the picture surface, as the architectural frame does in the scene below. In its general composition, the *Baptism* echoes the famous panel by Verrocchio, with Leonardo's intervention, painted for the monastery of San Salvi and now in the Uffizi.[9] Probably begun in the 1460s, but not completed until the mid-1470s, the panel was certainly known to Ghirlandaio, who seems to have been keenly aware of the most innovative work taking place in Florence. In addition to Baldovinetti and the Pollaiuolo brothers, Verrocchio was engaged in prestigious projects during this time, such as the bronze *Christ and St Thomas* group for Orsanmichele.[10] We might also remember that Tommaso di Currado chose Verrocchio as godparent to Domenico's sister Alessandra in 1475 – that is, at just the time the sculptor was working for important patrons. Although details in Ghirlandaio's mural, such as the poses of the angels on the left and the position of Christ's hands, correspond to those in Verrocchio's picture,

11 Domenico Ghirlandaio, *The Virgin and Child with Sts Sebastian and Julian*,
c. 1470, fresco, Sant'Andrea a Brozzi, San Donnino.

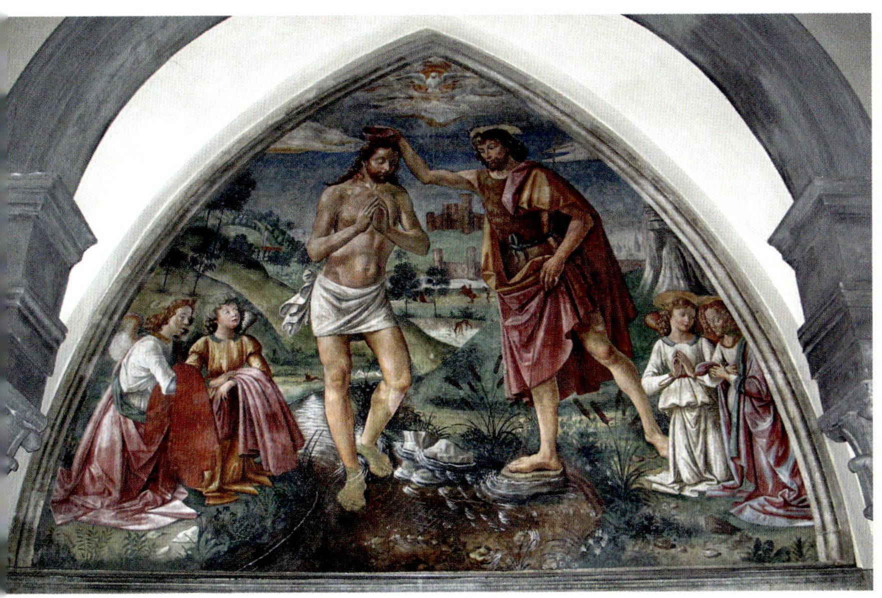

others point to alternative models.[11] That Ghirlandaio was absorbing ideas from many sources reflects the vibrant cultural milieu of Florence about 1470.

A closer look at the figure style suggests how Ghirlandaio assimilated aspects of his models to form an individual style. As we know from the earliest writings about art that emerged during the fifteenth century, developing a distinctive style – a signature or 'look' – was celebrated by critics. About 1400, Cennino Cennini echoed novel ideas about literature that emerged in the fourteenth century, writing:

> If you follow the path of one [master], by continuous practice your mind would be completely flabby not to get some fodder from it. You will then find, if nature has endowed you with a modicum of imagination, that you will end up taking on a style all of your own . . .[12]

12 Domenico Ghirlandaio, *The Baptism of Christ*, c. 1470, fresco, Sant'Andrea a Brozzi, San Donnino.

In this statement, Cennini echoed Petrarch, who likened the creative process to bees gathering nectar: 'Let us write,' Petrarch wrote, 'neither in the style of one or another writer, but in a style uniquely ours although gathered from a variety of sources.'[13] This was not just an aesthetic goal but a commercial imperative. In a competitive marketplace, as Florence was in the late fifteenth century, an artist had to stand out. Building a reputation – *buona fama* – depended on what economists call 'product differentiation' to increase market share.[14] St Sebastian and St Julian in Ghirlandaio's mural bear some resemblance to the saints of the Pollaiuolos' altarpiece in their active poses and elegant hand gestures, but their figural proportions and especially their drapery are markedly different. The Pollaiuolo brothers rendered the rich surfaces of brocade and velvet in an oil medium, while Ghirlandaio painted in fresco, forgoing surface details for a sculptural effect. At the same time, Ghirlandaio's figures bear little resemblance to Baldovinetti's seated figures in the San Miniato chapel apart from their voluminous drapery, which, however, falls in soft, curvilinear folds rather than Ghirlandaio's jagged pleats.

Verrocchio was another artist who shaped Ghirlandaio's early style. The Brozzi St Julian, brandishing his sword in his right hand and resting his left hand on his hip, imitates the poses and drapery style of Verrocchio's sculpture. Ghirlandaio copied the vigorous plasticity and dramatic chiaroscuro of Verrocchio's sculpted and painted figures, though he simplified them to harmonize with Baldovinetti's linear style. Already in the Brozzi murals, therefore, Ghirlandaio was well advanced in his search for a distinctive look.

Ghirlandaio's Brozzi murals also show that he had already mastered the arduous techniques and procedures of wall painting. Fresco (fresh) painting was a method of painting in colours on a wall covered with wet plaster. As described by painting manuals such as Cennini's *Libro dell'Arte* from around 1400, a lower level of rough plaster – called the *arriccio* – was spread over the entire surface to be painted.[15] The top layer of fine plaster to which colours were applied was called the *intonaco*. Since plaster dried relatively quickly, only as much plaster was spread as the artist could paint in a single day, forming patches called *giornate* (from the word *giorno*, or day), which comprise the *intonaco*. Colours were mixed with a slip made of water and lime that, as the *giornata* dried, bonded chemically with the plaster, forming a durable surface of chalky hues and matt tones.

Before the *intonaco* was laid, the painter had to partition the wall into areas for individual scenes according to a drawing of the whole composition, probably a small-scale drawing on paper. Cennini described the process of using plumb lines to fix horizontal and vertical axes, and to adjust the scale of figures and background to the area to be painted. He then described drawing on the *arriccio* in charcoal and diluted red paint to fix his design. Restoration of many murals in the late twentieth century revealed drawings on the *arriccio*, called *sinopie* (from sinoper, the red earth pigment used to draw them).

Ghirlandaio's *sinopia* for the *Baptism* was revealed during restoration and offers insights into his procedure (illus. 13).[16] He drew the *sinopia* freehand with a wide brush over a charcoal sketch. The Christ figure, done in swift strokes that set the major contours, and areas such as where the arms cross his torso, have been anticipated and suggest that Ghirlandaio drew it in reference to a small-scale drawing on paper. The angels at the sides, however, are messy and show changes; the head of the angel just to the right of Christ was drawn three times in different positions, and her arms overlap the lines of her torso. Ghirlandaio must have made a detailed drawing for the Christ but left the poses of the angels to be worked out on the wall in the *sinopia*.

As the artist painted the top layer of plaster, he gradually plastered over the sinopia on the *arriccio*, so for each *giornata* the artist had to paint from memory the design he had just covered up. By the fifteenth century, with the increased demand for life-like figures and settings, 'cartoons' were devised to transfer the designs to the *intonaco* to guide the final execution. The cartoon was a drawing on paper in full scale. Along the major contours, the artist pricked the paper with a needle; this formed holes that, when the drawing was laid onto the wall, were dusted with chalk or charcoal (a process called pouncing or *spolvero*), thus transferring the designs to the surface beneath. The artist needed only to connect the dots to have his design before him. Restoration of the *Baptism* revealed the lower layer of the *intonaco* (called a *secondo strappo*) showing rows of dots along the contours of the angels' faces, a tell-tale sign of cartoon use (illus. 14). He used cartoons in the *Virgin and Child* in the pillow on the Virgin's lap and the body of the child. Another method of transfer was to set the drawing on the soft plaster of the wall and trace the major contours with a pointed object like a stylus.

The mural of the *Virgin and Child* (illus. 11) shows that Ghirlandaio executed the architectural settings by directly incising lines in the wet *intonaco* guided by plumb lines and straight

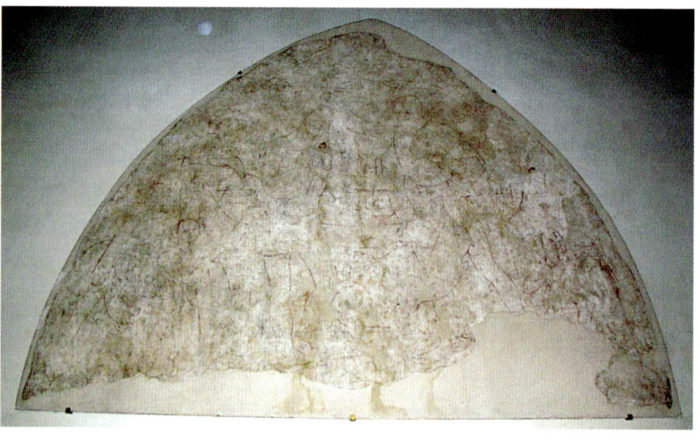

13 Domenico Ghirlandaio, *The Baptism of Christ*, c. 1470, sinopia, detail, Sant'Andrea a Brozzi, San Donnino.

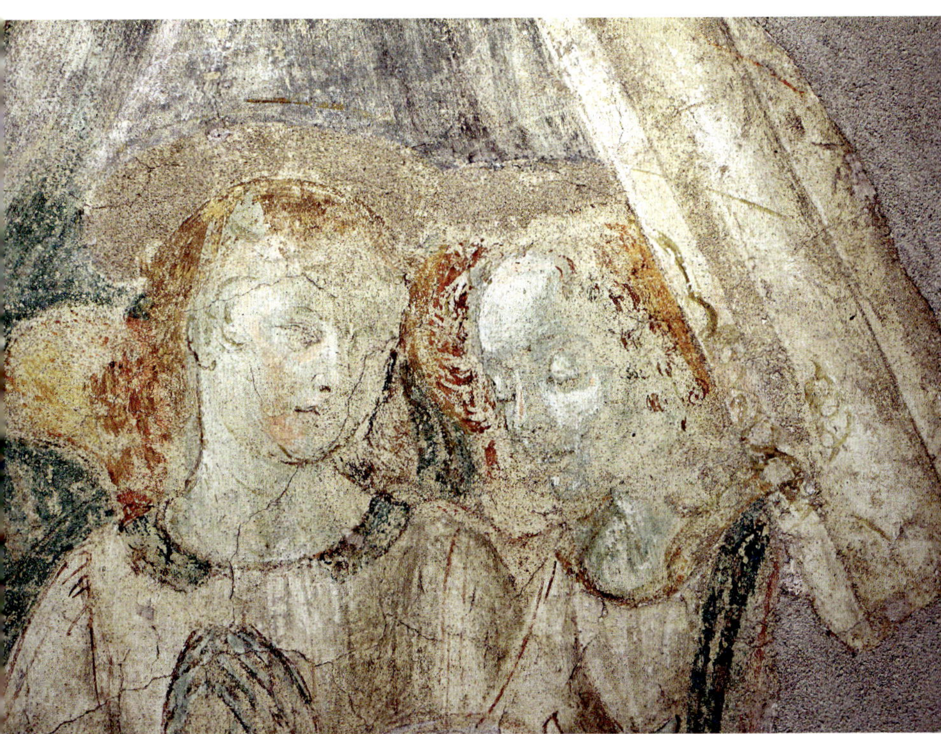

edges. We can see holes where nails were inserted in the wet plaster, and a plumb line stretched between them, leaving diagonal
marks of the twill cord on the surface. The raw incisions where a
straight edge guided a stylus are also visible. These marks do not
cross the contours of the figures, however, suggesting that their
placement in the architectural setting had been fixed beforehand
in a drawing of the whole composition and transferred to the
wall in a *sinopia* on the lower *arriccio* layer. Ghirlandaio may have
used direct incisions in the Virgin's drapery as well, although the
pigment here appears to be repainted and the incisions have
flattened owing to the transfer of the *intonaco* during restoration. Baldovinetti used direct incisions in the drapery of the San

14 Domenico Ghirlandaio, *The Baptism of Christ, c.* 1470, *secondo strappo*,
detail, Sant'Andrea a Brozzi, San Donnino.

Miniato figures, and Ghirlandaio may have been imitating his master's method. If so, he soon abandoned it. Ghirlandaio used different kinds of preparatory drawings – small-scale drawings, *sinopie* and full-scale cartoons – to execute this mural, though only the sinopia survives.

Once Ghirlandaio had transferred his design to the wall, he began laying in the paint. His murals were done in a technique that applies some colours in fresco – that is, on the wet plaster – and some after the plaster had dried. The reason for this is that the alkalinity of the lime in the plaster degrades some pigments, so these were applied after the plaster had dried. Ghirlandaio's pigments were made from a wide variety of materials: animal, vegetable and mineral. Those best for use in fresco include the earth-based pigments red and yellow ochre, lime white and the cobalt-based smalt. Copper-based pigments, such as azurite and malachite, had to be done on dry plaster. Costly ultramarine, made from lapis lazuli imported from Afghanistan, was also frequently applied in secco. Gilding, too, had to be done on dry plaster. The *secondo strappo* from the *Baptism* angels shows the lower layer of *intonaco* before the topmost layer of the paint film was applied. The underdrawings for the angels were done in dark red or a green-brown mixture of yellow ochre, black, white and pink (*verdaccio*), and the underpainting for faces in St John's white (*bianco di San Giovanni*) and the green earth pigment called *terra verde*.[17] The upper layer of paint, using mixtures of red and white in the flesh tones and a range of pigments for draperies and landscapes, were applied in discrete strokes of varying width and direction. Faces were done in a mesh of parallel and crossed strokes, while broad areas of drapery or background with sweeps of a wider brush. In the Brozzi murals, these surface effects are muted, while in his well-preserved murals, such as those that survive from the 1480s, brushstrokes reveal lively execution and vibrant colours.

Ghirlandaio probably painted the apse at the head of the right aisle in the church of Sant'Andrea at Cercina at this time (illus. 15).[18] Though more compact than the Brozzi work, the curving wall presented a challenge, and here Ghirlandaio's architectural frame unites the figures and ties them directly to the spectator standing in the space. The side figures, Jerome and Anthony Abbot, occupy shell niches, while St Barbara stands in a barrel vault at the centre. As at Brozzi, fluted pilasters support an entablature with a foliate frieze. By placing the central figure in the deep barrel vault, with the shallower niches at the side, Ghirlandaio allies the fictive space with the actual space of the apse. The lighting emphasizes this rich ambience: it falls from the left onto the left niche but from the right for the central and right niches, where the figures cast shadows. Barbara tramples the recumbent Dioscorus, her pagan father and tormentor, whose hands jut out over the lower moulding, casting shadows beneath and emphasizing the illusion of bulky figures occupying space. The shell niches, barrel vault and architectural frame again evoke Giuliano da Maiano's sacristy, where the same motifs, light effects and illusionism recur. The male saints were taken from a painting that was produced in Verrocchio's workshop but today is untraced: a *Crucifixion with Sts Jerome and Anthony Abbot.* The St Barbara, however, derives from a panel painted by Cosimo Rosselli for the Confraternity of St Barbara in 1468–9. As at Brozzi, Ghirlandaio interpolates figures drawn from entirely different sources forging them into a distinctive design that integrates statuesque figures into a perspectival space keyed to viewers' location.

If an artist's signature style was a crucial component in making an artistic career, patrons willing to employ him were another.[19] We do not know who employed Ghirlandaio for these early works in provincial sites. At Brozzi, the prominent Florentine family of Ugolino Mazzinghi were patrons of the church, and it is reasonable to think they commissioned Ghirlandaio's fresco.[20] Indeed, a

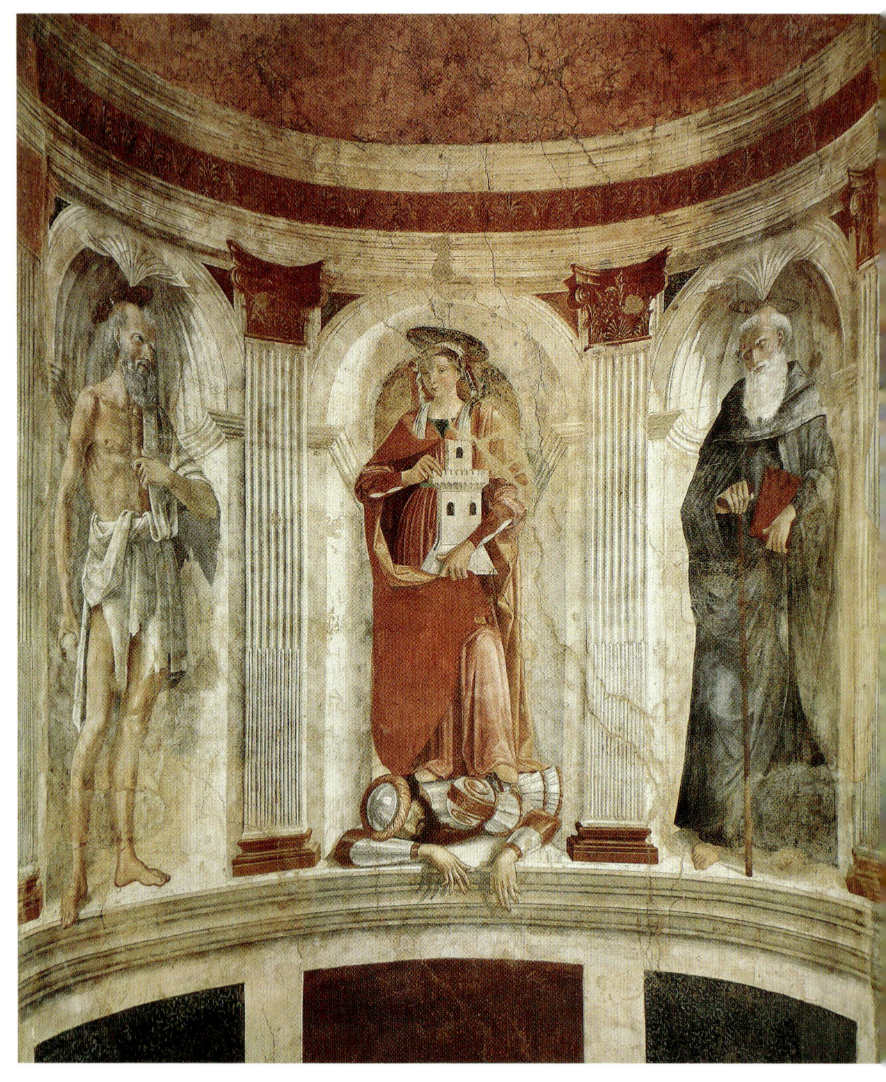

15 Domenico Ghirlandaio, *Sts Jerome, Barbara and Anthony Abbot*, *c.* 1472, fresco, Pieve di Sant'Andrea, Cercina, Sesto Fiorentino.

grandson of Ugolino named Giuliano (b. 1438) has his name saint depicted in the mural. At Cercina, we are on slightly firmer ground, as we know that land adjacent to the church had come to the Ghirlandaio family before 1469 in a dowry. The church itself, despite its remote location, housed a miraculous wooden sculpture of the Virgin, the object of veneration by a lay confraternity, which staged an annual procession from Florence, with prominent figures such as the archbishop St Antoninus (1389–1459; r. 1446–59) taking part. It was from these rather humble beginnings that Ghirlandaio began to forge links with patrons in his early career.

Ghirlandaio painted his first public work in Florence in these same years. A frescoed altarpiece of the *Pietà* with the *Madonna della Misericordia* in the church of Ognissanti adorns the altar of the prominent notary Ser Amerigo Vespucci (1394–1472).[21] The extended family had several chapels in the church, but Ser Amerigo's line, the most recent to arrive in Florence, only gained patronage and burial rights to their chapel just before Ser Amerigo's death. By the terms of a further agreement in November 1473, Ser Amerigo's sons – Ser Nastagio, Bartolomeo and Giorgio Antonio – agreed to erect the chapel in a different location, though still along the right wall of the church, and to follow the design of the chapel of the merchant's guild in the church of San Pier Scheraggio. This Romanesque church was where city officials were elected before the construction of the adjacent Palazzo della Signoria. As the church was largely destroyed, we have no idea what this chapel looked like. Bartolomeo Vespucci was a merchant and may have been the one to stipulate it as a model. Today, Ghirlandaio's murals in Ognissanti, framed by an arched *pietra serena* aedicule, are fragments, but originally they must have been united by a painted architectural frame, as were the murals in Brozzi and Cercina. The subject of the *Madonna della Misericordia* mural was determined by the previous dedication of the original space, and it was retained for the new chapel. The younger Vespucci

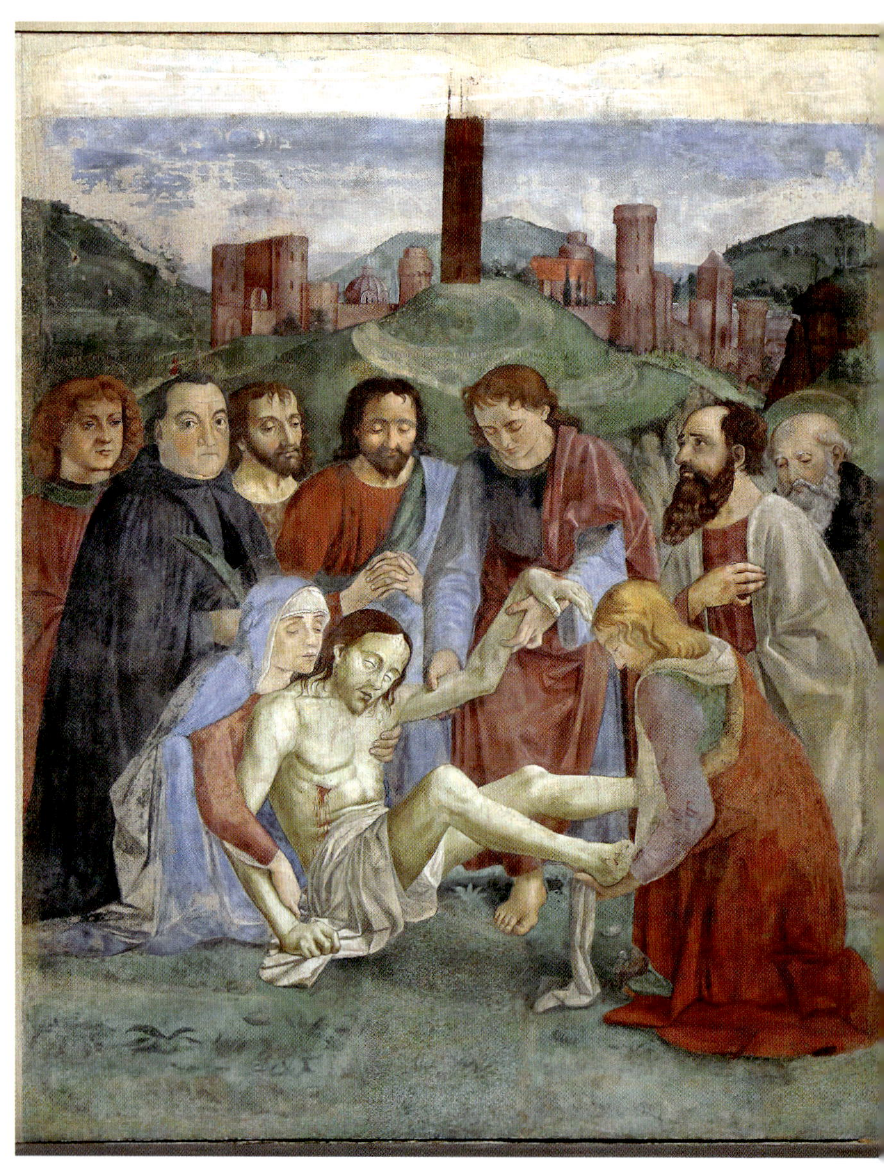

16 Domenico Ghirlandaio, *Pietà*, 1474, fresco, Ognissanti, Florence.

were Ghirlandaio's patrons, then, but we do not know how they came to know the young artist. Why they did not turn to Sandro Botticelli, the up-and-coming artist and their neighbour in Ognissanti, for the chapel's decoration, is also unknown.

If Ghirlandaio looked at Florentine models for his works in Brozzi and Cercina, at Ognissanti he reached much further afield. The *Pietà* depicts the Virgin cradling her dead son, who has been lowered to the ground following the Crucifixion (illus. 16). Mary Magdalene, her long blonde hair uncovered, steadies His feet, while the young St John the Evangelist raises His left arm. Flanking St John are kneeling male figures, including St John the Baptist, Nicodemus and Joseph of Arimathea; the figure in black with a halo clutching a palm may be St Anastasius, name saint of Ser Nastagio. In the distance, the base of the cross and the city of Jerusalem loom. Unexpected is the posture of Christ, who is placed awkwardly on the ground, his legs splayed and fist clenched, recalling His torture on the Cross. His pallor contrasts with the reds and blues of adjacent figures. Few precedents exist in Italian art for this depiction. Instead, Ghirlandaio took as models Northern European images of the subject, such as the painting of the *Lamentation* by Rogier van der Weyden in the Uffizi, which may have been in the Medici collections (illus. 17).[22] The posture of Rogier's Magdalene seen diagonally from behind is echoed in Ghirlandaio's figure, as is her sash, which falls across her back in Rogier's image but encircles her shoulders and falls to the ground in Ghirlandaio's. Tears streaming down the Virgin's cheek emphasize her extreme grief. The compressed figural arrange-ment mimics the flattened effects of Netherlandish spatial schemes. Florentines recognized the affective appeal of these images as distinctive to Northern European art, so it is not surprising that Ghirlandaio would turn to such models, especially for the subject of the *Pietà*. In this case it might have been the patron who directed him. Of the Vespucci brothers, the younger son, Giorgio Antonio,

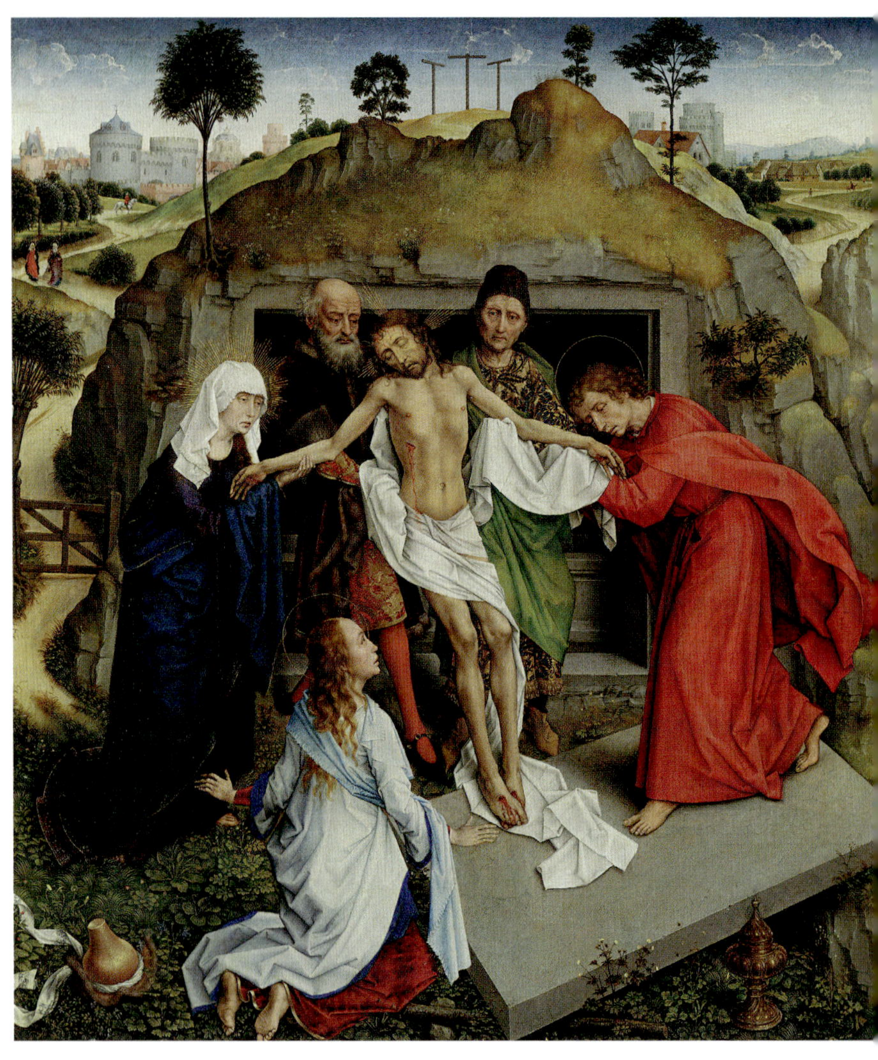

17 Rogier van der Weyden, *Lamentation, c.* 1450, oil on panel.

was a distinguished humanist and tutor, who later became a Dominican friar. Noted for his piety, he perhaps desired a striking image of the *Pietà* in the Flemish manner. Through his scholarly associations and elite students, he might have had access to Northern European images in private collections and arranged for Ghirlandaio to see them.

The *sinopia* for the *Pietà* suggests that Ghirlandaio prepared full-scale figure drawings and assembled them on the wall's surface, as we suspect he did at Brozzi (illus. 18). Ghirlandaio carefully drew the figures on the *arriccio*, probably over a charcoal sketch, for they show greater detail than the Brozzi figures. Inconsistencies in the placement of the figures (where the young St John's leg crosses over the leg of Christ) suggest that their relationship had not been worked out in detail in a cartoon of the whole composition but was resolved only in the *sinopia*. The *spolvero* dots in the draperies of the Virgin and Christ are evidence of cartoon use on the *intonaco*. A drawing of a man's head in the Uffizi shows pricked contours and might be an unused cartoon for this scene. It corresponds to the figure second from the left in the *sinopia* that was replaced in the finished mural by another beardless man who gazes directly at the spectator, possibly St Anastasius. This figure, perhaps a portrait of the patron, was painted on a single patch of plaster and was likely a late addition.

For the image of the *Madonna of the Misericordia* above, Ghirlandaio followed a traditional Florentine composition (illus. 19). The Virgin extends her arms, her expansive cape held up by two angels, offering shelter to the kneeling figures around her. Her elegant stance and the rapt gazes of the worshippers visualize intense piety, while the low viewpoint and the spatiality of the figure group forms a distinct contrast to the scene below. The blocky figures, seen through the cascading, triangular folds of their drapery, seem sturdier than the figures from the Brozzi murals and suggest a slightly more mature and confident artist. Much speculation has centred on the identities of the figures in the *Madonna della Misericordia*. Several of them seem to be portraits, most logically of Vespucci family members, the men on the left and the women on the right, but they are difficult to identify. The man at the far left dressed in the red, fur-lined robe and tall hat of a Florentine patrician might well be Ser Amerigo (he was the notary to the Signoria for many years); or is he the balding man at centre left seen from behind? Is Ser Nastagio, also a notary, the figure at the far left? And, as has been suggested, is Giorgio Antonio the youngish man next to him (he would have been about forty years old when the picture was painted)? The old woman at the far right is a widow, her white veil marked with the identifying black stripe, so she can't be Ser Amerigo's wife Nanna, who predeceased him, nor is she likely to be Ser Nastagio's wife Lisabetta, who was about forty years old at this time and not yet a widow. The figure with the bishop's mitre in profile at

18 Domenico Ghirlandaio, *Pietà*, 1474, sinopia, Ognissanti, Florence.

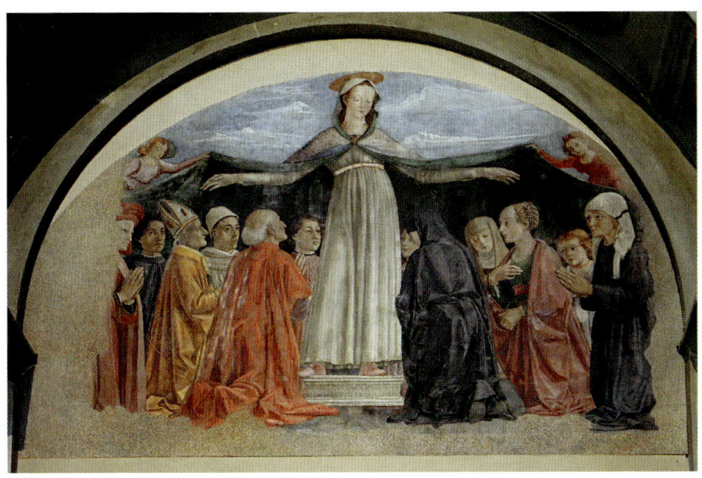

the left has been thought to be Archbishop Antoninus, but he had died in 1459 and any close connection to the family is unknown. The visage of the famous explorer Amerigo (b. 1454) is sometimes identified in this image, but since he was a grandson of Ser Amerigo and this image seems to depict the generation of the chapel's patrons, it is unlikely that he was included.

The Vespucci murals, Ghirlandaio's first for a prominent Florentine patron, are an important marker for his artistic persona in the early 1470s. As we know from contemporary writings, an artist's distinctive look, or style, was thought to have proceeded from two parts: first, his skill (in Latin *ars*, in Italian *arte*), meaning his facility in deploying the specialized operations of his craft; and second his talent or creativity (*ingenium, ingegno*), that is, his capacity for inventing new designs. Cennini would say around 1400 that painting required imagination (*fantasia*) coupled with manual skill (*l'operazione di mano*).[23] Based on the Vespucci murals, we might say that Ghirlandaio's mastery of the technique of fresco was evident, but so was his command of perspective, especially in arranging the blocky figures of the *Madonna della Misericordia* in a

19 Domenico Ghirlandaio, *Madonna della Misericordia*, 1474, fresco, Ognissanti, Florence.

semi-circle around the Madonna and foreshortening the group
to accord with the low viewing point of the spectator. The *Pietà*
in its original condition no doubt showcased his ability to transcribe surface detail and light effects in the Flemish manner. Both
would have shown off his talent for portraiture. His creativity in
re-imagining scenes of the *Pietà* and *Madonna della Misericordia* in
novel and compelling designs must have been appreciated by the
Vespucci, who employed him on later commissions. And these
aspects of his personal style propelled his emerging reputation.

Ghirlandaio probably painted these murals during the first
half of 1474, after the minimal structural work for the chapel
had been done. He had likely finished by September 1474, when
the attendance records of the Company of St Paul, which he had
joined in 1470, recorded a three-month absence.[24] His brother
Davide was also absent, and it is likely that they were engaged in
commissions outside Florence. We have no evidence of what these
might have been, but that Davide was with Domenico indicates
that their long collaboration had begun.

The brothers Ghirlandaio next appeared in Rome, where on
28 November 1475 Domenico was paid 10 gold ducats by the
librarian of Pope Sixtus IV, Bartolomeo Sacchi, known as il Platina
(1421–1481), for paintings in the library, which had been founded
by Pope Nicholas V in 1451 to house Greek and Latin books.
Further payments to his brother Davide extend to May 1476.
These payments were for the eight lunettes with busts of classical philosophers, Latin church doctors, St Thomas Aquinas and
St Bonaventure (whom Sixtus canonized in 1482) that decorated
the Latin library in the Vatican Palace (illus. 20).[25] Though these
murals, like those already discussed, are in sadly reduced condition,
their impact in the small space of the Latin library is striking. The
chamber, divided into groin-vaulted bays, is lit by windows and
was most likely filled with desks. The lunettes, formed by the
intersection of the walls with the vaults, were high above the

viewers' heads, the painted figures set against blue sky, their names inscribed beside them. Framed by painted swags of oak leaves, referring to the emblem of the della Rovere pope (the word *rovere* means oak), the figures hold banderoles filled with quotations from their writings. Their scrolls flutter over balustrades ornamented with classical mouldings and a wide acanthus frieze, surmounted by classical urns filled with foliage. Some of the figures lean over the balustrade to engage the spectators below; Aristotle, for example, leans to his left, his banderole proclaiming: 'The roots of education are bitter, but the fruit is sweet.'

Aspects of the design of the murals indicate challenges the artists faced. The architecture and figures are drawn as if seen head on, but several figures lean forward to address spectators below, and the flanking vases are foreshortened. Some figures are oddly different in scale from others. The technique – tempera, in which pigments are bound with egg, over a priming layer of fresco – is unlike Ghirlandaio's earlier murals, and the top layer of plaster is mixed with *pozzolano*, the volcanic ash found in Rome. The scale and position of the murals, high on the walls, is also unlike that of earlier projects. The different materials of the

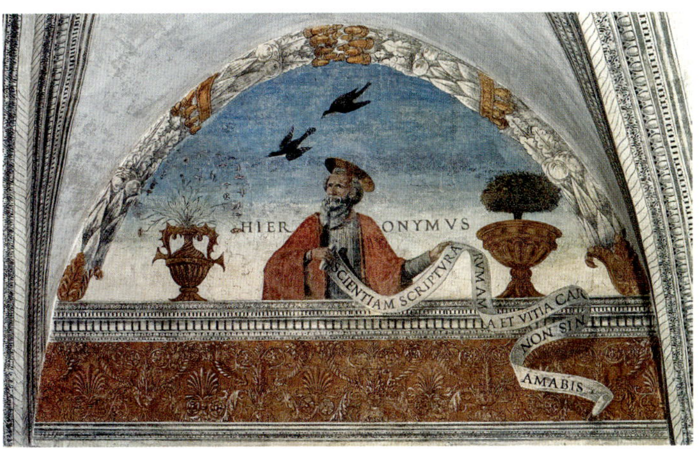

20 Domenico Ghirlandaio, *St Jerome*, 1475–6, fresco, Vatican Apostolic Library.

Roman walls and the execution of the paintings during the colder months – between November and May – required painting on dry plaster. What's more, the payments suggest that Davide primarily carried out the painting based on Domenico's designs. Evidently the brothers were adjusting to a new way of working together, strictures imposed by the site and the Roman milieu. Domenico's collaboration with Davide probably did not begin until after December 1472, when the younger artist's apprenticeship with the banner painter Bartolomeo di Giovanni Masini ended, so it was still new.

In addition, the brothers could not fail to take account of the intellectual and visual traditions of Rome. At the Vatican, Sixtus IV's campaign to restore the glory of ancient Rome pervaded all new ventures, including the library, which referenced the great libraries of antiquity. Pliny described the Roman library of Asinius Pollio (76 BCE–4 CE) as sumptuously decorated with portrait busts of ancient authors. The humanist outlook of members of the papal court such as Platina also shaped the imagery, which visualizes the union of ancient learning with Christian thought. The overwhelming presence of antiquity in Rome could not fail to impress the young artists and is seen in the rich vocabulary of architectural ornament in the murals. The monumental scale and grandeur of Roman remains shaped the figures too, which are more ponderous than earlier figures, even in their reduced state. The daring illusionism of Roman late quattrocento painting, examples of which were near to hand in the Vatican palace – the Roman settings of Fra Angelico's murals for Nicholas V's Vatican chapel (1448), the architectural fantasies of the adjacent Greek library (1454) and possibly lost works by the consummate perspectivist Piero della Francesca in the papal apartments (1458–9) – could not fail to impress the young painters.

The library murals, while less than successful artistically, had a decisive impact on Ghirlandaio's art and career. Surely working in Rome at the Vatican was a plum opportunity for the artist's career. Platina managed the library project and was likely his employer.[26] How did he meet the young Florentine? We have seen that Ghirlandaio's earlier works were for provincial sites, and the only Florentine patrons we know of were the Vespucci brothers. The youngest – Giorgio Antonio Vespucci – was, however, a humanist and bibliophile who had since the 1450s been building an impressive library.[27] In addition, during these years, Giorgio Antonio was an active teacher whose students were sons of the Florentine elite, including the Medici. Perhaps Platina's ties to the social and intellectual elite in Florence brought Ghirlandaio to his attention?

Ghirlandaio had left Rome by June 1476, when he and Davide were painting the *Last Supper* in the refectory of the Vallombrosian monastery at Passignano, south of Florence in the Val di Pesa (illus. 21).[28] The monastery – where Giovanni Gualberto (*fl.* 985–1073), founder of the Vallombrosian order, spent his later life – had been expanded during the tenure of the abbot Isidoro del Sera (r. 1445–85), who constructed the refectory and cloister. How the Ghirlandaio brothers came to the abbot's attention, we can only surmise. The convent was an important holy site that was richly endowed, and del Sera was an associate of political elites in Florence. He may have heard of the Ghirlandaios' work in the Vatican from them or from members of the papal court. The very short interval between the Roman work and the commission in Passignano argues for a connection through the clerical elite in Rome or Florence.

The mural was painted quickly between late June and 1 September 1476. Payments show that the brothers divided the work similarly to their arrangement in Rome; Domenico was present at the first and last payment and on 5 August, having 'done the faces' (*fatto e visi*), he returned to Florence. We can imagine that Domenico was responsible for the overall design of the mural

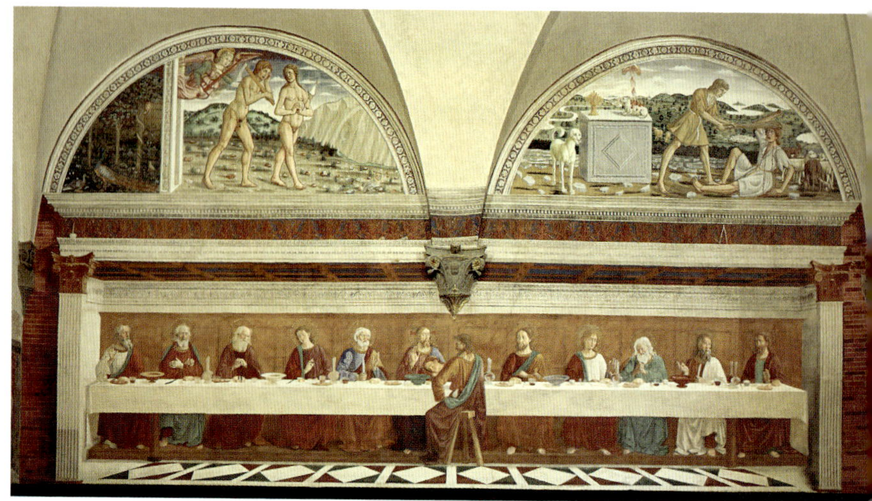

and the execution of the cartoons (whose traces are visible on the wall), and Davide for the rather stiff execution. The faces, however, confirm evidence of the payments: the apostles' animated expressions, painted by Domenico, contrast with their wooden gestures and monotonous drapery, most likely Davide's handiwork (illus. 22). The recent cleaning of the mural has revealed telling details, such as reflections on the glass carafes and tiny vignettes of a compass, a plumb line and an inkwell resting on painted architrave. The elegant architectural details, particularly the palmette frieze of the entablature and the inlaid wood wainscoting of the apostles' bench, show the new sensitivity to classical ornament that Ghirlandaio developed in Rome. These are coupled with an increase in the weight of the figures, with broad shoulders and voluminous drapery, compared to the Vatican library busts. Ghirlandaio has subtly altered the Florentine template for the *Last Supper*, a mural by Andrea del Castagno in the convent of Sant' Apollonia (*c.* 1447), by depicting it as a space separate from but continuous with that of the refectory, filled with a diffuse but

21 Domenico Ghirlandaio, *Last Supper*, 1476, refectory, Badia, Passignano, Tavarnelle Val di Pesa.

directed light that creates atmosphere. His drive for spatial clarity and links between real and depicted space recalls earlier works in Brozzi and Cercina, but here they are realized with greater consistency and on a larger scale.

Ghirlandaio's first murals that survive in good condition are in the funerary Chapel of Santa Fina in San Gimignano.[29] The tiny hill town, halfway between Florence and Siena, was part of the Florentine territorial state but retained its proud cultural identity in the fifteenth century. Central to that identity was its local patron saint, Santa Fina, a young girl whose piety and asceticism exemplified Franciscan ideals. Santa Fina died in San Gimignano at the age of fifteen in 1253 and was buried in the *pieve* (baptismal church) called the Collegiata. She was beatified in 1481 but never canonized. In 1457 the city fathers decided to build a new chapel for her tomb as part of a plan to remodel the Collegiata, but the work was not carried out until much later,

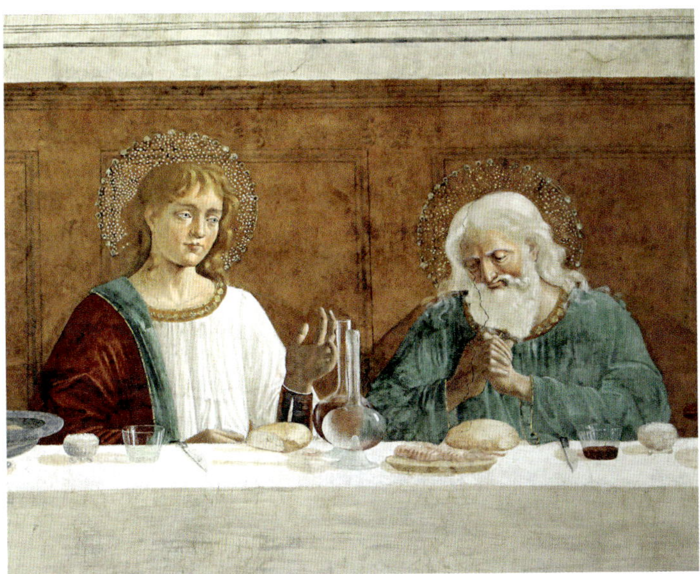

22 Domenico Ghirlandaio, *Last Supper*, detail.

between 1468 and 1473 according to a design by Giuliano da Maiano. The combined tomb and altar were begun by Giuliano's younger brother Benedetto in the autumn of 1475 and finished by 30 November 1477, when it was immured. Ghirlandaio then painted the side walls of the chapel with scenes from the saint's brief life. He must have finished by 23 May 1478, when the Opera (the governing board) allocated funds 'to satisfy those to whom it owes money for painting of the chapel and construction of [Santa Fina's] tomb', and when Domenico and Davide were working again at Passignano.

How Ghirlandaio came to the attention of the communal officials in San Gimignano is not known, but Baldovinetti, Ghirlandaio's probable master, had supplied blue pigments to the *operaio* (administrator) of the *pieve* for painting the vaults of the nave in autumn 1474, and Domenico might have been one of the artists paid for this work in February 1475. That Baldovinetti recommended the young painter is likely. Ghirlandaio would have participated in the nave painting in the *pieve* after the paintings in Ognissanti in Florence, which were finished by autumn 1474, and before the Vatican library commission, which were begun in November 1475. The *operaio* responsible for the projects in the *pieve* was Onofrio di Pietro, who was well connected with Florentine officials and may have heard about Ghirlandaio from them.[30] He may also have been in contact with elite clerics such as Abbot Isidoro del Sera in Passignano or Platina in Rome.

A recommendation may also have come from the da Maiano brothers. They were, as mentioned above, well acquainted with Ghirlandaio through family and professional ties; in particular, Benedetto – Domenico's near contemporary – was building his career in parallel with the painter. Giuliano, primarily a wood-worker in his early career, by the 1460s had expanded his activity to include architectural design, of which the San Gimignano projects were among the first. Benedetto, ten years Giuliano's junior and trained in the family workshop, also gained initial fame as a woodworker. In 1473 he made an elegant daybed (*letuccio*) for the banker Filippo Strozzi to give as a gift to King Ferrante of Naples. As related by a contemporary, Benedetto – who had also trained as a sculptor – then decided to give up woodworking and turn to marble sculpting. Benedetto's decision was confirmed by his enrolment in the guild of the masters in stone and wood in 1473 and the enlargement of the family workshop the same year. The San Gimignano tomb was among his first commissions for large-scale marbles. Paralleling Ghirlandaio's turn from goldsmithing to painting, Giuliano's pivot to architecture and Benedetto's pursuit of work in marble suggest that, when building their reputations and careers, ambitious artists sought the prestige attached to monumental public works in durable materials.

As crucial as patrons were to building artists' careers, professional collaborators such as, for Ghirlandaio, the da Maiano brothers were equally key. Commissions such as the Chapel of the Cardinal of Portugal and the cathedral sacristy were showcases of superb artistry and decorative unity where, as we have seen, teams of artisans worked in concert. Patrons relied on artists to bring in their équipes competent assistants and trusted suppliers of specialist materials. Networks of professionals, such as we have seen Ghirlandaio building in his early career, underlay the production of luxury cultural products that dominated the Florentine artistic scene in the 1460s. San Gimignano was the first instance of Ghirlandaio participating with Giuliano and Benedetto da Maiano on a monumental project but would not be the last, and it locates him at the centre of this world of elite artisanship.

Giuliano da Maiano designed the Chapel of Santa Fina as a smaller, less opulent version of the Chapel of the Cardinal of Portugal. A Greek cross plan with shallow projecting arms, it occupies the northwest corner off the nave, adjacent to the north transept (the Collegiata had its main chapel in the west and facade in the east). Pacing through the medieval body of the church, visitors to the chapel must have been startled by its classical architectural vocabulary and rich ornament (illus. 23). Fluted pilasters with Corinthian capitals flank the entrance arch. The elevation is repeated on the three sides of the chapel, with the altar and tomb on the north wall and the murals on the east and west walls. The entablature, showing heads of seraphim and cherubim in the frieze, unites the three sides. Instead of the stone inlay of the San Miniato chapel, the floor was covered in glazed terracotta tiles, sadly no longer extant, and the vault frescoed rather than ornamented in terracotta.

Ghirlandaio painted his murals in the arched fields formed by shallow recesses: the *Annunciation of the Death of Santa Fina* on the right and the *Funeral of Santa Fina* on the left, both incidents taken from the rich hagiographic literature (illus. 24–5). On the right, the saint reclines on a wooden plank, her head held up by her nurse Beldia; her ascetic life led to bodily weakness such that she could not move and so she rested on the plank as a form of penance. St Gregory the Great, pope from 590 to 604, appears in a mandorla of seraphim, raising his hand in blessing and announcing her death on his feast day eight days later, 12 March. Her death is also shown, her soul borne aloft by angels and the oak plank sprouting flowers, in accordance with legend. While Beldia gazes at St Gregory's apparition, her companion stares blankly, alluding to another incident in the saint's life when she saw the Devil but others could not. The contrast in awareness underscores the miraculous nature of the saint's vision. By conflating three different moments – the vision, her death and her soul's ascent – Ghirlandaio adopted a traditional mode of visual storytelling. From early Christianity the church permitted depictions of Christ's and saints' lives as the 'bible of the illiterate', in St Gregory's formulation, and throughout the Middle Ages narrative imagery

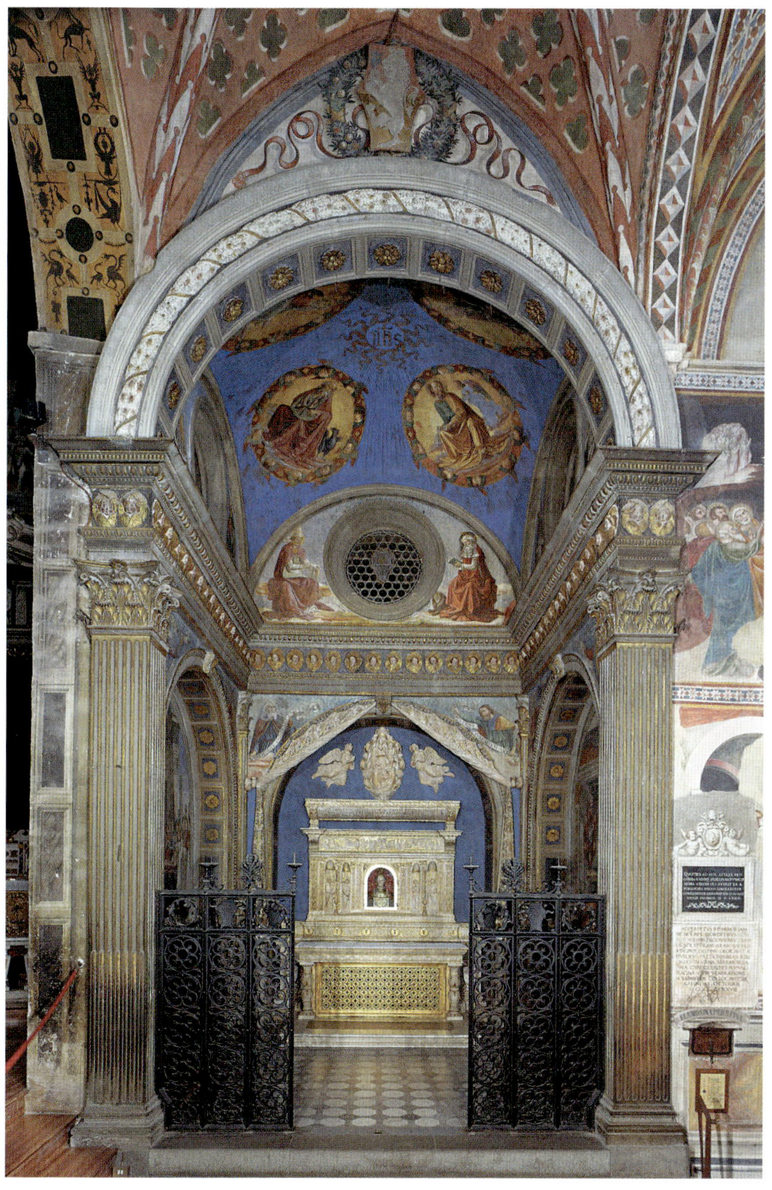

23 Chapel of Santa Fina, 1468–77, Collegiata, San Gimignano.

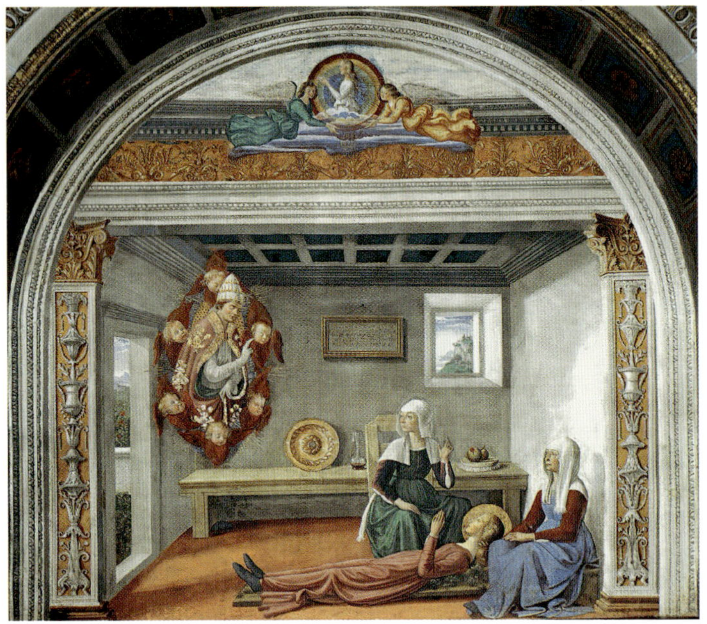

proliferated. In the *Annunciation of the Death of Santa Fina*, Ghirlandaio depicts multiple incidents that prompt viewers to recall the full account of Santa Fina's life. And yet, the figures occupy a room that appeals to viewers' everyday experience. A salver, carafe and pomegranates atop a circular box rest on a low bench, while roses bloom in a garden glimpsed from the door on the left; through the window on the right, we see a lush landscape. Light streams through the door and window, illuminating the scene and contrasting with the gilded rays from St Gregory's mandorla. The clearly designed space and the solid figures make the miraculous events concrete for viewers. The quotidian objects resonate with deeper meanings. Their prominence also recalls Flemish conventions of symbolism. The plank evokes Christ's cross, and the salver and carafe the bread and wine consecrated in the Mass. The pomegranates signify the Resurrection, their dark red colour

24 Domenico Ghirlandaio, *Annunciation of the Death of Santa Fina*, 1477–8, fresco, Collegiata, San Gimignano.

resembling blood. Each detail emphasizes parallels between the saint's and Christ's life, suffering and death, presenting Fina as *alter Christus* – another Christ – as was St Francis of Assisi. At the same time, the inscription on the plaque on the wall urges the saint: 'Prepare yourself, my daughter, for on my feast day you will join our company, and with your bridegroom you will be celebrated forever.' The reference to the bridegroom implies that Santa Fina is the bride of Christ and her death is her reunion with her spouse, drawing parallels between Santa Fina and the Virgin Mary, widely understood at the time as the bride of Christ. The glimpse of the walled garden filled with roses at the left is also an allusion to Mary.

In the *Funeral of Santa Fina*, the saint lies on a bier covered with gilded brocade, flanked by citizens and clerics, including the

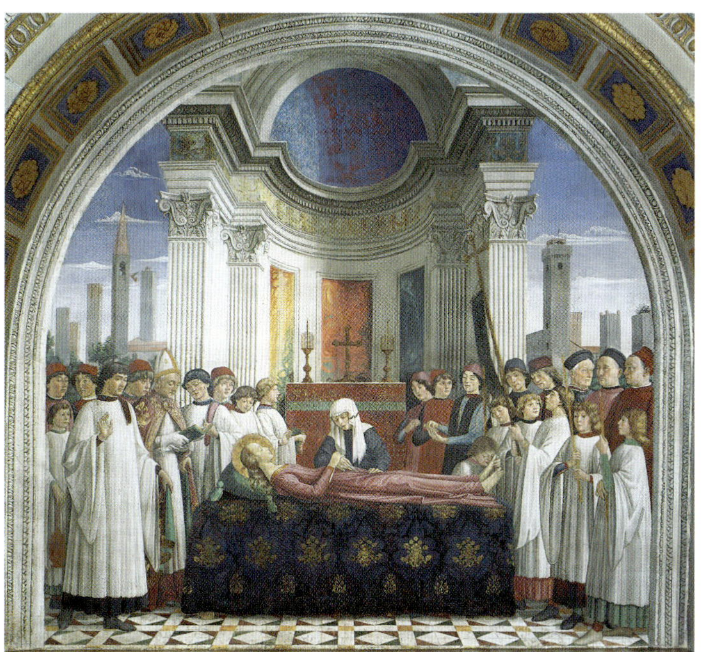

25 Domenico Ghirlandaio, *Funeral of Santa Fina*, 1477–8, fresco, Collegiata, San Gimignano.

bishop who conducts the funeral rite. A massive apse-like structure shelters an altar with a crucifix and candelabra. At left and right, the distinctive towers of San Gimignano appear against a blue sky. Once again, Ghirlandaio draws from the legends of Fina's life in showing miracles she performed (the funeral itself is not described in her biographies). The saint strokes her nurse Beldia's withered hand, healing it, while the blind child who caresses her foot is also cured. In the left distance an angel flies towards a bell tower, alluding to the spontaneous ringing of bells at the saint's death. The youth counting points made in argument perhaps refers to the commune's contemporary effort to canonize the saint, which was ultimately unsuccessful. The three men standing at the far right are likely portraits; the one in the centre of the group has been identified as the *operaio* Onofrio di Pietro, who commissioned the chapel and its furnishings. In both scenes, the almost motionless figures seem suspended in time, absorbed in contemplation. The emphasis on the miracles in the saint's brief and uneventful life is entirely appropriate, as are the references to contemporary figures and events. In what is probably his first monumental cycle, Ghirlandaio thus crafted a distinctive narrative voice that visualizes sacred historical events and endows them with immediacy and authenticity.

In the framing and depicted architecture, Ghirlandaio responded to Giuliano da Maiano's classical architectural vocabulary. In the *Death of Santa Fina*, piers with classicizing urns supporting an entablature with palmette designs in the frieze frame the scene. In the *Funeral*, the massive apse structure again mimics the elevation of the chapel itself. In each, the painted frame of the picture field crops the architecture, suggesting expansive space beyond the spectator's view. In the chapel vault, Ghirlandaio placed seated Evangelists encircled by heads of cherubim, with St Bernardino's emblem – the letters IHS (Jesus, Saviour of Men) on a blazing sun – at its centre. In the lunettes, church fathers flank the round windows, while in the spandrels on either side of the arched recesses, Old Testament prophets unfurl scrolls. Inscriptions, taken from their writings, underscore themes of Santa Fina's chastity and faith. The church fathers, including St Geminanus, holding in his lap a model of the walled city, and St Augustine, author of *The City of God*, present San Gimignano as a holy city.[31]

By the time Ghirlandaio had finished the San Gimignano chapel murals in late spring of 1478, his name was becoming known in other towns of central Italy. Though in a minor site, they demonstrated Ghirlandaio's technical skill and his inventiveness in visualizing holy stories and rendering them vividly in paint. Between December 1478 and February 1479, he was working in Pisa for the Opera del Duomo, painting in the '*sala grande dell' Opera*' images of the Madonna and Child and the Coronation of the Virgin.[32] The Opera in Pisa, the board of works that managed the cathedral complex – the cathedral, baptistery, bell tower and cemetery – occupied the Casa dell'Opera in buildings along the northeast perimeter of the Piazza del Duomo. The *sala grande* was the large meeting room on the first floor where deliberations likely took place. The artist was paid a nominal sum, the equivalent of about 6 florins, over a period of two months, so the two works were probably wall paintings that no longer survive. Comparison with the payment for the *Last Supper* in Passignano, about 18 florins excluding materials over two months, suggests that these works in Pisa were not extensive. They may have been part of an on-going campaign to beautify the room.[33]

Although the *sala grande* paintings no longer exist, Ghirlandaio's work for the Pisan Opera del Duomo is significant. The Opera was at this time headed by the administrator Antonio di Jacopo dalle Mura, who was trained as a goldsmith and was charged with supervising the myriad projects in the cathedral complex. Appointed in 1461, he had often employed Florentine artists and had excellent relations with officials in Florence, to whom, as a part of the Florentine territorial state, Pisa was answerable.[34] So, although he is not documented as working for the Opera in Pisa again until the 1490s, Ghirlandaio's connection to the *operaio* was perhaps useful to his career.

During this first stint in Pisa, Ghirlandaio may also have painted altarpieces for a local church. Vasari, the sixteenth-century biographer, describes two pictures by Ghirlandaio in the church of San Girolamo dei Gesuati. Two panels in the Museo Nazionale di San Matteo in Pisa, both showing the Madonna and Child with standing saints, are likely the pictures that Vasari identified. These are among the first of Ghirlandaio's surviving altarpieces, and they reveal his emerging personal style and panel painting technique. Most of his surviving early works are wall paintings, as we have seen, leading scholars to assume that he specialized in murals, and this might have been a prevailing view among contemporaries. Ghirlandaio may have undertaken monumental and public paintings on walls to build his reputation; but as we will see, paintings on panel – especially altarpieces as foci of devotion in important churches – were equally prestigious works with important audiences.

The *Madonna and Child with Sts Catherine of Alexandria, Stephen, Lawrence and Dorothy* (illus. 26), the better preserved of these two paintings, is a *sacra conversazione* (sacred conversation), an image type developed in the earlier fifteenth century in Florence.[35] It depicts the holy figures occupying a unified pictorial space: the Madonna and Child sit on a throne, while standing saints cluster at the sides. The panel signals Ghirlandaio's continued engagement with the workshop of Andrea del Verrocchio, first noted in his mural in Brozzi from about eight years before. Ghirlandaio's Christ child, resting on a cushion balanced on his mother's knee, reaches towards her with both hands as she offers him a rose. The Virgin's drapery shows the deep wedge-shaped folds

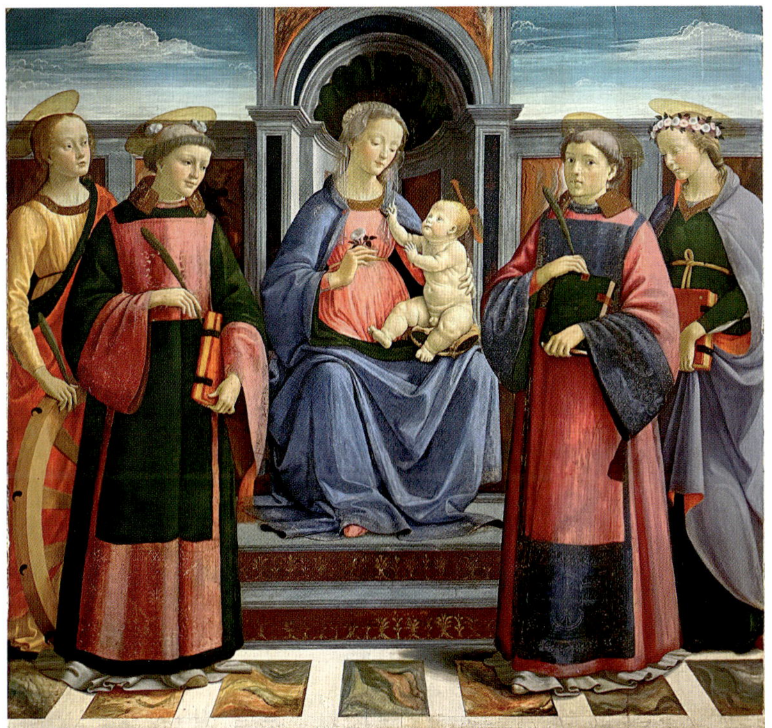

seen in the figures in Passignano, sculpted by light falling from
the right. The figures' poses seem inspired by a picture by the
young Leonardo da Vinci (Verrocchio's famous pupil), the *Virgin
and Child with a Carnation*, where the Virgin and Child interact in
the same way. The pudgy Child is also like Leonardo's. Leonardo's
bulky figures and focused chiaroscuro are, however, foreign to
Ghirlandaio's picture.[36]

The church of San Girolamo dei Gesuati, which no longer
exists, was the seat of the Gesuati order in Pisa.[37] Founded in the
fourteenth century, the order supported its pious works by producing herbal medicines and other concoctions, among them
pigments for painting and stained glass.[38] We know that, later in

26 Domenico Ghirlandaio, *Madonna and Child with Sts Catherine of Alexandria,
Stephen, Lawrence and Dorothy* (?), 1478–9, tempera on panel.

his career, Ghirlandaio purchased pigments from the Gesuati in Florence and Pisa. At this date, however, we do not know how he might have come to the attention of members of the order or its supporters. Very likely, the *operaio* Antonio di Jacopo dalle Mura recommended him. The completion of two altarpieces for the order's new church might have also led to another altarpiece commission, that for the church of the order's seat in Florence: the church of San Giusto fuori le Mura.

Before we consider this important work, however, we must turn to another altarpiece painted at about the same time as the two Pisa pictures (illus. 27). The picture, again a *sacra conversazione*, we know was painted for the church of San Martino in Lucca sometime after July 1476, when the patrons – cathedral canon Fra Pietro di Lorenzo Spada and Fra Clemente del fu Antonio Andrucci – founded an altar in the church.[39] It may have been part of a campaign by the *operaio* of the cathedral, Domenico Bertini, to systematize the church interior by commissioning new altars along the aisles. They procured a panel for the painting only on 2 December 1478, so Ghirlandaio must have painted it only after he finished work in Pisa in February 1479. The panel, slightly larger than the Pisa picture but oriented vertically, was moved to the sacristy at an unknown date and placed in a marble frame in 1853. The Virgin and Child occupy a tall throne, flanked by Sts Peter and Clement on the left, the name saints of the patrons in the place of honour, and Sebastian and Paul on the right. Unlike in the Pisa picture, the saints occupy different levels: Peter and Paul on the foreground pavement, Clement and Sebastian on the step behind. The Child stands on a pillow perched on the Virgin's knee, as at Brozzi. The most striking aspect of the painting is the gold brocaded silk curtains that hang from a rod at the top edge of the panel and are pulled to either side behind the saints. Crafted in gold leaf with tooling and red glazes in a pomegranate pattern, the drapes evoke the finest luxury silk textiles, for

which Lucca was a historical centre of production.[40] The striped
carpet that unfolds down the steps to the Virgin's throne might
also recall local textile production. Glimpses of landscape and
blue sky flank the Madonna's throne, creating a sense of deep
space, but the spatial configuration of the foreground is confusing.
The back of the Virgin's throne is behind the curtain, while the
saints stand before it. They pivot towards the Virgin, but seem
constrained by the shallow space, delimited by the curtain, carpet,
steps and inlaid pavement. Their placement on different levels
emphasizes the flat surface of the panel, so strongly asserted by
the curtains. Such spatial ambiguity is unlike the clear stereometry
of Ghirlandaio's approximately contemporary works, such as the
Death of Santa Fina mural in San Gimignano of 1477–8. Yet the
soft glow of light, which falls from the left, engulfs the figures in
a warm atmosphere, clarifying their relationship to one another.
The fine modelling of the figures, minutely transcribing changes
in tone as the lighted surfaces turn into shadows, and the rounded
folds of drapery signal a retreat from the dramatic lighting and
jagged fold vocabulary of earlier works such as the *Virgin and Child*
at Brozzi. It is likely that the patron requested the prominent
textiles in the painting to display the luxury silks made in Lucca
or, as has been suggested, to reference the famous Volto Santo
housed in the church of San Martino. The Volto Santo crucifix,
sculpted in wood, was thought to have been made by Nicodemus,
who was present at the Crucifixion. As a true image of Christ, it
was the focus of processions on feast days, when it was dressed in
special garments. The curtains in Ghirlandaio's image, tied back
to reveal the holy figures, evoke these festive events centred on
the Volto Santo.

We know that Ghirlandaio returned to Florence from Pisa
on 20 February 1479, the day after his last payment from the
Opera, because on that day he collected the dowry for his marriage to Costanza di Bartolomeo di Nuccio.[41] We do not have

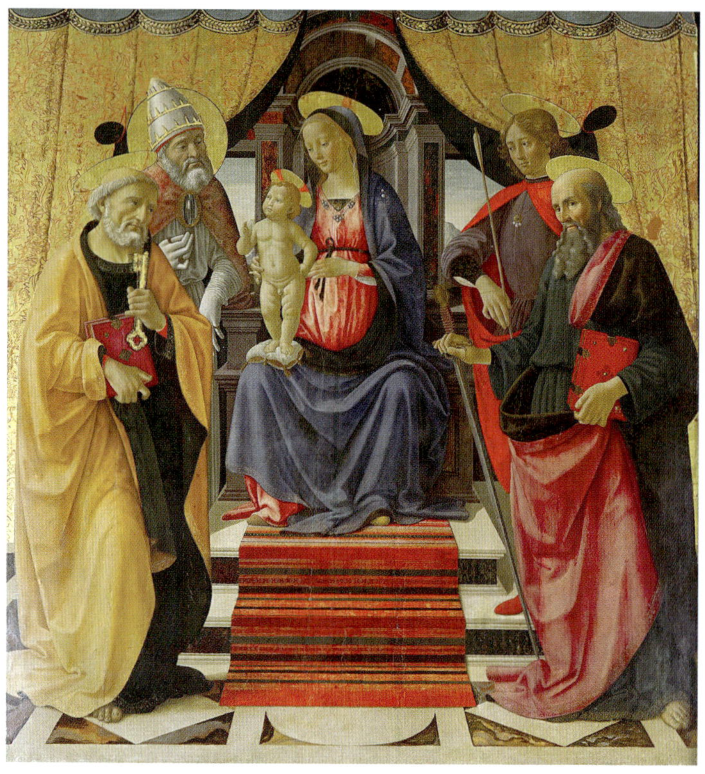

documented activity for Ghirlandaio during the next two years, but we assume he was in and out of Florence, and he may have produced a number of works during this time. One is the Gesuati altarpiece mentioned above, now in the Uffizi (illus. 28). Noted in early guides to Florence, Vasari saw it only after it had been moved following the destruction of the church and convent of San Giusto during the siege of Florence in 1529. Vasari also described the monastic complex, which was extensive and lavishly decorated by wall paintings and panels by Pietro Perugino and others.[42] Ghirlandaio's high altarpiece depicts the Virgin and Child seated in a jewel-bedecked throne, flanked by Sts Michael

27 Domenico Ghirlandaio, *Virgin and Child with Sts Peter, Clement, Sebastian and Paul, c.* 1479, tempera and gold on panel.

and Raphael, with St Justus of Volterra, patron saint of the church, and St Zenobius, a patron saint of Florence, kneeling in the foreground. Before the Madonna, an elaborate Anatolian carpet with geometric motifs unfolds, on which a vase of flowers rests.[43] Angels holding lilies cluster around the throne. An arcade with a straight entablature supported on carved balusters extends to either side; beyond, orange trees flower and fruit, and distant vistas reveal blue sky and hilly terrain. St Michael, perched on the step just below the Madonna's throne, turns gracefully to view the Madonna, while Raphael looks out towards the spectator. The bishop saints kneel on the foreground pavement and gaze reverently upwards at the holy figures. The light falls from the left yet is suffused, and figures cast shadows on the pavement; St Michael's left arm casts a shadow on his adjacent thigh.

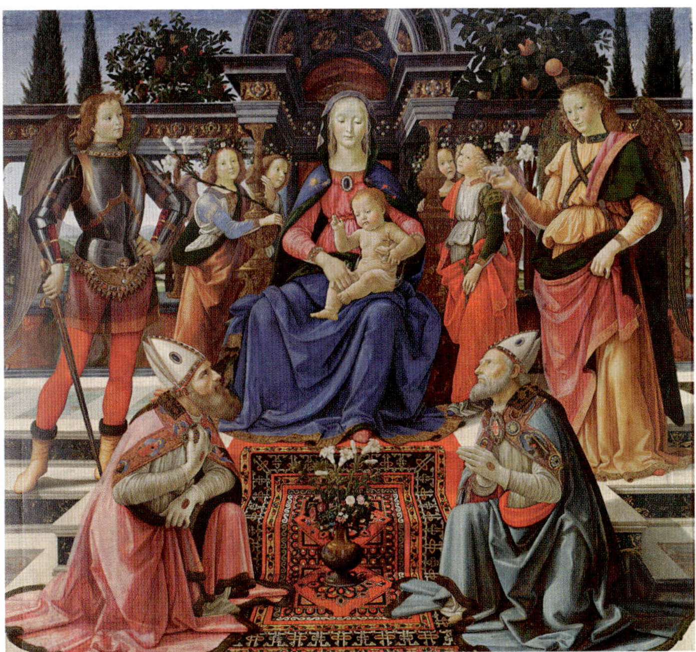

28 Domenico Ghirlandaio, *Virgin and Child with Sts Michael, Justus, Zenobius and Raphael, c.* 1480–81, tempera on panel.

In its spatial design and detail, the composition reflects yet another work from Verrocchio's shop: an altarpiece painted for an oratory in Pistoia cathedral.[44] The oratory was constructed at the behest of Bishop Donato de' Medici and the altarpiece commissioned by the executors of his estate after his death in 1474. Verrocchio designed the painting, called the *Madonna di Piazza*, between 1474 and 1479, and he may have begun painting it – but only about 1485 did his faithful pupil, Lorenzo di Credi, finish it. The design and execution reveal Verrocchio's desire to distil the *sacra conversazione* image type to its essentials. The space is ample, defined by the classicizing throne and flanking entablatures, the landscape views, the tiled pavement and especially the carpet that spills down the steps before the Virgin, its fringe lapping over the foreground edge. At the left, St John the Baptist extends his right foot forward, pointing to the Virgin, while at the right St Donatus turns, his hand on his breast. An atmosphere of suffused light softens the ample draperies, while the rich colours and glittering highlights on the carpet, on the capitals of the throne and on the flowers in the urns atop the entablature enliven the scene. Ghirlandaio's picture by contrast celebrates descriptive richness, especially of the throne with its gilded, pearl-studded frieze and the intricately embroidered robes of the bishop saints. Yet the surfaces of the faces and drapery are more abstract and almost sculptural compared to those of Verrocchio's painting.

Vasari praised Ghirlandaio's ability to replicate in paint light effects on metal surfaces; and he especially praised St Michael's armour, in which reflections of the light source at the left and of his red leggings are seen. Ghirlandaio's training as a goldsmith is evident in the variety of jewelled brooches worn by the Virgin and kneeling saints, by the jewelled edging of St Michael's breast-plate and the gem-studded bishops' mitres. The picture was an important commission for a prestigious convent, and Ghirlandaio lavished attention on every part, showcasing his skill, creativity and distinctive look. It marks the end of almost a decade of Ghirlandaio's independent activity, and it sets the stage for the altarpieces of the 1480s and '90s.

Ghirlandaio's panel paintings from the 1470s show mastery of technique distinct from wall painting, owing to their smaller size and different materials. They reveal that Ghirlandaio followed the traditional steps for preparing panels as described by Cennini.[45] The panels themselves were often assembled and planed by woodworkers, but they were prepared for painting in the artist's workshop. Poplar wood, used by most Italian painters, is rough and absorbent, and so a preparatory ground had to be applied before paint or gold leaf. Cennini described how to make animal skin glue and mix it with gypsum (hydrated calcium sulphate) for the ground layer, called *gesso*. It was normally applied in two stages, a coarse form, *gesso grosso*, and a fine form, *gesso sottile*, forming a smooth, white surface for painting and gilding. Onto the *gesso* ground layer, the artist sketched his design freehand or transferred it from a cartoon, using either the *spolvero* or incised method. Ghirlandaio generally used a brush and a liquid medium containing carbon black, as described by Cennini, for these drawings. Sometimes the underdrawings are visible with the naked eye in places where the paint has become translucent with time, as often happened with red lake, a pigment derived from insects.

No cartoons for Ghirlandaio's panel paintings survive, but we can be sure that he made them throughout his career. Evidence of his preparatory process can be found in the lowest layers of his paint film. These layers can be investigated using scientific techniques developed from the twentieth century. Infrared reflectography has revealed underdrawings beneath the paint film of several of Ghirlandaio's panel paintings. Infrared reflectography uses the part of the electromagnetic spectrum beyond visible light.[46] Opaque paint, when examined under the long wavelengths of the infrared spectrum, becomes transparent, revealing the layer

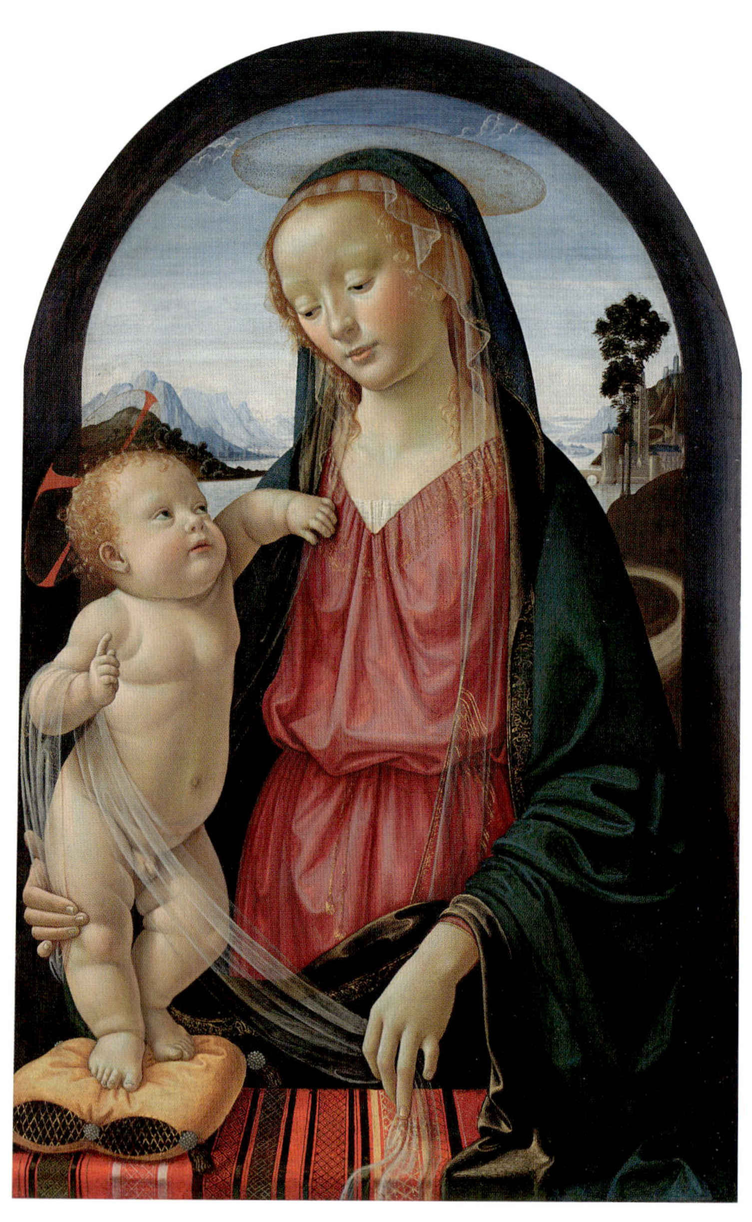

29 Domenico Ghirlandaio, *Virgin and Child*, *c.* 1478, tempera, oil and tempera grassa on panel.

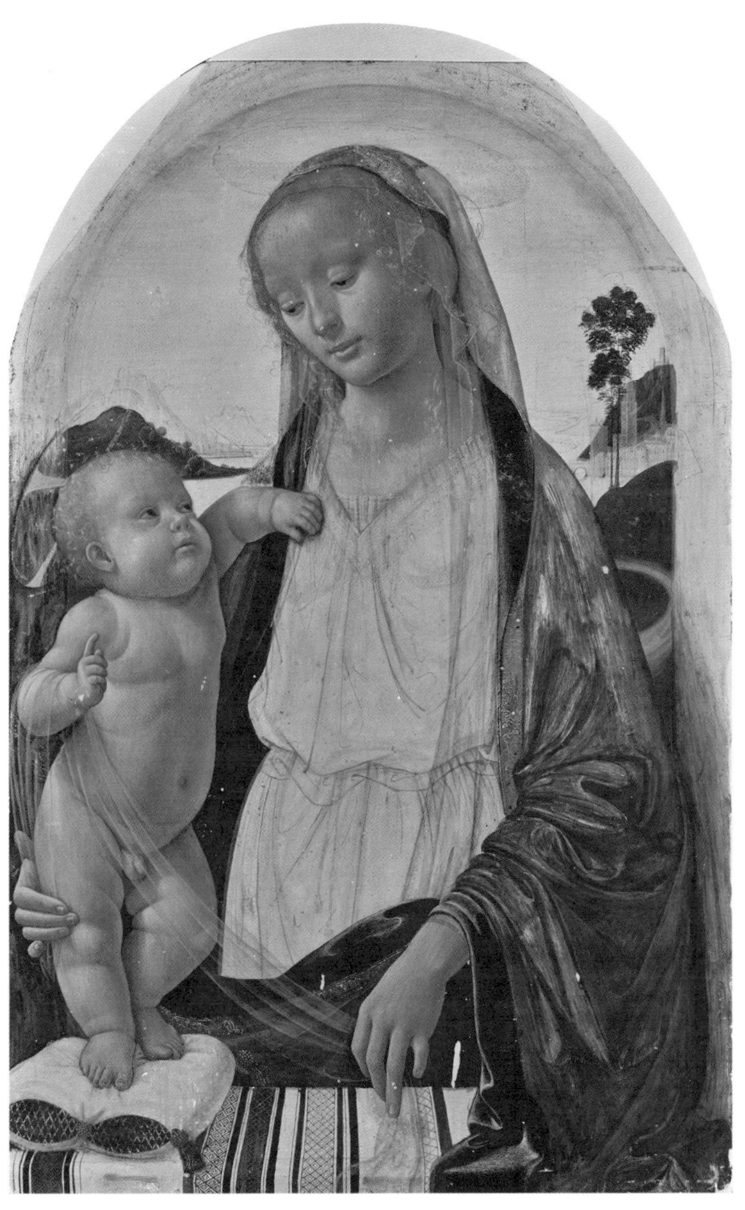

30 Domenico Ghirlandaio, *Virgin and Child, c.* 1478, infra-red image showing underdrawing.

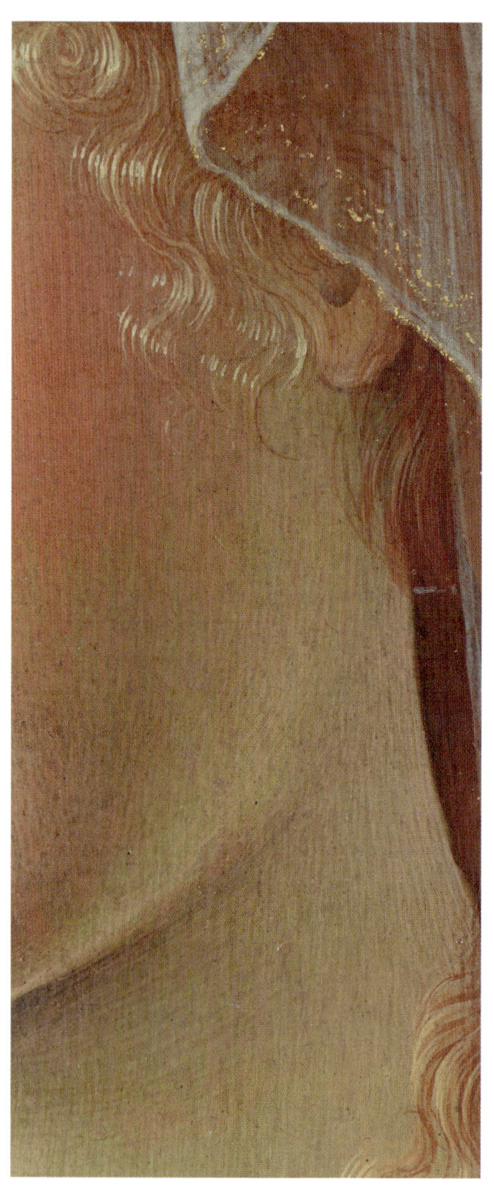

31 Domenico Ghirlandaio, *Virgin and Child*,
c. 1478, detail.

of the underdrawings. Some materials, however, such as copper-based pigments and certain kinds of ink or chalk, are not revealed by infrared. Moreover, since infrared penetrates several layers of the paint film, it can be difficult to tell which markings belong to which layer, leading to misinterpretation.

The panel of the *Virgin and Child* from about 1478 currently in the National Gallery, London, shows an underdrawing executed freehand in brush with long, curving strokes to indicate drapery folds (illus. 29–31). The strokes are occasionally doubled to make slight adjustments to the contours of the figure, but the under-drawings do not show extensive hatching or undermodelling in wash. These underdrawings are likely abbreviated in nature because the design had already been worked out in a fully mod-elled version on paper and transferred to the panel. The artist then made further changes while applying the paint. The landscape underdrawing is looser and more improvised, suggesting, as with the *sinopia* for the *Baptism* in Brozzi, that the preliminary drawings concentrated on the figures.

The underdrawing for the San Giusto altarpiece, executed a year or two later than the London picture, shows a similar exe-cution. The drapery was drawn with continuous strokes of the brush, perhaps over a pounced cartoon. Although no residue of the charcoal dust dots has been detected, they may have been erased after the brush drawing was done, as Cennini recommended. These underdrawings are functional tools for transfer and play little part in the creative evolution of the design, and they have limited aesthetic appeal in themselves.[47] As such, they are not indicative of Ghirlandaio's basic approach to form. In the finished painting, draperies especially do not always follow the under-drawing, as is visible with the naked eye for the red draperies of the saints.

Ghirlandaio's painting technique was traditional, but it evolved from his early works to the later ones to embrace new materials, especially the use of oil as a medium.[48] While figures were transferred by cartoon, the backgrounds were done using direct incisions made with the aid of a straight edge in the soft *gesso* ground, as they were on walls. Ghirlandaio usually mixed his pigments with egg, forming egg tempera. Egg yolk is an emulsion of fatty material suspended in egg protein in water. Because the water evaporates quickly after the paint is applied, it cannot be blended or worked when wet, nor can it be applied thickly to build up a textured surface. Instead, colours must be mixed before they are applied to the panel in discrete brushstrokes laid side by side to form thin layers. When dried, the paint forms a smooth, durable surface of opaque colours with a chalky sheen.

When well preserved, the surfaces of Ghirlandaio's panels – such as the National Gallery, London's *Madonna and Child* from 1478 – reveal his meticulous touch. He painted skin tones over a traditional layer of green earth, covered with a thin, transparent brown layer in the shadows (probably green-brown *verdaccio*) or mixed with lead white in the light areas. The flesh tones were applied with the point of the brush in long, hatched strokes, creating a loose web through which the green earth is visible. White and pink flesh tones were a mixture of lead white and vermilion, and they retain their vibrancy. In the draperies, Ghirlandaio used red lake mixed with lead white for the Virgin's tunic and azurite in a medium of walnut oil for her mantle. The red lake of the striped cloth covering the foreground balustrade was applied in a mixture of oil and egg, and the green of the striped cloth was also mixed with oil. Ghirlandaio's use of oil medium is rare at this date, but it must have been chosen to impart a greater richness to the blue, which has unfortunately darkened with time. It shows that Ghirlandaio treated each colour area individually to achieve the visual effect he wanted. Tempera painting facilitated this approach as colour areas are strictly defined with sharp contours, akin to the patchwork of *giornate* that comprise a fresco.

The *Madonna and Child* from about 1476, now in the National Gallery in Washington, DC, is less well preserved, but it shows subtle variations in the depiction of gold and metal threads (illus. 32).[49] Since Ghirlandaio was trained as a goldsmith, sensitivity to the effects of gold – either real gold leaf (beaten into thin sheets) or simulated in paint – is not surprising. The Washington panel's original background, now replaced, used gold leaf, and traces of the original gold are detectable under the contours of the Virgin's and Child's heads. Shiny metallic gold leaf applied over a mordant (a sticky material applied with a brush) is also used in the cuff of the Madonna's right sleeve and in the Child's curls. In her mantle, painted in ultramarine, gold is simulated using lead tin yellow (an opaque yellow pigment) on the border, while mosaic gold is used in the dark green brocaded lining. Mosaic gold (made of tin sulphide) was not as shiny as mordant gilding and shows that Ghirlandaio carefully deployed his materials to vary subtly their luminous effects.[50] The use of mosaic gold, unusual but found in paintings attributed to Verrocchio, is a strong argument for Ghirlandaio's proximity to Verrocchio's workshop in the mid-1470s, when this painting was likely completed.[51] Verrocchio's versatility and prestigious commissions drew up-and-coming artists to his shop, and Ghirlandaio was likely among them. Also indicative of his closeness to the older master is the violet tunic and twisted striped sash of the Child as well as the pearl-studded brooch of the Virgin, props that recur in paintings from Verrocchio's workshop.

Around 1480, Ghirlandaio was again working for the Vespucci family in the church of Ognissanti in Florence. The *St Jerome* was probably painted for Giorgio Antonio Vespucci, the humanist and cleric, so the choice of the saint who translated the Bible into Latin is not a surprise (illus. 33).[52] We might also recall that in June 1481 Ghirlandaio named Giorgio Antonio Vespucci as a godparent for his first child, Bartolomeo.[53] The picture formed a pendant to

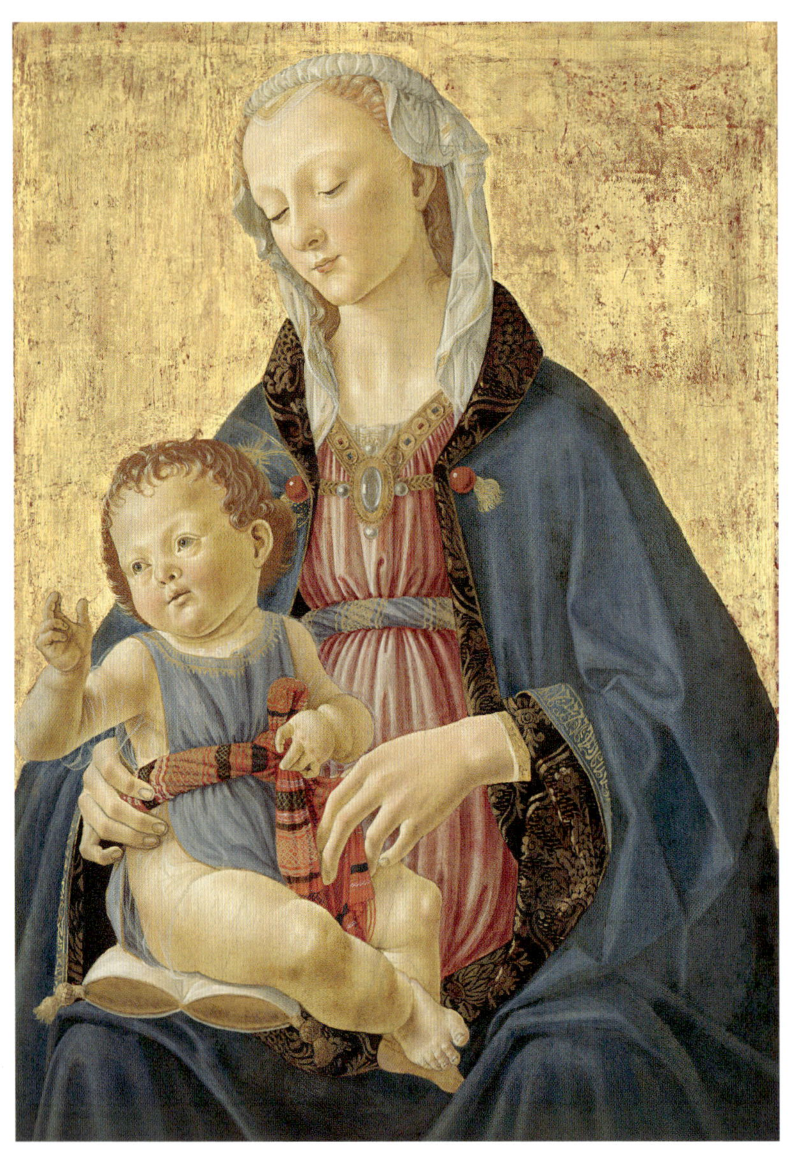

32 Domenico Ghirlandaio, *Virgin and Child*, *c.* 1476, tempera and gold on panel, transferred to board.

the *St Augustine* by Botticelli, which shows the saint in rapt attention, perhaps hearing Jerome's voice at the moment of Jerome's
death, according to popular accounts (illus. 34). The two pictures
flanked the central portal of the rood screen that separated the
nave from the choir. They were cut out of the wall when the rood
screen was disassembled in the sixteenth century, preserving the
upper layer of plaster and part of the lower layer, and hence the
painted surfaces are intact. Ghirlandaio's picture is dated 1480
in Roman numerals carved into the side of the writing desk;
Botticelli's picture is crowned with the Vespucci coat of arms,
further evidence for Vespucci patronage of Ghirlandaio's *Jerome*.

The saint sits in his study, surrounded by books, pens, inkwells
and other scholarly paraphernalia, his arm poised on his writing
desk, his right hand holding a quill pen. A thick Anatolian carpet
covers the desk, its long fringe catching the light. Inscriptions
in Greek, Hebrew and Latin underscore the saint's relationship
to texts and authorship; the Latin inscription in the frieze above
demands: 'Illuminate us, O radiant light, otherwise the whole
world would be dark.' The saint stares down intently at the viewer
(the mural was placed above eye level). Ghirlandaio took as his
model a painting by Jan van Eyck then in the Medici collections.
The earlier Vespucci *Pietà* was also inspired by a Northern European model, so the family must have admired these popular
imports. Although painted in fresco, the *St Jerome* is closer in size
to a panel painting (184 × 119 cm). Recent restoration revealed
that the picture was painted in twelve *giornate*, relatively many for
such a small surface. The costly ultramarine pigment indicates
its special status.[54] Ghirlandaio imitates the descriptive detail and
effects of light and texture for which Flemish pictures were prized.
Short, densely packed brushstrokes describe the woodgrain of
the lectern and the soft nap of the carpet. Propped up on the side
of the writing desk, a straight edge tool, scissors and spectacles cast
shadows. The shelf above is cluttered with the cardinal's hat,

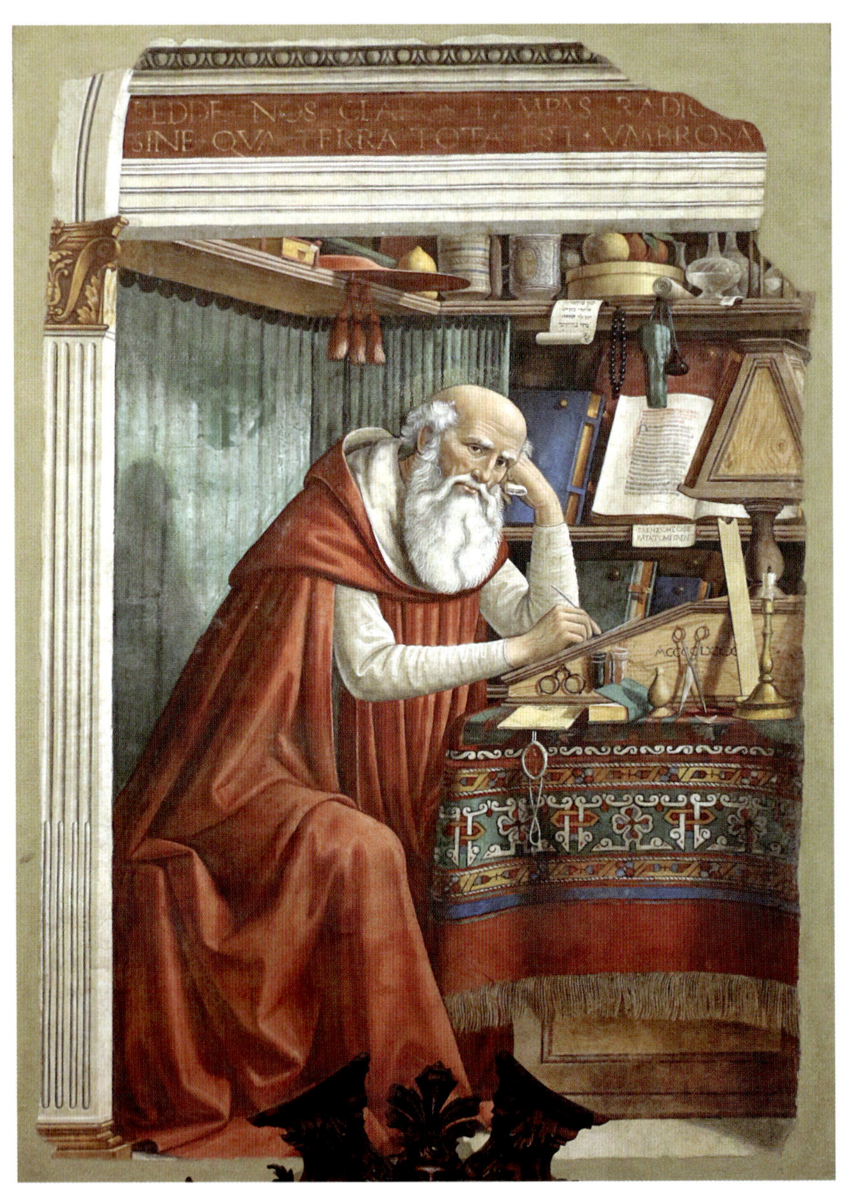

33 Domenico Ghirlandaio, *St Jerome in His Study*, 1480, fresco, Ognissanti, Florence.

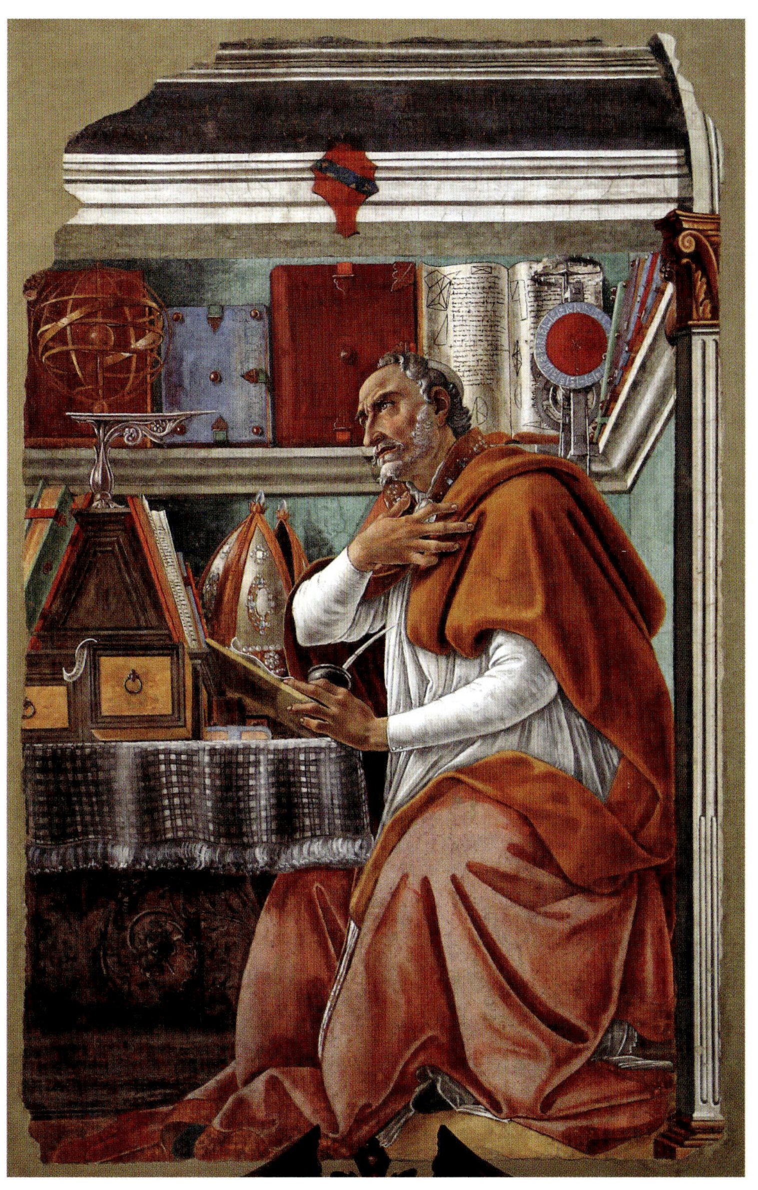

34 Sandro Botticelli, *St Augustine*, 1480, fresco, Ognissanti, Florence.

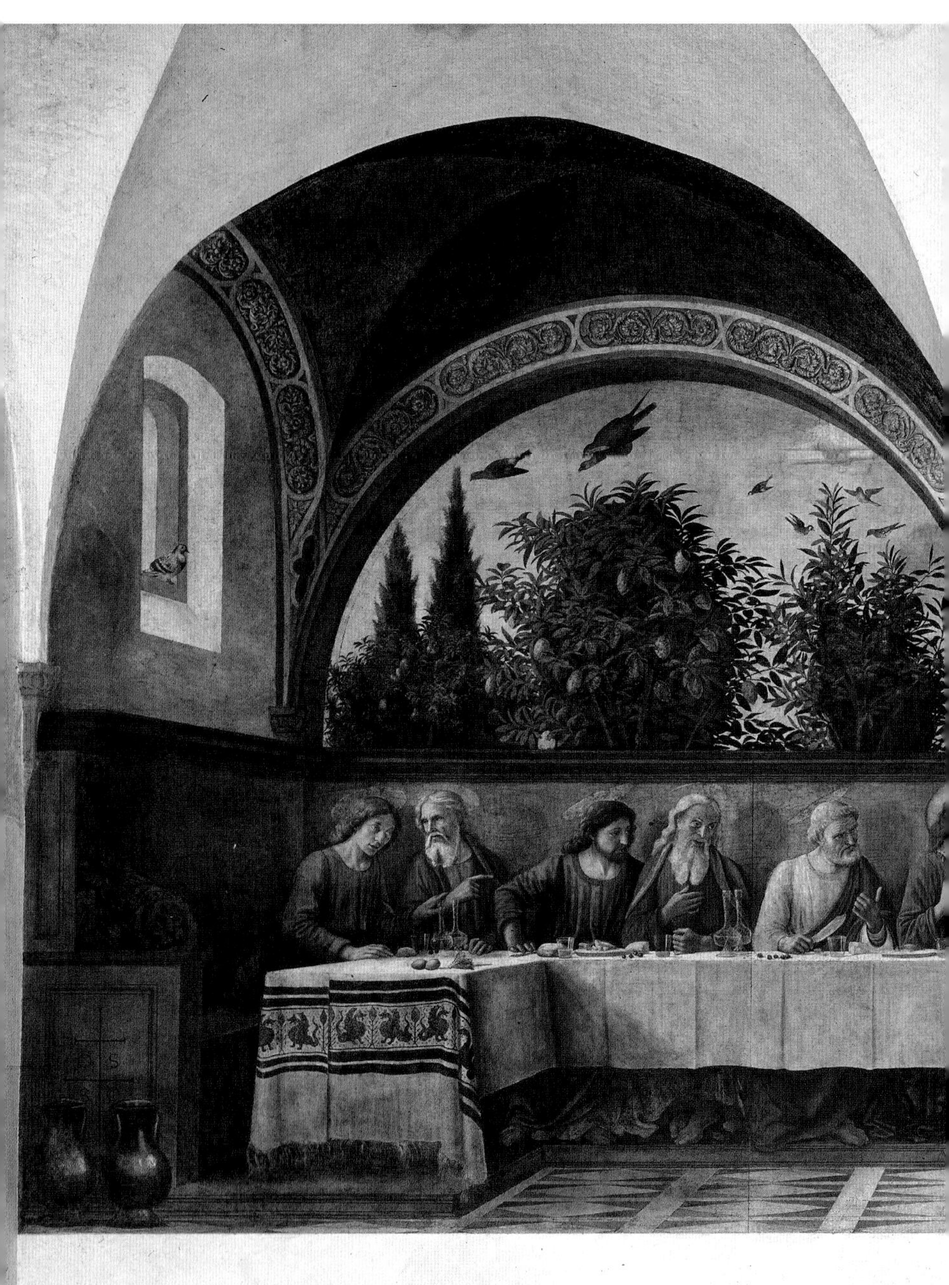

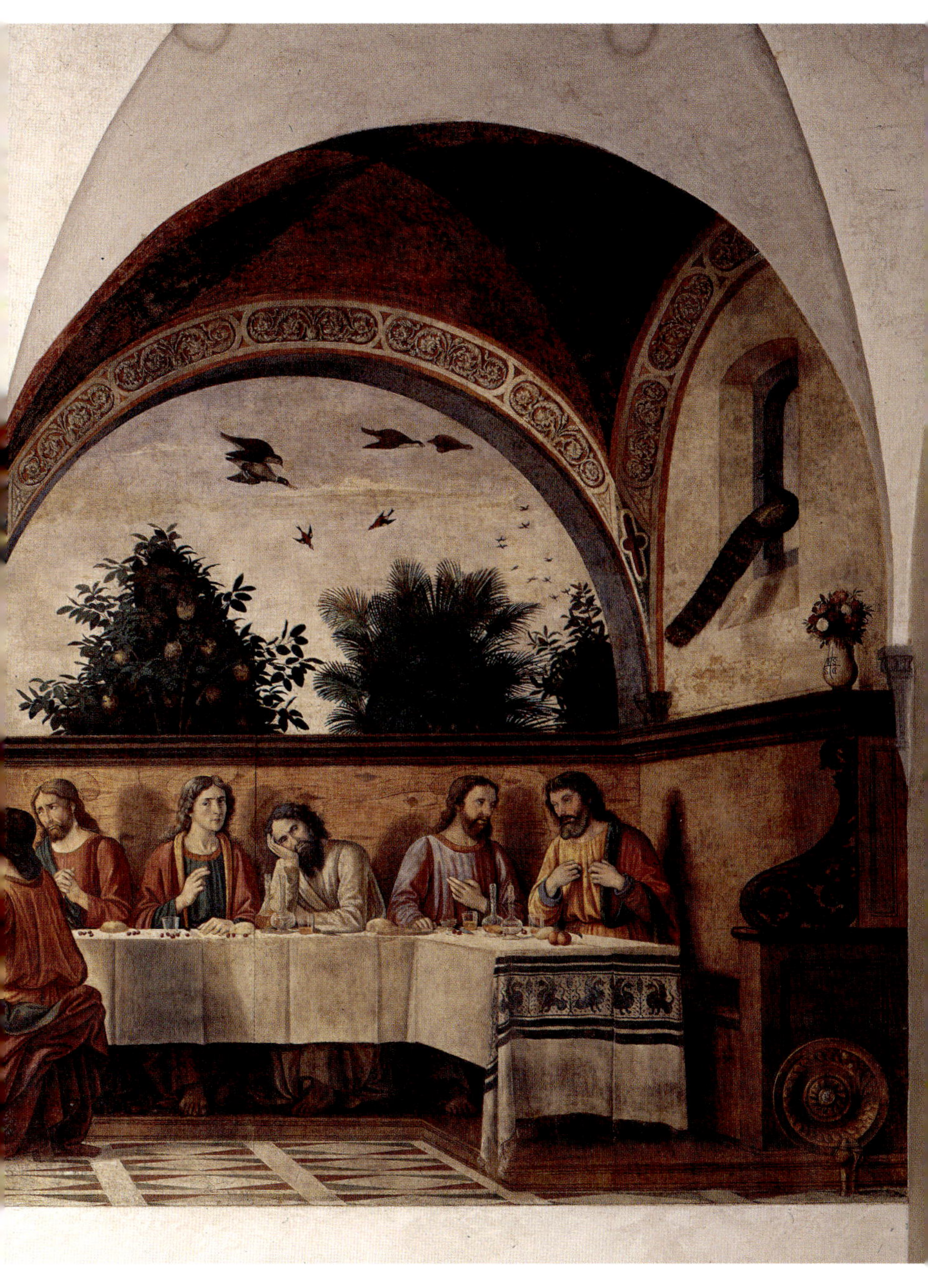

35 Domenico Ghirlandaio, *Last Supper*, 1480, fresco, Ognissanti, Refectory, Florence.

apothecary jars, an hourglass and a half-filled crystal carafe. Ghirlandaio endows Jerome with a rich physicality that held viewers' attention.

Ghirlandaio also painted another version of the Last Supper on the end wall of the refectory in the monastery adjacent to Ognissanti (illus. 35).[55] In this case, the monks likely commissioned him, apparently satisfied with his work in the church. The refectory, newly constructed in 1480 as part of a renovation to the complex, is a groin-vaulted space of five bays. Ghirlandaio depicted the event in a similarly vaulted room that appears to be an extension of the viewer's space. The actual corbel that is incorporated into the design enhances the illusion of spatial continuity. At the Last Supper, Christ gathered with his disciples in an 'upper room' to celebrate the Passover Seder, as recounted in the gospels. The blessing and distribution of the bread and wine during the meal, known as the institution of the Eucharist, became the central ritual of the Mass, in which the faithful receive communion and re-enact Christ's sacrifice on the Cross. It was during the Last Supper that Christ announced that one of the disciples would betray him. In the gospel accounts, Judas identifies himself by incriminating gestures, and in traditional depictions he is isolated spatially from the other disciples. In the Ognissanti mural, he occupies the near side of the long table and clutches a money pouch in his fist, but his erect bearing gives away no emotion. The other figures react in character to Christ's announcement of betrayal by turning towards each other, pointing, beating their breasts or slumping in resignation.

Light floods in from the left as the figures cast shadows and the tableware and glasses glint with reflections. Carefully orchestrated accessories allude to the multiple meanings of the *Last Supper*. The supper itself consists of bread, wine, platters of sliced lamb, cherries, apricots and oranges. The lamb is a traditional symbol of Christ; cherries, deep red like the blood of Christ, recall the joys of heaven; and apricots signify sin and redemption. The pheasant perched on the window at the right is a symbol of the Resurrection, while the dove on the window opposite is an emblem of peace. Flying above the trees in the garden beyond are birds of prey attacking a duck, an early Christian sign of heavenly joy, and goldfinches, symbols of the Passion and Resurrection. The trees – cypress, palm, orange and lemon – also carry meaning. The cypress refers to death, the palm to martyrdom and eternal life, the orange and lemon trees to the Virgin. The vase of roses perched on the cornice at the right – inscribed with the Ognissanti monogram, a double-armed cross and the letters OSSCI – also alludes to the Virgin. Compared to the mural in Passignano, the space is more ample, the illusion more complete and the figures more animated.

The *sinopia* for the *Last Supper* in Ognissanti survives and shows an evolving mural technique (illus. 36). A larger surface than either the Brozzi or *Pietà* murals, the Ognissanti *sinopia* included both figures and setting. Ghirlandaio marked out the architectural backdrop using a compass, plumb lines and straight edges, replicating a design that must have been carefully prepared beforehand.

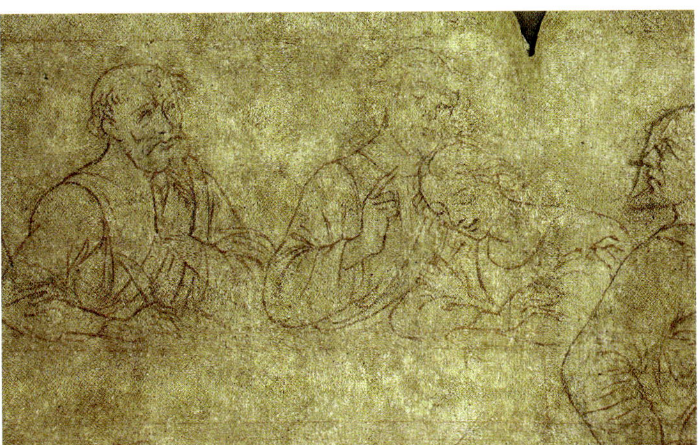

36 Domenico Ghirlandaio, *Last Supper*, 1480, sinopia, detail, Ognissanti refectory, Florence.

The depicted space appears to be a continuation of the actual space of the refectory, so it was crucial that the perspective be accurate. The figures were then drawn freehand over summary indications in charcoal and include details of pose, drapery and facial expression, indicating that the artist was working from detailed drawings of the individual figures. It was probably only when drawing the *sinopia* that the individual figures and setting were united on the wall itself. Unlike the *sinopia* from Brozzi or the *Pietà*, however, there are no hesitations or inconsistencies in figure pose or placement.

The works in Ognissanti and San Giusto signal Ghirlandaio's rising reputation. His peripatetic career in the 1470s might confirm Vasari's assertion, in reference to Perugino, that,

> it is true, indeed, that when a man has learnt there [Florence] as much as suffices him, he must, if he wishes to do more than live from day to day like an animal, and desires to become rich, take his departure from that place and find a sale abroad for the excellence of his works and for the repute conferred on him by that city.[56]

Ghirlandaio's father acknowledged his wide-ranging activity in his tax return in 1480, stating that his son did not have a workshop.[57] Murals, of course, were executed on-site, while panels such as the ones from Pisa were likely painted in temporary workshops. When he was in Florence, painting a picture such as the Gesuati altarpiece, he may have had access to space in another artist's workshop. Ghirlandaio's closeness to Verrocchio in the mid- and late 1470s, seen especially in the Gesuati picture, might signal that he was part of that vibrant workshop during this time. However, Ghirlandaio's art – which concentrated on firm contours, precise transcription of surfaces and clear disposition of volumes in space – is distinct from that of Verrocchio's many pupils. Perhaps these aspects of Ghirlandaio's style stem from his training as a goldsmith, crafting three-dimensional objects, elaborating surface detail and manipulating colour, sheen and texture of gold, silver and gems.

Travel expanded artists' contacts and built their client base, but it also developed their skills. They had to adapt to local customs and visualize local legends, and they had to collaborate with local artisans and suppliers. Ghirlandaio's adaptability, in addition to his emerging distinctive style, solid craftsmanship and inventiveness, honed during the 1470s, shaped his reputation and formed the basis for his productive career in the 1480s, the subject of the next chapter.

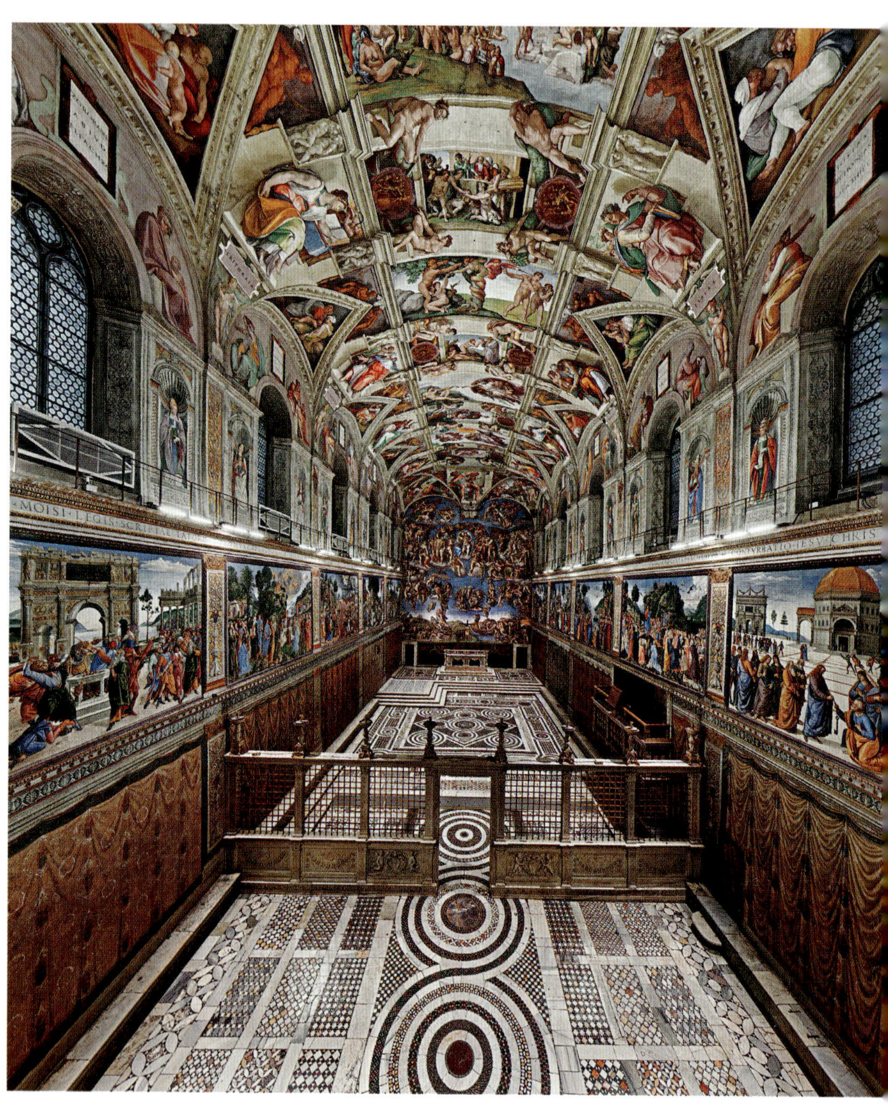

'A Good Master on Panel and Even More So on Walls': Paintings for the Pope, the City and the Merchant Elite

Ghirlandaio's peripatetic career during the 1470s prepared him for his most challenging – and, for his career, his most important – commission yet in the early 1480s: the decoration of the Great Chapel, now the Sistine Chapel, in the Vatican Palace (illus. 37). Pope Sixtus IV (b. 1414, r. 1471–84) had rebuilt the palace chapel, which contemporaries reported to be in disrepair, between 1477 and 1481.[1] The Great Chapel was designed to be decorated with paintings. The vast wall surfaces were interrupted only by windows and two cornices, demarcating three broad fields beneath the vault, which was painted with stars against a blue background. Ghirlandaio arrived in Rome in September 1481, joining a group of painters assembled to complete the work. These included the Florentines Sandro Botticelli and Cosimo Rosselli, as well as Pietro Perugino, Umbrian by birth but active in Florence during these years. A contract of 27 October 1481 between these artists, their assistants (*familiares suos*) and Giovannino de' Dolci, the superintendent of the Apostolic Palace, provided for ten 'histories with their curtains' that had already been begun, starting from the altar wall.[2] Presumably the first two murals on the altar wall had already been painted by Perugino, while of the remaining eight scenes, the four artists

37 Sistine chapel, 1477–81, Vatican City.

were to paint two scenes each. A deadline of 15 March 1482 was fixed, with a penalty of 50 papal ducats if not met. The price was to be set by arbitrators, who assessed the artists' first four murals, including the narratives, framework, curtains and standing popes, at 250 ducats each, as recorded in a further document of 17 January 1482.

The documents are confusing because, while providing for ten murals, the decorations comprised sixteen narratives: two each for the entrance and altar walls and six on the north and south walls. It is likely that the first ten murals referred to in the October 1481 document were those on the walls enclosing the area around the altar, which was separated from the entrance space by a marble screen, and it is possible that the last six murals were commissioned in a contract that no longer survives. The later murals were the work of artists not among the original four who were likely brought in to speed the project to completion. There is evidence that the painters met the deadline of 15 March and that the chapel was substantially complete by May 1482.[3]

Still, there is much we do not know. How, for instance, was the work divided among the four artists? And who, apart from Giovannino de' Dolci, was in charge? A common narrative style – including multiple episodes, consistent figure scale and horizon line, a harmonious colour scheme and an abundant use of gold – suggests that the artists hewed to pre-established norms that guided their individual designs. Perugino, who had worked in the Vatican just before the Sistine commission, was most likely the group leader.

Nor is the chapel as we see it today as originally planned. Michelangelo repainted the ceiling between 1508 and 1512 and the altar wall between 1534 and 1541, walling up the original windows and destroying the narratives, papal portraits and the frescoed altarpiece. The entrance wall collapsed in 1522 and was repainted in 1571–2. The marble rood screen, originally enclosing the chancel and abutting the singing gallery set in the right wall, was moved towards the entrance in the sixteenth century. Nonetheless, as it does today, the fifteenth-century chapel presented a magnificent spectacle to viewers when consecrated on the feast of the Virgin's Assumption, to whom the chapel was dedicated, on 15 August 1483. A contemporary rhapsodized over the chapel's 'interior walls draped in tapestries and gold and its gilded railings coursing over those transverse marble sculptures'. He asked, 'But does not the pavement of your chapel with its marble, not baked, tiles and multi-coloured ones at that, marvellously and so skilfully arranged, with their complicated intertwining swirls, which make for beauty, easily surpass in the opinion of all every capacity of its makers'? Indeed, the chapel visualized the pope's magnificence and power to the privileged audience on important ceremonial occasions.

This assembly, called the *Capella Papalis* (Papal Chapel), met with the pope at prescribed events during the liturgical year, sometimes in the designated Vatican Palace chapel but at times in other sites. The group, numbering about two hundred in the late fifteenth century, included the College of Cardinals, the generals of the monastic and mendicant orders, the resident theologian (called the Master of the Sacred Palace) and members of the papal bureaucracy. Other attendees included those directly involved in the sacred ceremony – the celebrants, deacons and Master of Ceremony – as well as members of the papal chorus and servants of the cardinals. Secular members included the senators and conservators of the city of Rome, the diplomatic corps, visiting royals and the captain of the papal guard. During ceremonies, attendees were organized according to rank, seniority and level of participation. The pope, who presided over the mass, sat in the papal throne, raised on a dais and sheltered by a baldachin against the south wall, just below the altar. Within the chancel, cardinals, bishops, ambassadors, senators, conservators, Roman aristocrats, dukes and princes, and the pope's chamberlains and doctors stood or were seated on benches, chairs, stools or on the steps and floor. Outside the chancel, servants, monks, visitors and other attendees stood in a random order, attended by papal guards. This audience was largely a well-educated elite, versed in theology and with worldly experience. During the long sessions of the Papal Chapel, they had ample time to contemplate the dazzling spectacle that Sixtus's decoration set before their eyes and to absorb its timely message of papal primacy. After the election of Martin V (r. 1417–31), the papacy returned to Rome from France, but its authority was challenged by church councils, secular rulers, Roman barons and curial factions. Sixtus, through myriad building and beautification projects, reimagined Rome as the New Jerusalem and the popes as legitimate spiritual and temporal rulers, heirs of St Peter, who derived his authority directly from Christ. The new chapel was the most sumptuous and complete expression of this idea.

The histories on the walls of Sixtus's chapel comprised, again in the words of a contemporary, 'a picture of both laws'; that is, stories from the Old and New Testaments. On the south wall were scenes from the life of Moses, who received the tablets of the law from God, and on the north wall scenes from the life of Christ, who established the new Christian law. The scenes were paired across the chapel to bring out their parallel meanings; the acts of Moses served as prefigurations of the acts of Jesus in a way of thinking about the Hebrew Bible that had been established at the dawn of Christianity.[4] Typology held that the new law of Christianity fulfilled the prophecies of the old law of the Hebrew Bible, thereby supplanting and elevating it. Inscriptions in the frieze above each history make their typological pairing explicit, adopting in each case identical wording. The popes standing in niches on the window level above the narratives depicted the first thirty popes with identifying inscriptions, starting with Christ and St Peter on the altar wall, according to the *History of the Popes* written by the Vatican librarian Platina and presented to Sixtus in 1475. The learned audience would have been able to read these Latin inscriptions and to grasp their meanings, an effect surely intended by whoever devised the programme, most likely Sixtus himself. The pope was an accomplished theologian and philosopher and actively involved in the many projects initiated during his reign. The imagery promoted the role of the pope as lawgiver, ruler and priest, and it visualized his spiritual and temporal power as derived from Christ himself.

Ghirlandaio's participation in this project must have been for him, as for the other artists, a singular experience. While he had worked in the Vatican Palace before, decorating the papal library, the chapel was an incomparably larger and more significant space, and the imagery vastly more extensive and complex. He had collaborated with other artisans, most notably in the Chapel of Santa Fina in San Gimignano, but never with multiple famous painters and their workshops as here. And although he had designed narrative murals such as the *Last Supper* and the scenes from the life of Santa Fina, he had never invented multi-episodic scenes that were part of an extended mural cycle.

Ghirlandaio's surviving narrative scene is the *Calling of Peter and Andrew*, the third from the altar on the right or north wall (illus. 38).[5] He also painted the *Resurrection and Assumption* on the entrance wall, which was damaged and repainted by Hendrick van den Broeck in a sixteenth-century style that bears no hint of Ghirlandaio's design. The *Calling of Peter and Andrew* follows in order Perugino's *Baptism of Christ* and Botticelli's *Temptation of Christ* in the New Testament cycle, and it is followed by Rosselli's *Sermon on the Mount*. It faces Biagio d'Antonio's *Crossing of the Red Sea* on the Old Testament wall. The accompanying inscription to the *Calling* reads, 'Congregatio Populi Legem Evangelicam Accepturi' ('the assembly of the people who accept the evangelical law'), and to the *Crossing*, 'Congregatio Populi a Moise Legem Scriptam Accepturi' ('the

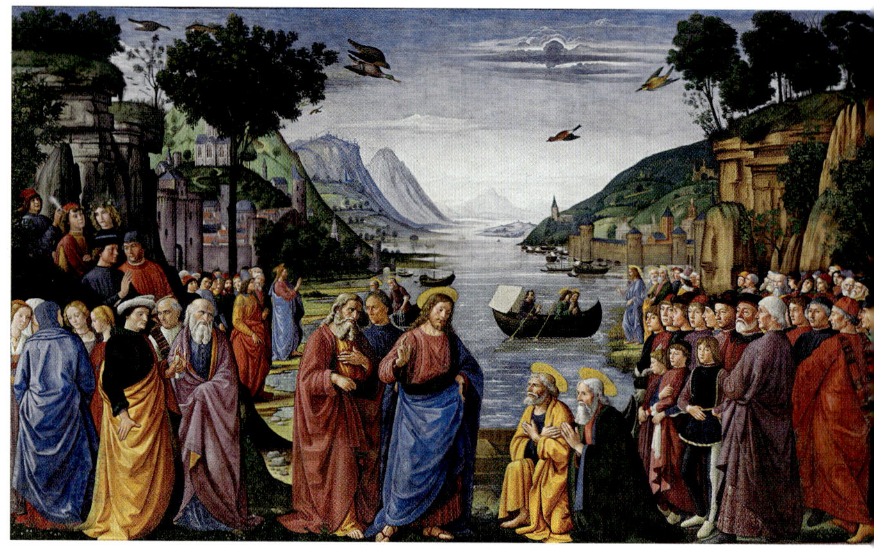

assembly of the people who accept the law written by Moses').
Hence the two scenes continue the central idea of the old and
new laws that govern the imagery of the entire decoration.

Ghirlandaio's scene is a symmetrical composition, as are those
of Perugino, Botticelli and Rosselli immediately adjacent to it,
with Christ in the centre foreground addressing his kneeling
disciples Peter and Andrew. The incident takes place before a
sweeping landscape with a vast lake and distant views of mountains, the shoreline populated with walled cities and shipping.
The image is drawn from the gospels of Matthew, Mark and
Luke; Matthew says:

> Jesus was walking by the Sea of Galilee when he saw two
> brothers, Simon called Peter and his brother Andrew,
> casting a net into the lake; for they were fishermen. Jesus
> said to them, 'Come with me, and I will make you fishers
> of men.' And at once they left their nets and followed

38 Domenico Ghirlandaio, *The Calling of Peter and Andrew*, 1481–2, fresco,
Sistine Chapel, Vatican City.

him. He went on, and saw another pair of brothers, James son of Zebedee and his brother John; they were in the boat with their father Zebedee, overhauling their nets. He called them, and at once they left the boat and their father, and followed him. (4:18–22)

Ghirlandaio's mural includes the actual calling of the first apostles in the middle ground left scene, where we see Christ standing on the shore, raising his hand as two haloed, bearded figures in a boat pull a fishing net. At the middle ground right, Christ blesses James and John, in a boat with their father Zebedee, as they glide to shore. In the central foreground group, Christ stands, his hand raised in blessing, addressing the kneeling Peter and Andrew. This incident is missing from Matthew's account but was perhaps inspired by the ending of Luke's account of the *Calling* (5:8–10): 'When Simon Peter saw this [a large catch of fish], he fell at Jesus' knees and said, "Go away from me, Lord; I am a sinful man!"' We recognize the first disciples from the left scene of their calling by their white beards, haloes and dress, although now Peter wears a yellow robe over his blue tunic and Andrew has donned a green robe over his red tunic. They appear similarly clad in the calling of James and John, where they lead a group of onlookers dressed in contemporary, not biblical, dress.

Ghirlandaio depicts the three incidents that make up the story of the calling of the first apostles as if they were all taking place at once within the scene. This way of telling a story in pictures, called 'continuous' narrative, has its roots in ancient painting, and it was a device familiar to audiences in the early Renaissance. Continuous narratives required figures to appear several times within the scene, in each case recognizable through consistent features and dress. Hence we see Christ with beard and halo wearing a red tunic and blue cloak in the centre, left and right incidents. Since we know from experience that a person cannot be in two places at once, if a figure appears more than once, we understand that it is shown at different moments in time. Ghirlandaio's vast landscape setting provides ample room for the enactment of the different episodes. And since viewers in the chapel – and most viewers at this time – knew the biblical stories by heart, they could mentally arrange the incidents into the proper sequence so that the story made sense. As we saw in the *Death of Santa Fina* mural in San Gimignano, Ghirlandaio depicted different moments in the same story within a unified space, but he did not repeat figures. By using the repeated figures in the Sistine murals, paintings, which are atemporal, can depict multi-episodic stories that take place in time. In addition, through continuous narration, the biblical incidents could be presented in all their richness and complexity.

All the narrative murals in the chapel use the device of continuous narration – some, such as Botticelli's *Temptation of Moses*, contain seven episodes of the story – and it must have been one of the compositional norms all the artists agreed to at the outset. In addition, the appearance and clothing of the principal figures – Moses in his long white beard, clad in a yellow tunic and green robe, or Christ with his red/purple tunic and blue robe – is consistent for all the murals, and was key to the visual and narrative coherence of the entire cycle. In this way the patron, ultimately Pope Sixtus IV, created a magnificent display and clearly communicated a message of papal primacy.

Luke begins his account of the *Calling*, 'One day as Jesus was standing by the Lake of Gennesaret, the people were crowding around him and listening to the word of God.' In addition, the mural's titulus, 'The Assembly of the People who Accept the Evangelical Law', would seem to demand a large group of figures. And indeed, aside from the protagonists of the story, Ghirlandaio has depicted throngs of figures whose roles in the story range from active participants to dispassionate bystanders. Clustered to the left and right of the central incident, the figures are of two types: those dressed in the loose robes of what was imaged to be the costume of biblical figures, and those clothed in contemporary dress. The biblical figures are the protagonists in the story, but they are far outnumbered by the contemporary figures. Who are they? The contemporary figures at the left in the foreground and in the two groups further back in space seem to be a mix of pointedly characterized figures that must be portraits of contemporaries and more generalized 'staffage', including all the women. For example, the balding figure with short white hair who looks to his companion at the left has an intensity of expression that suggests it is a portrait. The group of five figures above him to the left are generalized, but one sports a cap with a large pearl-studded brooch and ostrich feather; the other wears a garland of flowers. These figures may be Ghirlandaio's 'signature', the one a pun on his family's name, the other recalling their profession as goldsmiths and jewellers. Similarly, in the central scene, between Christ and the white-bearded patriarch, is a figure seen bust-length in contemporary dress. His features are distinctive enough to be a portrait, and his central position signals he was someone of importance – but who?

The rows of figures at the right of the scene, however, are most clearly portraits of contemporaries, some of whom are identifiable. Giovanni Tornabuoni (1428–1497), the head of the Rome branch of the Medici bank and depositary general (receiver of taxes due to the Apostolic Chamber) for Pope Sixtus IV, stands in the front row of elders third from the right.[6] His son Lorenzo (1468–1497), dressed in a fur-lined, brocade tunic, stands before him. To the right of Giovanni is a white-bearded figure identified as Giovanni Argyropoulos, the Greek émigré scholar who might have been the young Lorenzo's tutor in Greek, in which he became proficient. The others are unidentified, although they have been thought to represent the Florentine colony in Rome, of which Giovanni Tornabuoni was a conspicuous member. They must have been recognizable to the privileged audience in the chapel and therefore have been associates of the papal court. Yet viewers of the mural, painted probably in the autumn of 1481, might have recalled recent events. In the aftermath of the assassination attempt on Lorenzo de' Medici on 26 April 1478 in Florence cathedral, war had broken out between Florence and Pope Sixtus IV, who was implicated in the plot.[7] The war ended only on 3 December 1480, when a peace between Lorenzo and Pope Sixtus, brokered by King Ferrante of Naples, went into effect. On that day, a delegation of Florentines, of whom Giovanni Tornabuoni was one, begged the pope's pardon for Florentine transgressions, and the pope lifted the censures he had imposed. Indeed, the Florentine artists' work in the chapel may have been a conciliatory gesture to the papacy in the aftermath of the war. Lorenzo himself may have been the instigator of this pact, and the presence of Giovanni Tornabuoni (Lorenzo's uncle) in Ghirlandaio's *Calling* might support this idea.[8] During the war, Florentines had had to flee Rome, their possessions confiscated, with dire consequences for citizens and the Medici bank, whose loans to the papacy were repudiated. Florentines' return with peace, and their presence in this mural, would have been read as confirmation of newly restored relations and papal favour. What's more, Ghirlandaio may have worked for Tornabuoni in Rome in the late 1470s, decorating a funerary chapel for Giovanni's deceased wife, Francesca Pitti Tornabuoni (d. 1477), in Santa Maria sopra Minerva. It is thus not surprising that he and Florentine associates would appear prominently in Ghirlandaio's mural.

Artists had inserted contemporary portraits into narrative scenes since the fourteenth century, so this aspect of Ghirlandaio's mural, and those of the other Sistine artists, was not new.[9] While in the past they have been decried as secular intrusions into the sacred stories, these portraits occur with such frequency that we must assume that they were acceptable to patrons and audiences. Giovanni Tornabuoni and his retinue stand respectfully off to the right side of the central scene, distinguished from the holy figures by their position and dress. The three young boys and two full-length figures in the front row assume animated poses, their attention directed towards the encounter of Christ and his disciples. The other figures, seen from the shoulder up, stare intently ahead. Only the young Lorenzo Tornabuoni stares out towards the spectator, establishing a link between the events in the picture and the spectators in the chapel. In this way, past and present – biblical time and historical time – merge, reminding viewers of the great arc of salvation history, terminating with the Last Judgement, still to come.[10] Today, as then, spectators are reminded that the significance of these biblical events is still with us. The decorative scheme of the chapel, finished only in the mid-sixteenth century, illustrates this history from Genesis, on the ceiling, to Michelangelo's *Last Judgement* on the altar wall. The histories of Moses and Christ on the side walls depict two central ages – one under Moses's law and the other under Christ's grace – in this universal history.

As we have seen, the portraits in Ghirlandaio's mural were recognizable to the elite audience, and their presence confirmed Florentines' newly regained status at the papal court. But how else might they have been seen? Although they are more witnesses to – rather than active participants in – the sacred drama, they might be understood (along with the apostles) as part of the 'assembly of the people who accept the evangelical law' referred to in the titulus. As such, they declare their faith and model pious behaviour to the audience, who equally witness the sacred ritual taking place in the chapel. In addition, the portraits record appearances and preserve their memory for future audiences after their deaths. Leon Battista Alberti voiced the commemorative role of portraits in his book about painting, written in 1434: 'Through

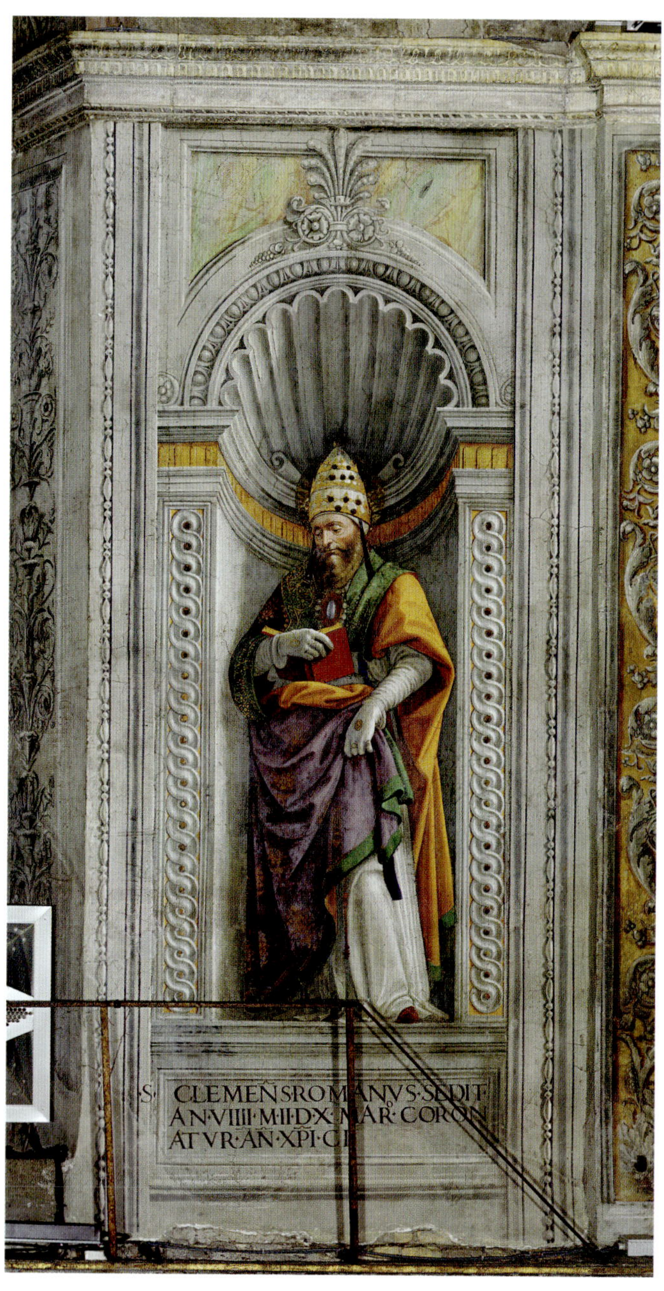

39 Domenico Ghirlandaio, *Pope Clement*, 1481–2, fresco, Sistine Chapel, Vatican City.

painting, the faces of the dead go on living for a very long time."[11] Giovanni Tornabuoni, with his son by his side, wished to remind viewers of his life and to signal the survival of his family into the future.

Pigment analysis of the Vatican's *Calling of Peter and Andrew* revealed unusually rich materials in keeping with Sixtus IV's courtly taste. Ultramarine and red lake, the expensive pigment derived from insects, were applied in secco, as was green over a base of *terra verde*. Abundant gold leaf, some of which has fallen away, denoted the reflections on drapery and foliage. For the first time Ghirlandaio used smalt, an inexpensive blue derived from cobalt, applied in fresco for the blue of the sea and sky.

Ghirlandaio's work in the Sistine Chapel also included papal portraits in the upper register flanking the windows. The portraits were, of course, imaginary. They vary in their facial expressions and postures, although they all wear the papal tiara and hold books or scrolls. Ghirlandaio's Pope Clement, the third pope following Peter, is in the southwest corner and, according to the inscription, he reigned for eight years (illus. 39). He stands swathed in an ample purple cope with a yellow lining and fixed with a jewelled morse; he bends his head, intently studying his open book. The series of popes, all decorously posed and luxuriently clad, linked Pope Sixtus, who had been depicted in the frescoed altarpiece on the altar wall, back to Peter and Christ and legitimized his powers before the intended audience. Positioned on the register between the starry sky above and the histories below, the popes acted as intermediaries between humans on earth and God in the heavens. Framed by scalloped shell niches, they form a series of heroic early Christian famous men, recalling perhaps Roman examples of *uomini famosi*, such as Masolino's decoration in Cardinal Giordano Orsini's palace in Rome, finished by 1432. Like the portraits in the histories below, they served as exempla to be praised and emulated.

Ghirlandaio likely finished his work in the chapel by May 1482. He returned to Florence endowed with a status and reputation he had not previously enjoyed. Serving the pope in such a prestigious location sent a powerful message to would-be patrons. But he had also learned valuable lessons from his co-workers that altered the course of his art. Painting large-scale, multi-episode stories required more helpers than just his brothers Davide and possibly the 24-year-old Benedetto, as is evident from close inspection of the mural surface, which reveals many hands at work. This was Ghirlandaio's first experience of directing a team. In conforming to narrative norms, Ghirlandaio had to adapt his approach to composition, especially in embracing continuous narrative. Adhering to the common palette, he tried out new applications of blues and greens, and gilded highlights with abundant gold leaf. Painting in close quarters with the other artists, on the same or adjacent scaffolds, fostered sharing of techniques and motifs. It has even been proposed that artists contributed to one another's murals. Did Botticelli add the garland to the youth in Ghirlandaio's *Calling* while at work on the neighbouring scaffold, as art historian Arnold Nesselrath suggests?

Ghirlandaio's Roman sojourn opened up new opportunities in Florence. Shortly after returning there, in September 1482, Ghirlandaio painted an image of St Zenobius in the Sala dei Gigli (Room of the Lilies) in the Palazzo della Signoria, the seat of the Florentine government (illus. 40).[12] This was his first civic commission, and it was in an important and highly visible location. How he came to be recommended to the Opera del Palazzo, the governing board for the Palazzo della Signoria, is not known. The da Maiano brothers, who had completed work there just before, might have recommended him, as we suspect happened at San Gimignano. Yet any of the influential Florentines on the Opera might have been aware of his work in Rome. Some scholars have suggested Lorenzo de' Medici was involved in the planning of the decoration, although he was not a member of the Opera when the Sala dei Gigli was painted, and there is no evidence in the documentation of his being involved. Others have proposed that, by hiring three of the artists active in the Sistine Chapel, the Sala dei Gigli project was Lorenzo's response to Sixtus IV's Sistine decoration. And yet, as we will see, Ghirlandaio alone began the project; the other artists were only brought in later, perhaps in a bid to finish the project quickly.

The Sala dei Gigli was one of three large chambers in the palace. The rooms were used for different purposes: the Sala del Dugento (Room of the Two Hundred), on the first floor, was where the Council of the People met, while the Sala dell'Udienza (Audience Chamber), on the second floor, was where the Signoria, the elected governing body, and its advisory committees met.

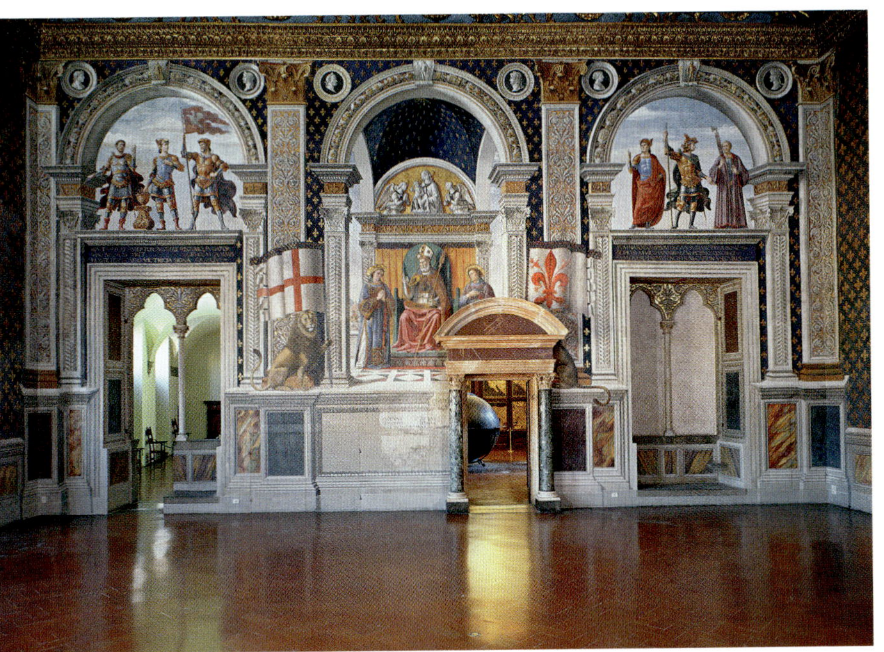

40 Domenico Ghirlandaio, *St Zenobius Enthroned with Sts Eugenius and Crescentius; Brutus, Mucius Scaevola, Camillus, Decius, Scipio and Cicero*, 1482–3, fresco, Sala dei Gigli, Palazzo Vecchio, Florence.

The Sala dei Gigli was adjacent to the Udienza and was where foreign ambassadors waited to be admitted to the Signoria's meetings and where state banquets were held. All three rooms were subject to a comprehensive restoration scheme beginning in 1470, in which the Sala dei Gigli was to be the most opulent and impressive. Between 1472 and 1477, each room was furnished with carved and gilded wooden ceilings displaying emblems of Florence: the *Marzocco* (lion) and banners of the people and the commune. Marble doorframes, complete with classical columns and statuary, were designed by Benedetto da Maiano and installed between the Sala dei Gigli and the Udienza in December 1480. The inlaid doors were designed by Giuliano da Maiano and the woodworker-architect Francesco di Giovanni, called il Francione (1428–1495) and were installed at the same time.

Ghirlandaio's murals on the east wall of the Sala dei Gigli were the first of an extensive wall decoration planned by the administrators, the Operai del Palazzo. As seen today, the wall takes the form of a triumphal arch with fictive pilasters on high bases supporting the carved and gilded entablature of the ceiling and dividing the wall into three arched bays. In the spandrels of each bay, profiles of emperors occupy roundels, while warriors with weapons grace the keystones. In the central space, St Zenobius – the first bishop of Florence (d. 417) and the most important patron saint of the city after St John the Baptist – sits on his cathedra flanked by his deacons, Eugenius and Crescentius. They occupy a vaulted portico, its blue vault studded with gold stars. A fictive enamelled terracotta relief of the Virgin and Child, set against a gilt mosaic ground, crowns the aedicule against which the saint sits. To the left in the distance, the Florentine baptistery, bell tower and cathedral are seen. In the sixteenth century, a door was inserted at the right, obliterating the lower part of the right deacon, the landscape and the seated lion holding a banner with the lily of the commune.

This central bay was only the initial phase of the decoration, which was greatly expanded on 5 October 1482. At the same time, Ghirlandaio and Botticelli were charged to paint the west wall, Perugino (later replaced by Filippino Lippi) and Biagio d'Antonio the north wall, and Piero del Pollaiuolo the south wall of the chamber, all according to the same terms as Ghirlandaio's commission. In the end, only Ghirlandaio finished the work. Barely a month later, on 8 November 1482, he was paid for the paintings. Originally two windows in the west wall had been filled in to allow for the mural decoration. However, they must have been reopened and the new paintings destroyed for, on 31 December, Ghirlandaio was compensated 5 florins for paintings 'near the said St Zenobius, which was afterwards destroyed'. By 18 April 1483, Ghirlandaio had finished the wall according to the new scheme (with windows in place) and he was paid in instalments, the last in February 1485. Restoration has confirmed the piecemeal execution of the mural as borne out in the documents. In 1490, the other three walls were decorated with fictive pilasters and gold fleurs-de-lys on a blue ground.

Today, the outer bays of the west wall show illusionistic doorframes on whose cornices Roman Republican heroes, identified by inscriptions, pose against a blue sky. The famous Romans probably replicate the decoration of a chamber that had been destroyed in the renovations of the 1470s. This small room was ornamented by a series of famous men that included Roman heroes and Florentine poets and statesmen. Doris Carl has suggested that the series in the Sala dei Gigli would have continued around the other three walls, depicting famous men from antiquity to the present day. Benedetto da Maiano's portal, surmounted by Florence's patron saint St John the Baptist, and the inlaid wooden doors, with images of its celebrated poets Dante and Petrarch, lend credence to this idea. Traditional imagery for town halls celebrated good government and virtues such as justice that foster the common good (*ben comune*). Portraits of famous men served as personifications of these virtues. Carl proposed that Ghirlandaio's heroes might have originally occupied a fictive loggia and that they were intended to be seen just above eye level. With the reinsertion of the windows on the west wall, however, Ghirlandaio had to repaint his figures much higher on the wall and on a smaller scale. This change resulted in the different scales of the St Zenobius in the central bay and the heroes at the sides.

In spite of its sporadic gestation, Ghirlandaio's decoration presents a unified conception that visualizes patriotic themes. The striking illusionism of his design is entirely compatible with his approach to mural painting from the beginning of his career. The viewpoint is ideal, much above a spectator's height, but the figures and framework conform to a consistent perspective scheme. Blue sky in the distance unites the images of all three bays. The depiction of St Zenobius echoes Giuliano da Maiano's design of the east wall in the cathedral sacristy, which, as we have seen, impressed Ghirlandaio as a youth. In addition, the details of ornament derived from classical sources, such as the Roman emperors' profiles in roundels and the military costumes, confirms Ghirlandaio's close study of ancient artefacts during his trips to Rome.[13] The Opera expressed their satisfaction with Ghirlandaio's work by commissioning from him again in May 1483 – just after he had finished painting the west wall for the second time – an altarpiece for the chapel of the priors in the Sala dell'Udienza. The act specifies neither the subject nor price of the altarpiece, only that Ghirlandaio should design it 'in such a way and form as it will be freely seen and pleasing to the great Lorenzo di Piero di Cosimo de' Medici'. If the Opera intended to entice Lorenzo's active support of the plan, they ultimately failed. Ghirlandaio never even began the work, most likely because by 1483 the money for the Palazzo renovations was diverted to other needs.

Close inspection of the Sala dei Gigli paintings shows what the documents suggest: that Ghirlandaio completed this mural project quickly. His brother Davide painted Zenobius's two deacons, and another assistant painted some of the famous men. Yet the conception is entirely the master's. The challenge Ghirlandaio faced as he was increasingly in demand was to exercise control over assistants' execution of his designs. That challenge loomed large as his commissions grew more numerous and complex through the 1480s.

The reason for Ghirlandaio's haste in completing the prestigious Palazzo Vecchio commission may have been his engagement during these same years in the decoration for Francesco Sassetti's burial chapel in Santa Trinita (illus. 41).[14] Sassetti (1421–1490) spent his entire career in the service of the Medici bank, first as general manager at the Geneva branch and from 1459 in Florence. His fortunes were tied to those of the bank, which, even before the death of Cosimo de' Medici in 1464, were in decline. Under Sassetti's leadership it continued to contract, although Sassetti enjoyed the support of Lorenzo de' Medici until his death. Sassetti's family had traditionally been buried in Santa Maria Novella, but by 1480 Sassetti had decided to build his funerary chapel in the church of Santa Trinita.

This decision resulted from fierce competition for the right to bury deceased family members in private chapels in churches. The practice became widespread in the late Middle Ages when prohibitions against burial inside churches, instead of in cemeteries or cloisters, were relaxed. It expanded with the growth of the mendicant (or begging) orders, many of whose churches were designed with private chapels, the money from which helped build and maintain the church. Families purchased the rights to bury their dead, and then invested considerable sums in tombs, liturgical furnishings, murals and altarpieces. They often paid for clergymen to say memorial masses for their dead,

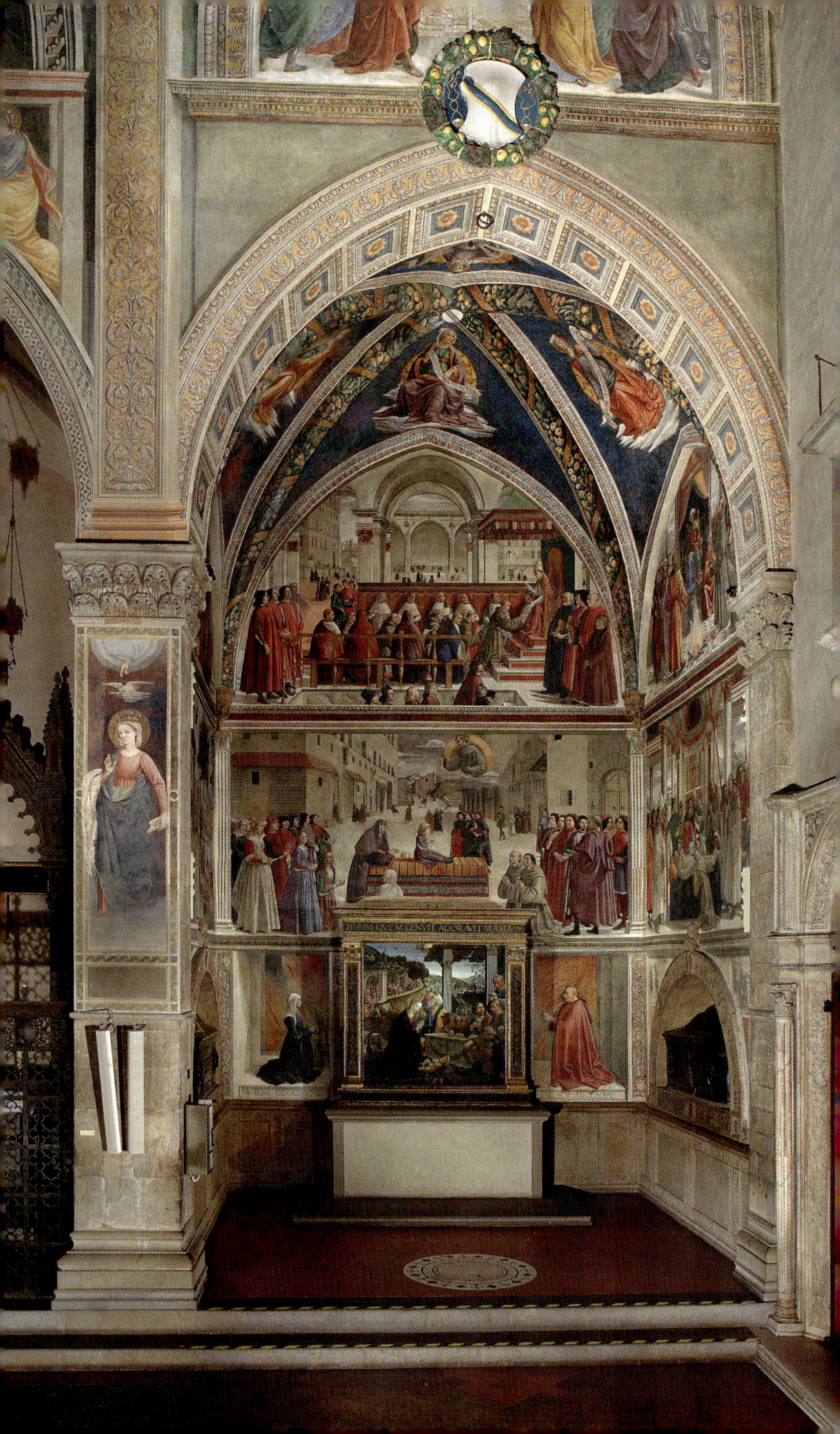

for, as explained by a thirteenth-century churchman, since the
dead cannot perform good works nor pray for themselves, 'For
those who . . . are in limbo, our prayers are favourable to them
or cause a softening of their sorrows.'[15] Location mattered as well,
as burial near the graves or relics of important saints was bene-
ficial; they could intercede on the soul's behalf and protect it from
demons. As quasi-public spaces, these chapels also signalled the
wealth and social standing of the family to others who frequented
the church. For this reason, family coats of arms were often placed
prominently on the exteriors of the chapels for all to see.

Sassetti family patronage of the high altar of Santa Maria
Novella dated to 1430, and Francesco Sassetti was recognized
as its patron in 1470. By 1486 the patronage rights to the chapel
and the altar had been transferred to Giovanni Tornabuoni,
Sassetti's colleague and competitor at the Medici bank. Although
Sassetti had resisted the transfer, he ultimately gave in to the richer
and wilier Tornabuoni, for by 1480 he had negotiated the rights
to build his funerary chapel in Santa Trinita, a smaller Vallombrosian abbey church in his neighbourhood. He was still smarting
years later; in 1488, upon leaving for a last attempt to rescue the
Lyon branch of the bank from bankruptcy, he penned instruc-
tions to his sons, which charged them, above all, to redress the
insult they had suffered from 'the animosity and rudeness of the
friars of that place'. He continued, 'I admonish you not to take
this lightly, because what is at stake is the honour of our house
and the proof of our antiquity.'[16] Sassetti thus summed up the
ultimate significance for him of his burial chapel. A later family
chronicler gives further insight; he asserted that Sassetti decorated
the chapel in keeping with a vow he had made, that is, in gratitude
to his patron saint and in hopes of further protection, thereby
confirming for us the devotional function of the chapel.

Ghirlandaio's decoration, which survives almost intact, with
its original murals, tombs and altarpiece, amply fulfilled Sassetti's

41 Sassetti chapel, 1483–5, Santa Trinita, Florence.

goals by visualizing ideas undoubtedly suggested by Sassetti and his friend the scholar Bartolomeo Fonzio. Sassetti was an avid humanist and collector of books and Roman coins. The chapel commission was the first time that Ghirlandaio was faced with designing an extensive narrative cycle with accompanying portraits, an altarpiece and decorative framework. While the execution took place between 1483 and 1485, preliminary planning including drawings must have begun after his return from Rome in 1482 and during the execution of the Sala dei Gigli murals.[17]

The chapel, a single groin-vaulted bay in the north transept of the church (whose facade is to the east and apse to the west), accommodated two tiers of murals on three walls depicting scenes from the life of St Francis, the patron's name saint. The lowest zones on the side walls house the elegant black marble sarcophagi of Sassetti and his wife, Nera Corsi Sassetti, under low arches that recall Roman burial niches (illus. 42). They are rimmed by carved reliefs with figures in roundels that allude to the deceased couple; among them frolicking Nereides and Tritons on Nera's tomb, and warriors and centaurs wielding slings on Francesco's, recalling Sassetti's personal emblem and coat of arms. Painted grisaille scenes drawn from ancient Roman coins flank the sides. On the altar wall, Ghirlandaio portrayed Francesco and Nera in life, kneeling in prayer, facing the centralized altarpiece with the *Adoration of the Shepherds*. The fictive niches in which the donors kneel seem to encompass the real space of the altar and indicate that they pray to the Virgin and newborn Christ depicted in the altarpiece.

Over the entrance arch of the chapel, the encounter of *Augustus and the Tiburtine Sibyl*, who interpreted the emperor's vision of the Virgin and Child as heralding an era of peace, fills the lunette (illus. 43). At the left is a fictive sculpture of David with the head of the slain Goliath at his feet, his shield bearing Sassetti's coat of arms and the sling nestling a stone, a pun on

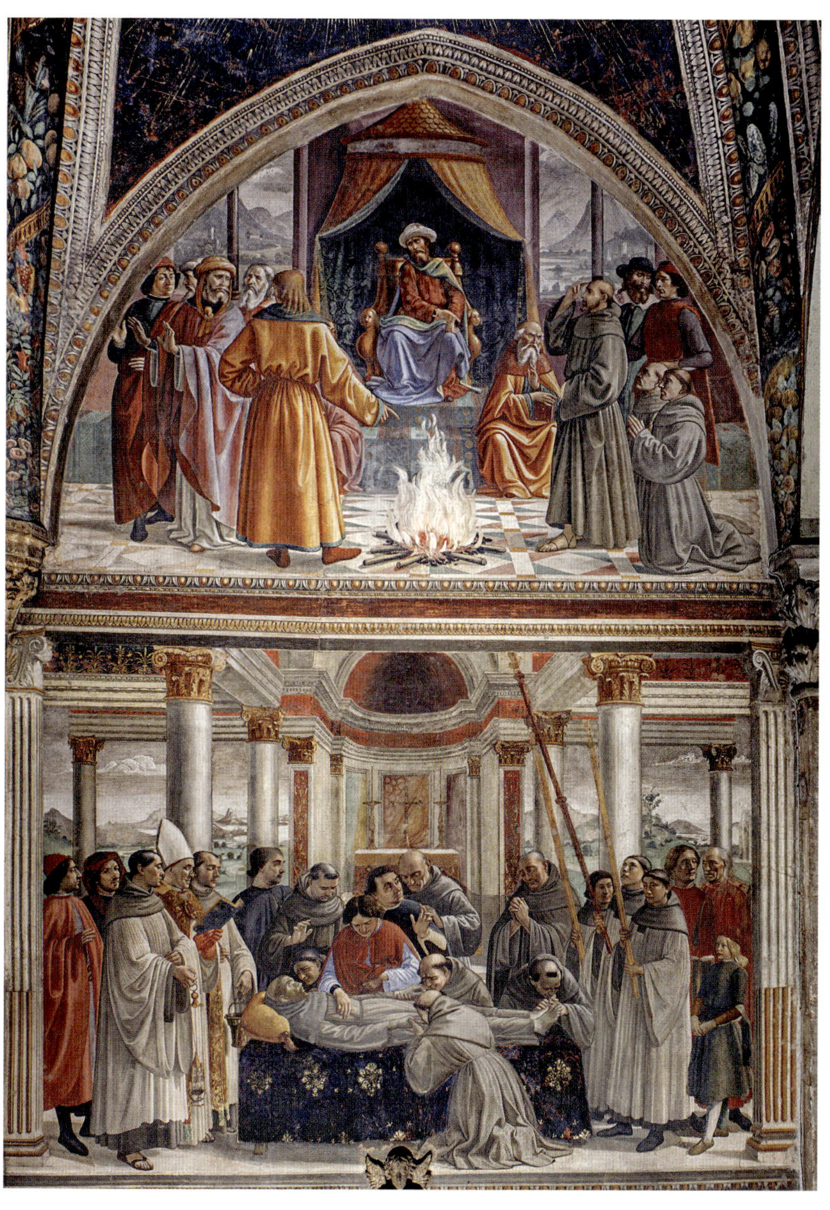

42 Domenico Ghirlandaio, *St Francis before the Sultan* and *Funeral of St Francis*, 1483–5, fresco, Sassetti chapel, Santa Trinita, Florence.

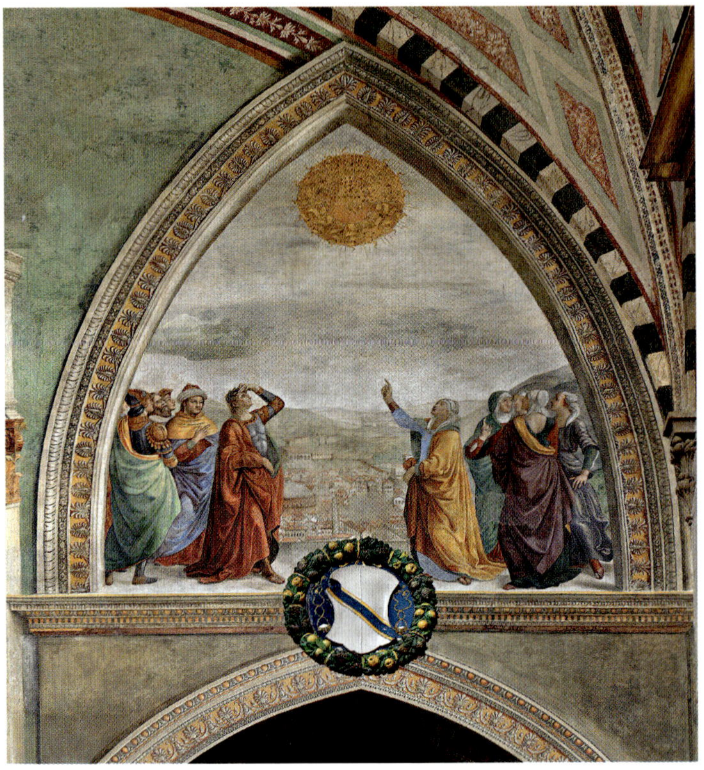

Sassetti's name ('little stones'). David also prophesied the birth
of Christ. Linking the lunette and chapel entrance arch is a
glazed terracotta garland encircling Sassetti's coat of arms flanked
by slingshots with stones. Drawing from antiquity, the Hebrew
Bible and Christian thought, the imagery celebrates prophecy,
birth and resurrection.

The theme of prophecy on the exterior mural continues in
the chapel vault, in which, for the first time in Florentine art,
four sibyls – classical augurs – hold scrolls foretelling the birth
of Christ. The narratives of St Francis' life on the chapel walls
follow traditional imagery of the saint's biography as codified in

43 Domenico Ghirlandaio, *Augustus and the Tiburtine Sibyl*, 1483–5, fresco,
Sassetti chapel, Santa Trinita, Florence.

earlier works. Ghirlandaio's designs consciously recollect Giotto's murals in the Bardi chapel in Santa Croce in Florence, but they bring the imagery into the present to evoke spectators' experiences. By invoking Giotto's hallowed designs, Ghirlandaio appealed to viewers' sense of continuity with past traditions, and he claimed remarkable stature for his own. They begin at the top of the left wall, with *St Francis Renounces His Worldly Goods*, then, on the altar wall, with the *Confirmation of the Franciscan Rule by Pope Honorius III* (illus. 45). On the upper right wall, *St Francis before the Sultan* is followed by the lower scene on the left wall, the *Stigmatization of St Francis*, and on the lower right the *Funeral of St Francis*. The lower scene just above the altar depicts a rare scene in the saint's life, a posthumous miracle: the *Resurrection of the Notary's Son*.

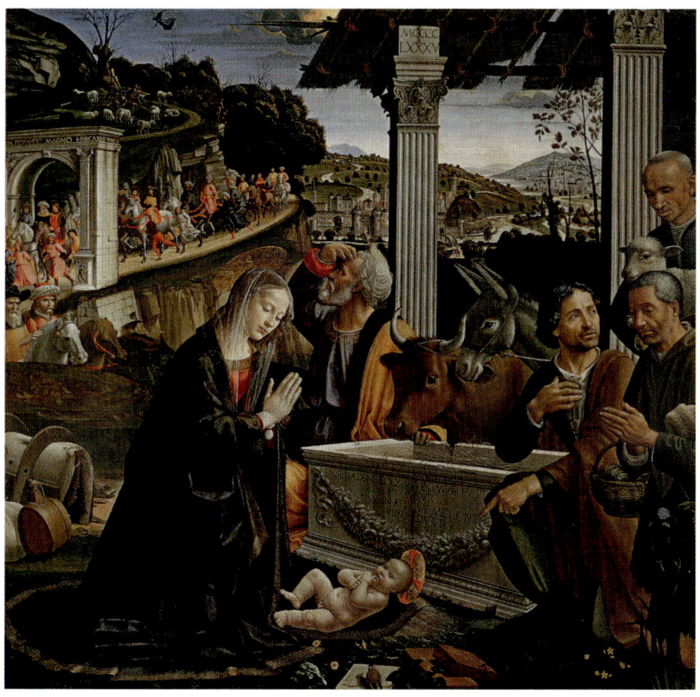

44 Domenico Ghirlandaio, *Adoration of the Shepherds*, 1485, tempera on panel, Sassetti chapel, Santa Trinita, Florence.

The altarpiece – the devotional and liturgical focus of the chapel – depicts the Virgin kneeling in adoration of the newborn Christ, as shepherds crowd in (illus. 44).[18] As such, it signals the dual dedication of the chapel to the nativity and St Francis. Christ's birth fulfils the sibyls' prophecies of the saviour's coming. An inscription on the sarcophagus declares: 'my tomb will produce a new deity'. Remarkable is the sympathetic portrayal of the rough-hewn shepherds, likely inspired by the triptych of the same theme by Hugo van der Goes, commissioned by the banker Tommaso Portinari for Sant'Egidio, the church of the Santa Maria Nuova hospital, and newly arrived in Florence. The exquisitely refined execution of the painting, which everywhere shows Ghirlandaio's meticulous brushwork, casts Flemish colour palette and oil technique into a Florentine idiom. The *Adoration of the Shepherds* thus unites themes of prophecy, birth and rebirth in the surrounding murals.

The theme of rebirth may explain the choice of the rare scene of Francis's *Resurrection of the Notary's Son* just above (illus. 46). This scene also had special meaning for Sassetti, for in 1478 or 1479 his eldest son Teodoro died, probably in Lyon, where he too worked for the Medici bank. Shortly thereafter, in May 1479, Nera Corsi Sassetti bore him another son, named Teodoro in memory of his brother, as was customary. The habit of 'remaking' a deceased family member through use of the same name was less a personal memorial than a way of perpetuating the identity of the family, as we recall from the naming practices of Ghirlandaio's own family discussed in Chapter One. Sassetti's choice of this scene reminded viewers of his family's antiquity and resilience. The scene takes place against a backdrop of the Piazza Santa Trinita, with the facade of the very church in which the chapel sits shown at the right, the tiny child falling from the window of the palace at the left. By setting the event in Florence instead of Rome, where it historically took place, Ghirlandaio encouraged

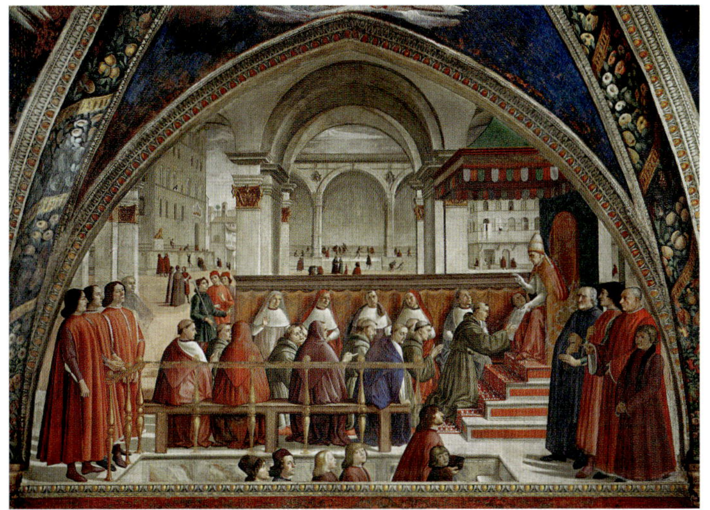

his viewers to imagine the event in terms of their own experiences. He also relocated the scene above, the *Confirmation of the Rule*, to Florence, with a view of the Palazzo Vecchio and Loggia della Signoria in the distance. He seems in this way to claim that Florence, not Rome, was the site for the new era of peace to come, as proclaimed by the Augustus mural on the entrance wall and the Nativity of Christ in the altarpiece. That this new era was in the Florence dominated by Lorenzo de' Medici and his circle, Sassetti included, was affirmed for spectators by the scenes before them.

As in the Sistine narratives, portraits populate the sacred scenes, especially on the altar wall. In the scene of the *Confirmation of the Rule*, just above the *Resurrection of the Notary's Son*, Sassetti stands at the right with his son Federigo; Antonio Pucci and Lorenzo de' Medici stand to the left. Pucci was a Medici ally whose son had married one of Francesco's daughters in 1483. Lorenzo raises his hand to greet his sons Piero, Giovanni and Giuliano, who mount the stairs led by their tutor, the humanist Angelo Poliziano.

45 Domenico Ghirlandaio, *Confirmation of the Franciscan Rule by Pope Honorius III*, 1483–5, fresco, Sassetti chapel, Santa Trinita, Florence.

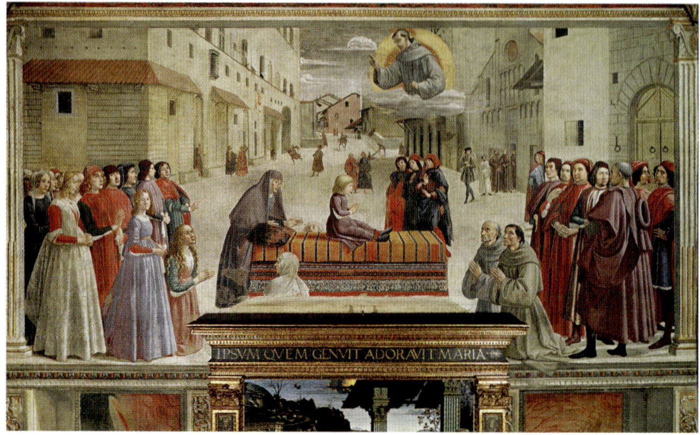

Sassetti's three other sons stand at the left. In the *Resurrection of the Notary's Son* just below, Sassetti's five daughters and their partners stand at the left. Ghirlandaio and his brother Davide are also shown at the right edge; Domenico, in a short blue tunic with red mantel, his arm akimbo, looks out at the spectator. His confident demeanour projects the status Domenico had achieved during the years he was painting this chapel, between 1483 and 1485. His reputation secured, the artist was emancipated from his father, and he established an independent household and his own workshop. The portraits of Sassetti and his family model piety and memorialize them for posterity while visualizing their social status and hopes for future salvation. The artist's self-portrait, we must assume, makes similar claims.

Ghirlandaio finished painting the Sassetti Chapel by the end of 1485, and the first mass was celebrated on 1 January 1486. Four months before, on 1 September 1485, Ghirlandaio and his brother Davide had contracted with Giovanni Tornabuoni to decorate his funerary chapel, the main chapel in Santa Maria Novella (illus. 47).[19] This plum commission, for a prominent patron in one of the largest and most important churches in Florence, must

46 Domenico Ghirlandaio, *Resurrection of the Notary's Son*, 1483–5, fresco, Sassetti chapel, Santa Trinita, Florence.

have been Tornabuoni's response to his rival Sassetti's opulent chapel in Santa Trinita, then nearing completion. It challenged the artist to surpass his achievement at Santa Trinita in a much larger space for a much richer patron. The surviving contract is notable for what it says as much as for what it doesn't say. Drawn up in Giovanni Tornabuoni's Florentine palace, the patron declared his purpose: 'as an act of piety and love of God, to the exaltation of his house and family and the enhancement of the said church and chapel'. The contract goes on to specify in detail what Giovanni required, and it reveals him as a man accustomed to getting what he wanted. The subjects – the lives of the Virgin, to whom the church was dedicated, and of St John the Baptist, the donor's patron saint – were utterly conventional, although the programme as executed celebrates Giovanni's family and his city above all. The inscription on the mural at the lower right of the east wall, among the last to be painted, celebrates the good fortune of the city in which Giovanni participates: 'In the year 1490, when the most beautiful of cities, famed for its deeds, victories, arts and buildings, enjoyed wealth, health and peace'.

In the contract, Tornabuoni stipulated that the vault should show the four evangelists; it then described the histories of the Virgin on the west wall, proceeding from the bottom up. They were the *Birth of the Virgin*, the *Betrothal and Marriage of the Virgin*, the *Annunciation*, the *Nativity and the Adoration of the Magi*, the *Purification of the Virgin*, *Christ in the Temple* and the *Death of the Virgin*. In the east wall, seven scenes from the life of St John the Baptist, again starting from the bottom, were to include *Zacharias in the Temple*, the *Visitation*, the *Birth of the Baptist*, *St John in the Desert*, the *Preaching of the Baptist*, the *Baptism of Christ* and the *Feast of Herod*. On the window wall were to be figures of Dominican saints, and above the windows the *Coronation of the Virgin*. Giovanni also specified materials, such as lapis lazuli for the figures and less costly German blue for the other parts, and the use of fine gold for decorative details. He also

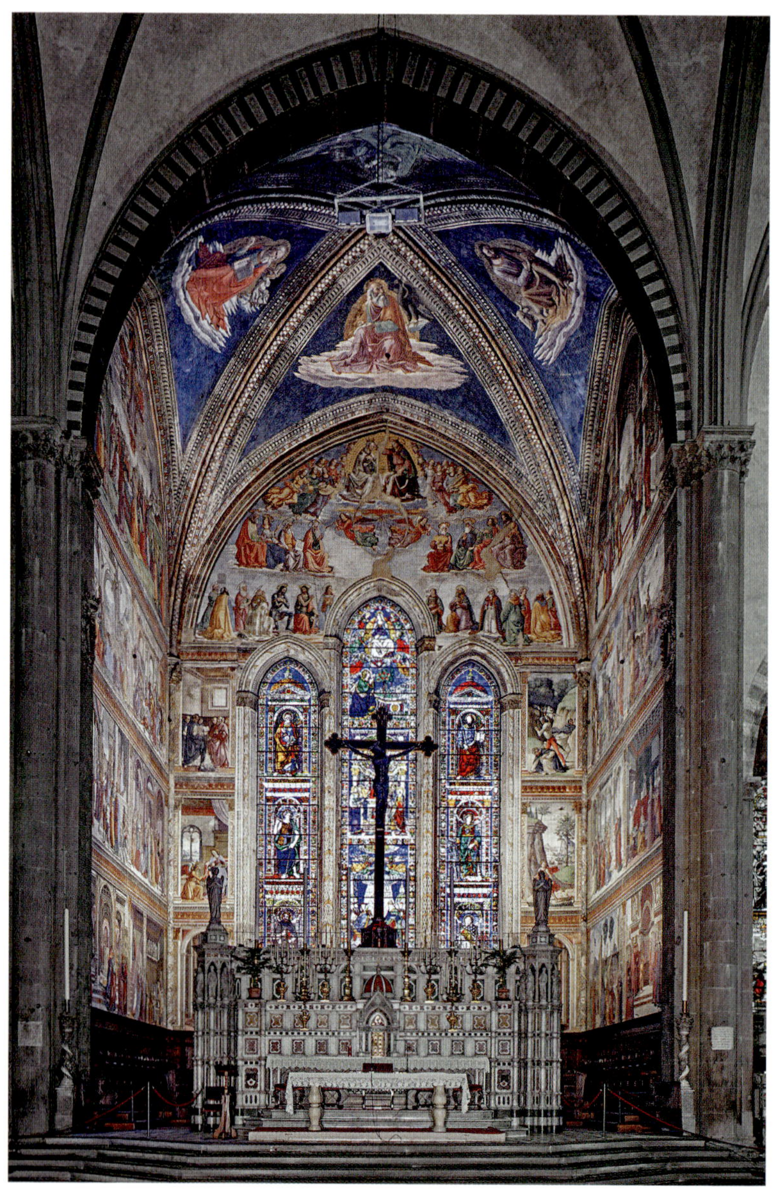

47 Tornabuoni chapel, 1485–90, Santa Maria Novella, Florence.

directed that the scenes should be painted in fresco with 'figures, buildings, castles, cities, villas, mountains, hills, plains, water, rocks, garments, animals, birds and beasts'. He required that the artists begin painting by May 1486 and that they finish in four years for a fee of 1,100 gold florins. The mandating of subjects, deadlines and materials is common to contracts, but Giovanni's stipulation of technique and lively descriptive style is unusual, especially as he was undoubtedly very familiar with Ghirlandaio's work. It lends insight, however, into what Giovanni valued about Ghirlandaio's work and his expectation that they would be 'noble, worthy, exquisite, and decorative paintings', as stated in the document.

Despite its details, the contract is silent on other aspects of the commission. The absence of any representatives from the church, who had ultimate authority for the main chapel, is surprising, and no responsibility was assigned for the structural modifications to the chapel (the filling in of an oculus on the window wall) or for building what must have been a large scaffolding. It is also notable because of its timing; although it states that Giovanni 'holds the rights of the indisputable patron of the great chapel', in fact it precedes by over a year the formal granting of those rights. He and his entire extended family received the patronage rights to the walls and the altar of the main chapel only on 13 October 1486 in a document signed in the chapter house of the church, the witnesses to which included the friars in the convent. Securing patronage rights was the culmination of a long campaign in which, as we have seen, he bested Francesco Sassetti and other rival claimants. The 1485 contract with the Ghirlandaio brothers may have been designed to impress the friars with his munificence and hint at more generosity to come. The paintings were probably already underway in the chapel at the time of the contract granting patronage rights, as proof of Giovanni's ability to deliver results. In addition, Giovanni's last will and testament, drawn up on 26 March

1490, provided for new choir stalls, stained-glass windows, an altarpiece costing 500 florins, candlesticks, embroideries, tombs and memorial masses, confirming that by this date he had secured burial and patronage rights to the entire chapel. The promise of a new altarpiece and stained-glass windows occasioned an expansion of the original decorative programme, so that what a visitor sees even today is a grandiose testament to Giovanni's piety and magnificence.

Responding to the vast wall space in the chapel, Ghirlandaio organized the murals on four levels, with fictive piers and entablatures dividing the walls into ample fields. Lavish antiquarian details ornament the painted architecture, with motifs derived from ancient decorative painting, newly discovered in Nero's Golden House in Rome in the 1480s. Gold leaf simulates mosaic tesserae, while the Tornabuoni emblem – three diamonds arranged in a triangle – repeats in the entablatures. This frame creates independent spatial zones for the narratives, which are organized around an ideal viewing point in the centre of the field. Only the painted piers respond to the viewpoint of the spectator below; they are foreshortened so that the capitals jut forward from the entablatures they support, while their bases recede into the depicted space where they cast shadows. In addition, the scale of the figures increases with their distance from the spectator to ensure visibility: the foreground figures on the lower tier are at a height of 160 centimetres (63 in.), while those in the highest scene are at 204 centimetres (80½ in.). Light in all the scenes falls from the direction of the window; that is, from the right for the west wall and the left for the east wall. Only on the window wall are scenes united by a shared perspective scheme.

The murals reveal Ghirlandaio's mature narrative style, the fruit of his experiences in the Sistine and Sassetti chapels. Lessons drawn from the Sistine cycle guided Ghirlandaio's designs, achieving decorative unity and legibility. The narratives begin on the lower

tiers and move from the outer side towards the window wall, the
Virgin cycle from left to right, the Baptist cycle from right to left.
The compositions centre the main action in the foreground, unite
figure and background using architecture, and deploy the full range
of pigments suited to application in fresco – red, blue, green,
yellow – thus achieving a luminous ensemble. As in the Sassetti
Chapel, Ghirlandaio avoided continuous narration with repeated
figures in favour of concentrated action set within clearly constructed spaces. If we look at the *Expulsion of Joachim from the Temple*,
we see these ideas at work (illus. 48). According to legend, Joachim,
the Virgin's father, went to the temple to offer a lamb for sacrifice.
His offering was rejected because he was childless. We see, in the
foreground right, Joachim clutching his lamb and looking quizzic-
ally at the robed figure who shoves him outside the temple, while
in the middle ground left the high priest welcomes another sup-
plicant's offering. The temple is imagined as an arched, flat-roofed
structure set in the centre of the picture field that frames the
complementary actions. Even if we did not know the story, we
perceive the foreground figures, through their size and placement,
as the protagonists. Ghirlandaio choreographed their action as

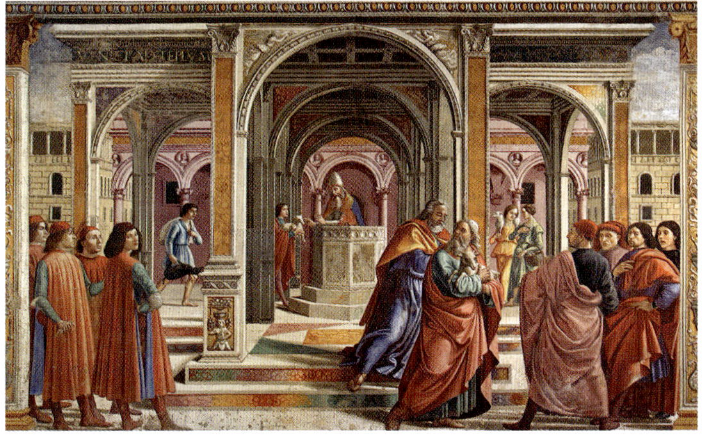

48 Domenico Ghirlandaio, *Expulsion of Joachim from the Temple*, 1485–90,
fresco, Santa Maria Novella, Florence.

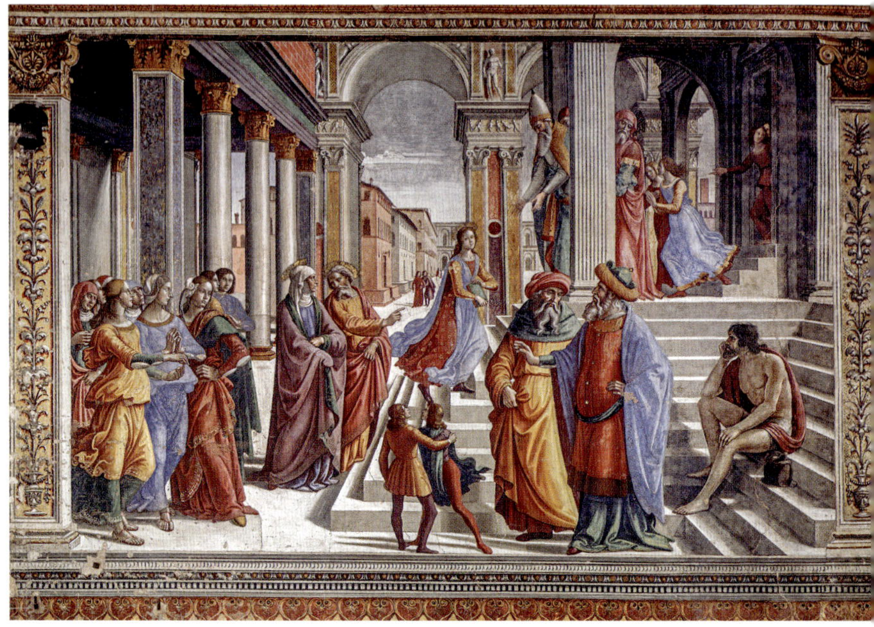

a potent encounter between two figures. As in the Sassetti Chapel murals, Giotto's rendition of the theme in the Arena chapel in Padua inspired Ghirlandaio's design.

The arresting action of the scenes is often set against imposing architectural backdrops that recall Roman buildings.[20] In the *Presentation of the Virgin*, the capitals of the colonnade on the left were likely drawn from a Roman model (illus. 49). The vaulted structure in the middle background resembles a triumphal arch, with illusionistic sculptures in niches and winged victories in the spandrels flanking the central arch. A triumphal arch reminiscent of the Arch of Constantine forms the backdrop of the *Massacre of the Innocents*, ornamented with reliefs taken from Roman coins and sarcophagi (illus. 50). The *Annunciation to Zacharias* takes place before a fanciful structure replete with classicizing architectural detail, coloured marble revetment and sculpted relief set against

49 Domenico Ghirlandaio, *Presentation of the Virgin*, 1485–90, fresco, Santa Maria Novella, Florence.

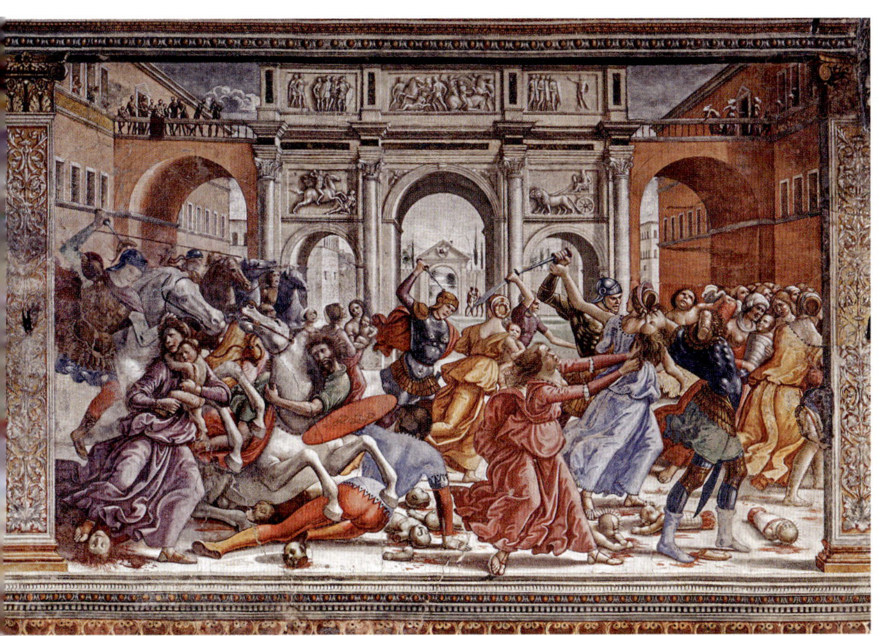

gilt mosaic fields (illus. 51). These imposing details are copies of
reliefs from the Arch of Constantine and coins. In the imagina-
tively luxurious interior of the *Birth of the Virgin*, ornaments derived
from Roman models cover almost every surface (illus. 52). The
central piers are decorated with motifs of vases and candelabra
(called grotesques) derived from the decoration of Nero's Golden
House, which we know Ghirlandaio had visited while in Rome.
They are crowned with capitals that are whimsical variations
on the ionic order. The grotesques recur in the inlaid panels of
the wainscoting behind, touched in gold, where Ghirlandaio has
recorded his family names: BIGHORDI and GRILLANDI. Just
under the cornice festooned with garlands and angels' heads, a
relief of cherubs playing musical instruments is painted in grisaille.
Its model was likely an ancient sarcophagus, but it also recalls
Donatello's singing gallery for the Florentine cathedral.

50 Domenico Ghirlandaio, *Massacre of the Innocents*, 1485–90, fresco, Santa
Maria Novella, Florence.

While similar details in the Sassetti murals recall the patron's interest in ancient artefacts and texts, Giovanni Tornabuoni was not known as a scholar. He was, however, aware of Medici adherents' pursuit of such studies, and, through his position at the bank, he procured ancient artefacts for Lorenzo de' Medici's collection during his long residence in Rome.[21] He also took care to educate his son Lorenzo in humanist studies. The splendid Roman settings of the Tornabuoni murals thus showcased his wealth, associated Tornabuoni with the cultivated elite and recalled his illustrious career in the Eternal City.

As in the Sistine and Sassetti murals, full-length portraits of the patron's family and friends stand as witnesses to the sacred events. In the scene of the *Annunciation to Zacharias*, in which an angel tells the saint that his elderly wife, Elizabeth, will give birth to the Baptist, ranks of figures stand to the left and right. Giovanni Tornabuoni occupies a position at centre left closest to the sacred

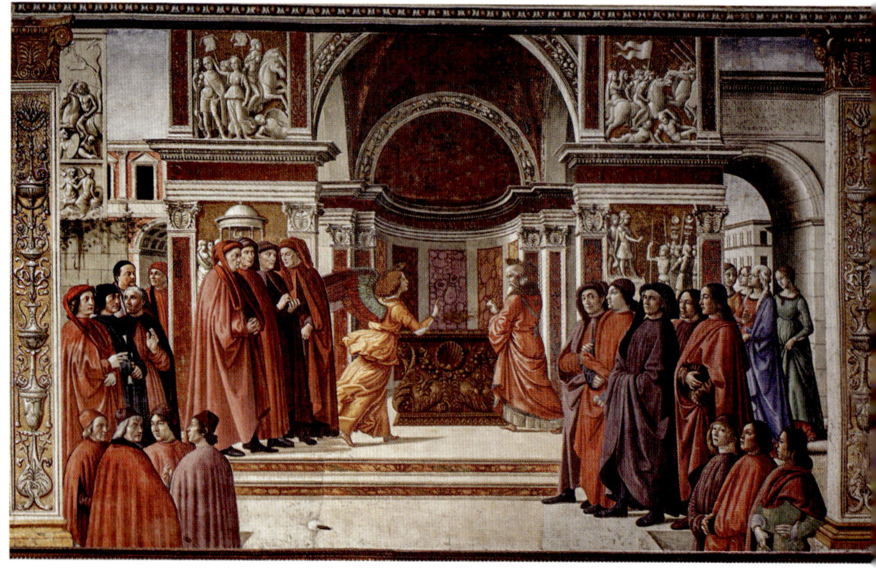

51 Domenico Ghirlandaio, *Annunciation to Zacharias*, 1485–90, fresco, Santa Maria Novella, Florence.

event, accompanied by members of his extended family, the Tornaquinci consortia. At the right, two steps down, are more Tornabuoni relatives. In the corners left and right stand figures seen in three-quarters view, including Florentine scholars such as Marsilio Ficino and Angelo Poliziano, and to the right Tornabuoni's Medici bank associates.

On the opposite wall, in the scene of the *Expulsion of Joachim*, at the left, Giovanni Tornabuoni's son and heir Lorenzo leads a group of young men, gazing over his shoulder towards viewers. Mirroring Lorenzo's pose at the right, Ghirlandaio rests his hand on his breast, a gesture that signals his humility but also his skill of hand. He seems to suggest that, while Tornabuoni's gift to the church is the chapel, he also contributed to it with his artistry. Seemingly a bold claim, it must be one that Giovanni Tornabuoni had approved. It is worth recalling that Santa Maria Novella was the major Dominican church in Florence, founded by Ghirlandaio's

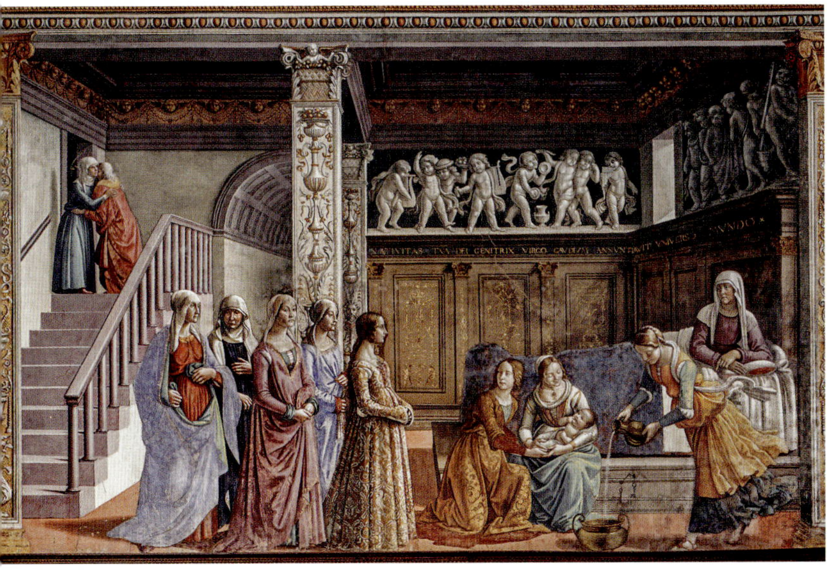

52 Domenico Ghirlandaio, *Birth of the Virgin*, 1485–90, fresco, Santa Maria Novella, Florence.

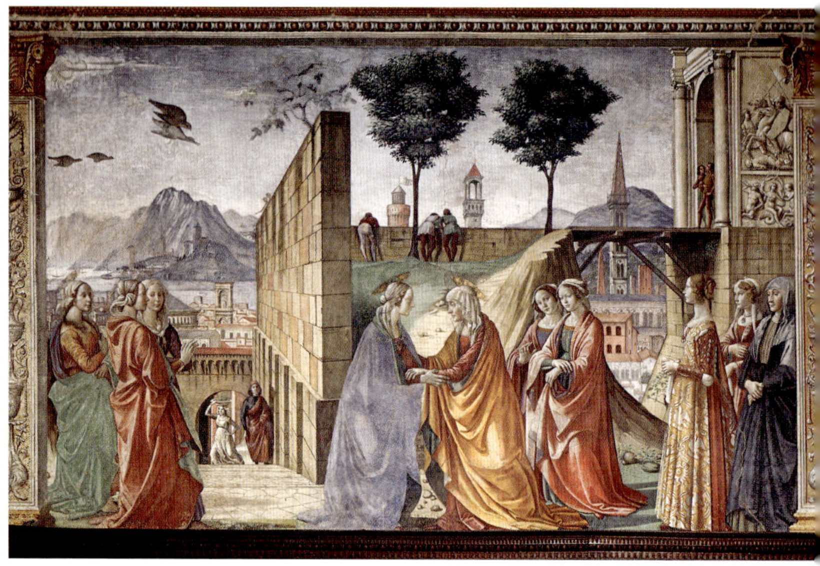

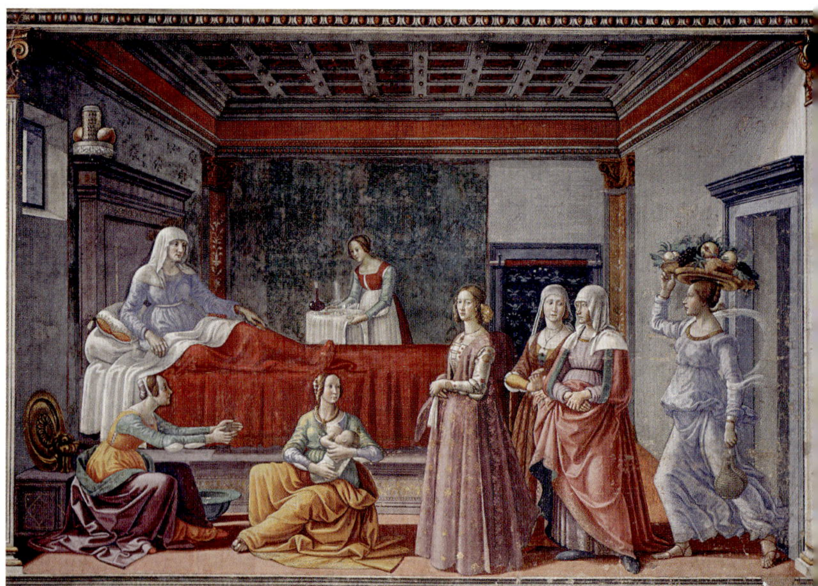

53 Domenico Ghirlandaio, *Visitation*, 1485–90, fresco, Santa Maria Novella, Florence.
54 Domenico Ghirlandaio, *Birth of the Baptist*, 1485–90, fresco, Santa Maria Novella, Florence.

name saint, and that his first wife and he himself would be buried in his newly purchased tomb in the cemetery, so the church had personal meaning for him too. Next to Ghirlandaio gather his brother Davide, seen from behind, his father Tommaso and brother Benedetto. As Giovanni had, Ghirlandaio demonstrated his piety and appealed to the saints for the protection of his family.

The inner scenes of the lowest tier feature female portraits. In the *Birth of the Virgin*, next to the *Expulsion*, a group of women visit St Anne, who reclines in bed as maidservants bathe the new-born Virgin. Ludovica Tornabuoni, the patron's daughter, leads the group, dressed in a richly brocaded gown and elegant jewellery signalling her status. Across the chapel in the scene of the *Visitation*, at the right is a group of three women, including Giovanna degli Albizzi Tornabuoni, Lorenzo Tornabuoni's first wife, who had died in 1488, dressed in a resplendent gown (illus. 53). She is followed by Lorenzo's second wife, Ginevra Gianfigliazzi, and an older woman, perhaps a posthumous portrait of Giovanni Tornabuoni's sister Lucrezia (1427–1482), the wife of Piero de' Medici. Giovanna appears again in the scene just above, the *Birth of the Baptist* (illus. 54). The portraits of women family members suggest that Giovanni Tornabuoni had considerable regard for his female relatives, as borne out by other aspects of his patronage.

As with Francesco Sassetti's chapel, the murals in Santa Maria Novella showcase Giovanni Tornabuoni's wealth, his extended family and his social position to viewers. But who were those viewers? In the fifteenth century, the nave in most large churches, including Santa Maria Novella, was divided by a rood screen, which sequestered spaces closest to the altar for the clergy's use. Most visitors, including during mass, had limited physical and visual access to the most sacred spaces. Maria DePrano establishes that, from most viewing positions in the church, only the upper scenes in the main chapel would have been visible, and even then at considerable distance. Only the friars attending mass in the choir or privileged viewers on special occasions such as feast days or funerals could have seen the lower tiers with all their portraits. As an advertisement to a worldly audience, then, the mural decoration had limited reach. DePrano suggests instead that the heavenly audience was primary. As in Sassetti's chapel, Tornabuoni's chapel housed family tombs, four of which were located in the most privileged place at the foot of the altar, and he had endowed memorial masses for the deceased. The portraits memorialized family members and invited the friars and others gathered in the apse and choir to pray for their souls to reduce their time in purgatory. As silent witnesses to sacred events, they appealed to the Virgin and saints for protection and aid in their journey to heaven.

In the Santa Maria Novella murals, Ghirlandaio used earth pigments best suited for painting in fresco, and smalt as a preparation for azurite and ultramarine. In his contract, Giovanni Tornabuoni specified azurite in the skies and ultramarine in the figures, but the smalt preparation, applied in fresco, would have speeded up the execution and minimized use of the more costly blue pigments.

Close examination of the murals during the restoration of 1983–91 revealed that Ghirlandaio applied his colours to fresh plaster in thin layers from darkest to lightest. In the flesh tones, he used *terra verde* and St John's white underpainting, just as he had in the *Baptism* at Brozzi. The upper layers were done with fine brushstrokes in white and light pigments in the highlights and reddish-brown lines to indicate features, while hair and beards were stroked more freely. The drapery was painted with broad sweeps of the brush, frequently ignoring the indications of contours traced from cartoons. Architectural backgrounds were painted freely but adhered to the often-elaborate guidelines incised in the wet *intonaco*. Smalt, applied in fresco, formed a base for azurite retouching in shadows, applied in secco. Gold leaf was applied to details of costume and setting; in the upper reaches, it was applied over wax bosses to catch the light more easily.

As in the Sassetti Chapel, Ghirlandaio supplied an altarpiece for the chapel, for which Giovanni Tornabuoni provided the generous sum of 500 florins in his testament of 1490. It was removed in the nineteenth century, and its parts dispersed. Reconstruction shows it was an enormous double-sided structure in the form of a triumphal arch, its main panel facing the choir and nave showing the *Madonna of the Apocalypse with Sts Dominic, Michael the Archangel, John the Baptist and Thomas*, the reverse towards the windows depicting the *Resurrection*. It thus served as the liturgical focus for the friars and male worshippers in the upper nave, and the Tornabuoni during memorial masses for family members buried there. These and side panels of standing saints in shell niches were encased in a colonnaded, gilded framework surmounted by an arched pediment housing a tabernacle for the Eucharist made by the woodworker Baccio d'Agnolo. The altarpiece thus functioned additionally as an altar of the Sacrament. The *Madonna of the Apocalypse* shows the Virgin seated on clouds nursing the Child, surrounded by bands of the firmament and heads of seraphim and cherubim (illus. 55). From behind, rays of light allude to her as the 'woman clothed with the sun' from the Book of Revelation (12:1). In accordance with the dedication of the chapel to the Assumption, and the imagery of the murals and stained glass that visualize her role as mother of God and queen of heaven, the *Madonna of the Apocalypse* exalts her immaculate status and signals the dedication of the church to her. The *Resurrection* recalls Christ's sacrifice, re-enacted in each mass, which reopened to mortals the doors to Paradise, closed since Adam and Eve's disobedience. It was a particularly appropriate image for a funerary chapel, where family members prayed for the salvation of their deceased. The altarpiece was begun after the murals were completed in December

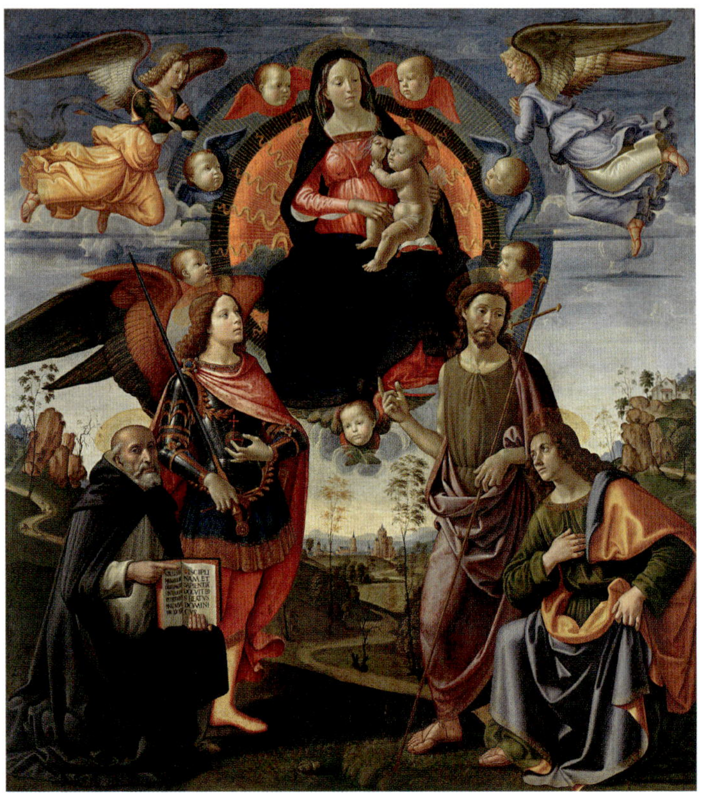

1490 and installed in April 1494, just months after Ghirlandaio's
death the preceding January.

Throughout the 1480s, while Ghirlandaio was deeply engaged
in mural decoration, he was also producing independent panels
for a wide range of patrons. Most impressive is the high altarpiece for the church of the Ospedale degli Innocenti in Florence,
the foundling hospital devoted then as today to the welfare of
children (illus. 56).[22] Founded in 1419, it began operations in
1445; in the 1480s, Prior Francesco Tesori undertook a renovation
of the church, Santa Maria degli Innocenti. On 23 October 1485

55 Domenico Ghirlandaio, *Madonna of the Apocalypse with Sts Dominic, Michael,
John the Baptist and Thomas (or John the Evangelist)*, 1490–94, tempera, oil and
tempera grassa on panel.

– that is, shortly after he signed his contract with Giovanni Tornabuoni for the murals in Santa Maria Novella – Ghirlandaio agreed with the prior to supply the painting by August 1488 for a price of 115 florins. In the end, it was finished in March 1489 and cost 122 florins. From surviving documentation, we know that the panel was housed in an elaborate gilded framework – based on the design of his own altarpiece in San Giusto in Florence – that included pilasters, freestanding columns and angels at the side, surmounted by a tabernacle for the host and flanking candelabra. This frame, which cost more than the painting, was sadly lost, probably during renovations to the altar in the sixteenth century.

Ghirlandaio adapted the popular theme of the Adoration of the Magi to its setting in the hospital. The Virgin and Child, seated before the manger, its rustic roof supported by magnificent classical piers, receive the gifts of the magi, the elderly magus kneeling to kiss the child's foot, the others offering precious vessels. At the left, St John the Baptist, patron saint of Florence, points to the Virgin while appealing to viewers. Before him a small innocent kneels, rays emanating from his head. At the right, St John the Evangelist, patron saint of the silk guild, under whose supervision the hospital operated, guides the devotions of another innocent. Past and future events are depicted in the middle ground: the annunciation to the shepherds at the right and the massacre of the innocents at the left. The association of the innocents of the hospital – foundlings, or *gittatelli* (little throwaways) – with the holy innocents slain by Herod's soldiers was made explicit by the relics of the child martyrs deposited in the altar at the dedication of the hospital church in 1451.

The picture is often judged to be one of Ghirlandaio's most beautiful, with brilliant colours and prodigious gilding. The refined touch of Ghirlandaio's brush is seen especially well in the little innocents, whose dark red wounds are glimpsed through

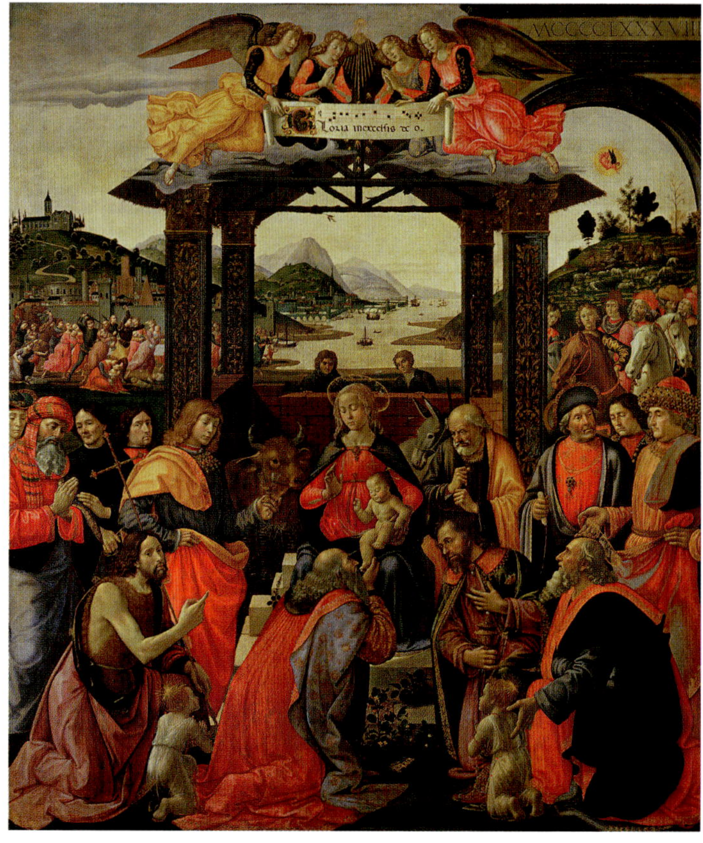

diaphanous white drapery (illus. 57). Visitors from the exotic
East, the magi were a pretext for the display of beautiful fabrics,
elaborate jewellery, precious metalwork and exotic costumes.
The older magus's robe is brocaded with stars, while the dress
of the younger magi sport jewels and embroidery. Three figures
at the right of St Joseph, one holding a scroll, are thought to be
portraits of consuls of the silk gild and are elaborately clothed.
The emphasis on opulent fabrics was also a reminder of the luxury production of guild members. Their presence in the cortège

56 Domenico Ghirlandaio, *Adoration of the Magi*, 1486–9, tempera on
panel.

of the magi advertises their generosity as patrons of the hospital and church. Behind the young magus standing at the left, portraits of Francesco Tesori (the patron and hospital prior) in black and of the artist himself in red show both participating in the worship of the newborn Christ.

Ghirlandaio repeated the theme of the Adoration of the Magi in a large round painting (*tondo*) for his faithful patron Giovanni Tornabuoni (illus. 58).[23] We know from a 1498 inventory of his large palace on the Via Tornabuoni that it was hung in the first-floor chamber belonging to his son, Lorenzo. The normally laconic inventory scribe added '*bello*' (beautiful) to

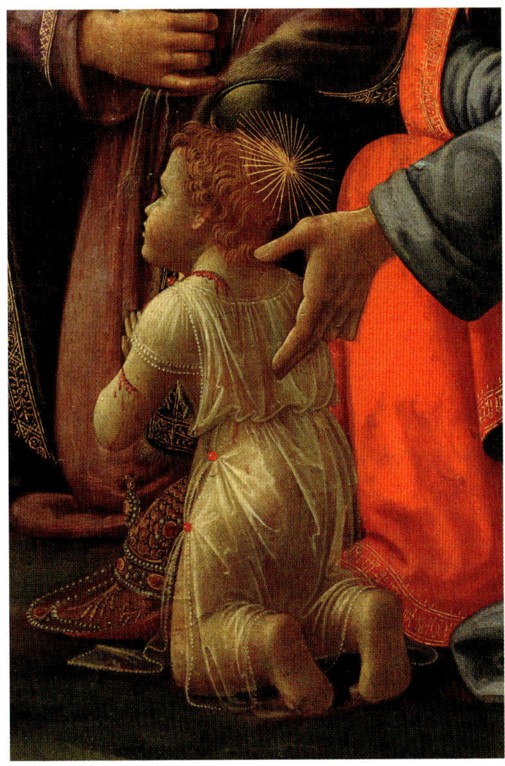

57 Domenico Ghirlandaio, *Adoration of the Magi*, 1486–9, detail.

the picture's description. The picture was in a large gold frame that made it stand out among the other furnishings, which included inlaid panelling with scenes from the legend of Jason and Medea, a chest with a marquetry '*prospettiva*' (view), two painted and gilded marriage chests, maps in gold frames and a bed finished in gold and silver. The *tondo* shows the magi, who offer gifts to the Child, accompanied by a throng of soldiers, servants and attendants. At the left middle ground, the angel announces Christ's birth to the shepherds, while in the distance is a port with ships. The *tondo* format was popular, especially for private devotional pictures, and it would not have been out of place amid the rich furnishings of the Tornabuoni palace. The subject was especially

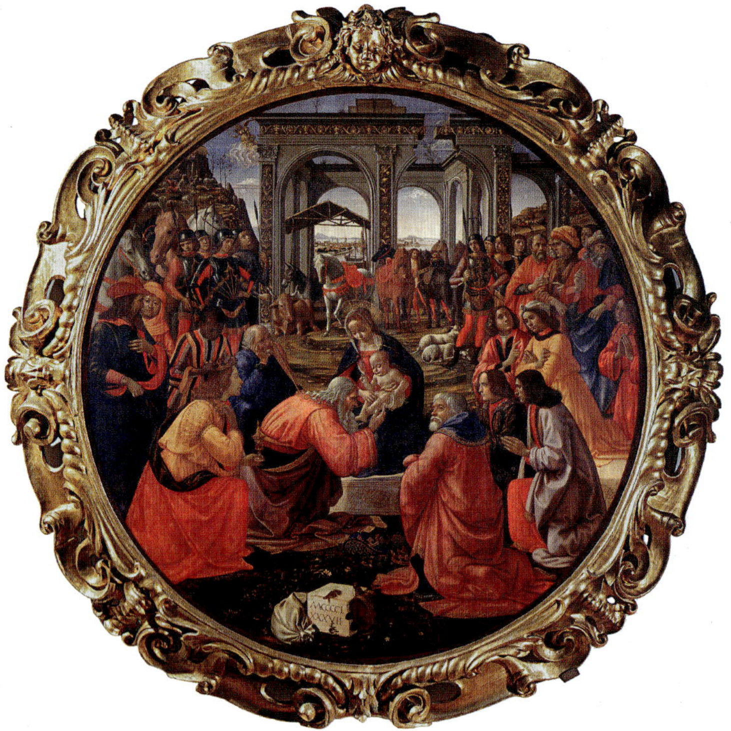

58 Domenico Ghirlandaio, *Adoration of the Magi*, 1487, tempera on panel.

dear to the Medici family, to whom of course the Tornabuoni were related, through their sponsorship of the Confraternity of the Magi, which re-enacted the magi's procession every year on 6 January, the feast of Epiphany. It was also an occasion for a virtuous display of opulence. Ghirlandaio arranged the figures in a circular cortège, which complements the shape of the panel. The classical motifs, such as the plinth with reliefs of putti on which the Virgin sits, and the palace ruins in the background, perhaps reflected Giovanni's interest in classical artefacts and appealed to Lorenzo's pursuit of humanistic study. The broken entablature of the unroofed classical structure reminded viewers that the coming of Christ swept away the paganism of the classical world. The picture bears the date of 1487, so it was underway at the same time as the murals in the Tornabuoni Chapel in Santa Maria Novella.

In addition to altarpieces and private devotional images, Ghirlandaio also painted portraits during this time, some of which are among the most well-known images of the Renaissance.[24] Unlike the portraits in his narrative murals, which are public statements of piety, the independent portraits are intimate keepsakes. The *Old Man and His Grandson* in the Louvre is an especially touching image of intergenerational rapport (illus. 59).[25] Seated in an interior with a landscape view through the window, the old man wears a fur-lined red robe (*lucco*), his headdress (*capuccio*), draped over his shoulder, of an upper class Florentine man, while the child sports a red cap and doublet.[26] The striking deformity of the old man's nose, a condition called rhinophyma, was derived from Ghirlandaio's portrait drawing in Stockholm of the old man on his deathbed. Ghirlandaio positioned the man with his head inclined to minimize the deformity. The poses of the figures – the old man looking fondly at the child and the child resting his hand on the elder's chest – visualize a tender intimacy in which the child ignores the disfiguring growth. Viewers grasp the virtue of the elder sitter, who commands the affection of the innocent child and imparts his wisdom to him. While we do not know the identities of the sitters, the portrait captures the emotions and mutual regard that bound families, the bedrock of society, together in Renaissance Florence.

Ghirlandaio's portrait of Giovanna degli Albizzi Tornabuoni (1468–1488), now in Madrid, was painted for her husband Lorenzo di Giovanni Tornabuoni, whom she married on 15 June 1486 at the age of seventeen (illus. 60).[27] In 1498 – long after her death and her husband's remarriage – it hung in the suite of rooms occupied by Lorenzo in the Tornabuoni palace, in the chamber of the golden beams (*camera del palcho d'oro*), adjacent to the room that housed the Adoration *tondo*. Described in the inventory as 'a painting with a large gold frame with the head and bust of Giovanna degli Albizzi', it shows the sitter in profile facing left. By the time this portrait was painted, the profile view was old fashioned, but Ghirlandaio may have posed Giovanna this way because when it was painted, she had already died, so he was unable to draw her from life. He likely based his design on one of her medals, created around the time of her wedding.[28] In addition, tradition sanctioned the profile view as the most efficient form to capture individual likeness, as sources from Pliny to Victorian silhouettes attest. Earlier fifteenth-century profile portraits of women had established ideals of feminine beauty derived from literature seen in Giovanna's portrait: her fair hair, curls gently framing her face, tied in a chignon at the back; a high forehead and long, slightly curving neck. Avoiding eye contact, the profile view also visualized society's expectations of women's behaviour, circumscribed as it was to roles as daughters, wives and mothers in the family palace. It also captures the remoteness and inaccessibility of the departed beloved. An epitaph Poliziano composed for her tomb read:

By beauty, child, wealth and husband
I was fortunate, and also by talent, character and mind.
But during the next birth and the next year of marriage
Alas! With my offspring not yet born I perished.
That I might die more sadly treacherous fate showed
      me so many favours
But did not bestow them.

The lines suggest she died during her second pregnancy; she left an almost one-year-old son, Giovanni di Lorenzo Tornabuoni. The date inscribed on the panel, 1488, probably refers to the date of her death, not the date of the picture's execution, which was about 1490.

The panel shows Giovanna standing erect before a shelf filled with objects belonging to her. Her clothing, jewellery and possessions telegraph her wealth and social position. Her figure includes a view of her waist, which is unbelted, perhaps alluding to her pregnancy. She is dressed in a sleeveless, richly brocaded gown (*giornea*), over a red dress (*gamurra*) with glimpses of her under blouse (*camicia*) in the front and at the sleeves. The gown shows diamonds, the Tornabuoni emblem and Ls for Lorenzo, firmly tying her to her husband's family, while her dress is adorned with small white flowers, emblematic of her purity. Suspended from a cord around her neck, she wears a pendant of a diamond, a ruby and three large pearls, which we know from Giovanni Tornabuoni's testament was a family artefact. On the shelves behind her, another brooch with a square ruby encircled with diamonds and pearls surmounted by a dragon alludes to Giovanna's purity, strength and prosperity. The dragon was an attribute of St Margaret, the patron saint of childbirth. The string of coral beads was thought to be protective from evil spirits, while the small book was likely a book of hours, alluding to her piety.

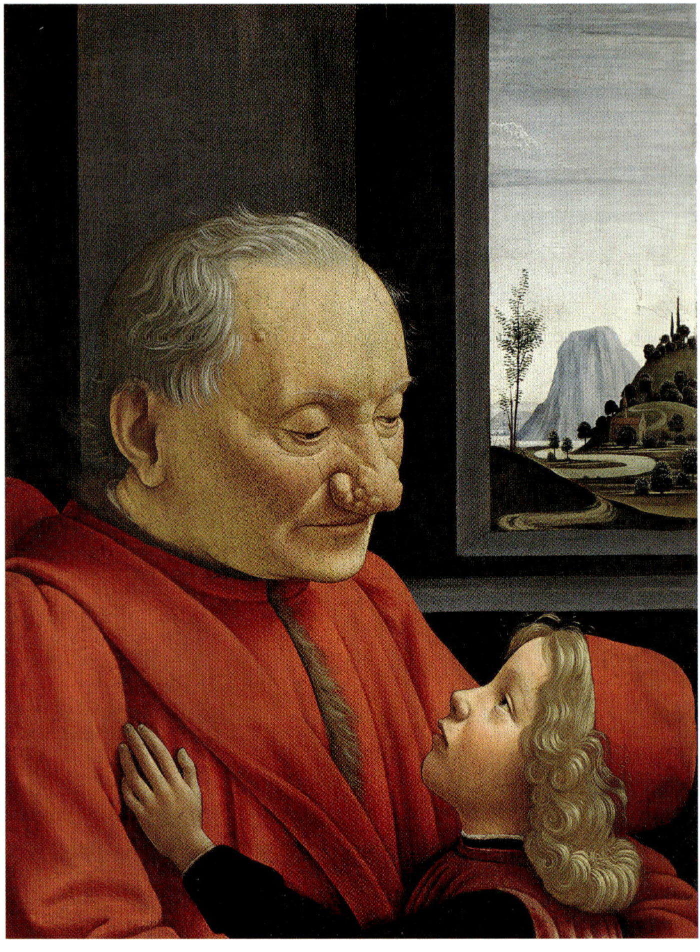

Pinned to the wall behind her is a piece of unfolded paper
on which is written: ARS UTINAM MORES ANIMUM QUE EFFIN-
GERE POSSES/PULCHRIOR IN TERRIS NULLA TABELLA FORET
MCCCCLXXXVIII (Art, if only you were able to portray character
and soul, no painting on earth would be more beautiful). The
inscription, based on one of the Roman poet Martial's epigrams,

59 Domenico Ghirlandaio, *An Old Man and His Grandson*, c. 1490, tempera on
panel.
60 Domenico Ghirlandaio, *Giovanna degli Albizzi Tornabuoni*, c. 1489–90,
tempera, oil and tempera grassa on panel.

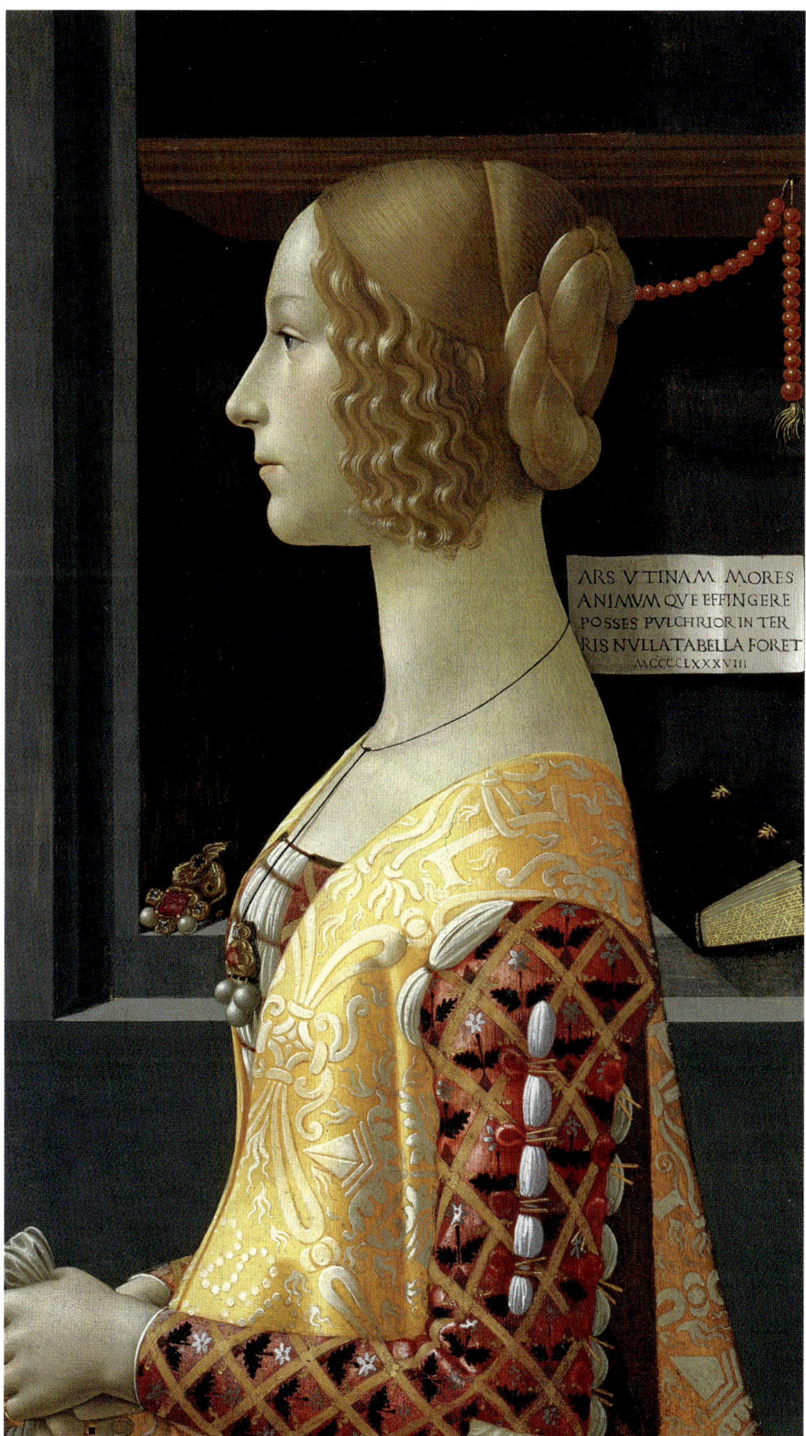

ARS VTINAM MORES
ANIMVM QVE EFFINGERE
POSSES PVLCHRIOR IN TER
RIS NVLLA TABELLA FORET
MCCCCLXXXVIII

was adapted by Lorenzo (or his tutor Angelo Poliziano) to lament the loss of the young wife, which even art – with all its power – could not bring back. It also implies that the task of portraiture was to record appearances and to depict something about the character of the sitter. Long expressed in literature, by the late fifteenth century this idea of portraiture had been embraced by the larger culture. We find it invoked in a legal document concerning a disputed price for one of Ghirlandaio's late altarpieces now in Rimini. The arbiter of the dispute found a reduced price justified because the portraits there, painted after Ghirlandaio's death, resembled their sitters 'neither in their character (person) nor their appearance'.[29] In Giovanna's portrait, the remoteness of the profile pose, and the longing and wistfulness expressed by the inscription, transform her image from a record of an individual to a feminine ideal of beauty and virtue.

Investigation of the portrait of Giovanna Tornabuoni revealed its highly refined painting technique, where different areas were done with different techniques to create brilliant effects of texture and surface.[30] The underdrawing and scoring in the *gesso* ground having established his basic design, Ghirlandaio lay in a base of lead white for the hair and clothing and a mixture of lead white and green earth for the flesh tones. For the background wall and niche, he applied a base layer of rich brown oil paint. For Giovanna's face and hands, over the green earth he applied the flesh tones in tempera enriched with oil (so-called *tempera grassa*), using a loose mesh of exceptionally fine parallel brush strokes, varying the thickness and opacity of each stroke to create thin layers in the shadows and dense ones in the highlights. The result is an almost shimmering, preternaturally smooth surface. In the hair, layers of fine strokes in *tempera grassa* mark every tress, done over a ground of lead white. For Giovanna's elaborate dress, the artist alternated layers of oil paint with enriched tempera. The red areas were done in oil paint over *tempera grassa*, with each detailed ornament shaped by deft strokes. The background was completed with the shelf containing the prayer book, brooch and coral beads; the fine details of these objects were touched with gold powder mixed in oil, called shell gold, and applied with a brush. Final highlights in the hair were applied in *tempera grassa*. This is perhaps Ghirlandaio's most refined and most meticulously painted panel, and its exquisite state of preservation allows us to see his technique at its best. Although he embraced the use of oil, primarily to add lustre and intensity to his colours, his handling of paint is compatible with the point of the brush application of pure tempera. He does not exploit the possibilities of oil paint, as did the Flemish painters, to create blended colours and glowing tones.[31] Indeed, although Ghirlandaio responded throughout his career to the allure of Flemish painting, as has often been pointed out, with its rich palette, sharp focus detail and virtuoso light effects, he never abandoned the fundamental procedures of the Florentine painting tradition.

In the 1480s, Ghirlandaio's most productive decade, his workshop painted murals and altarpieces distinguished by their scale, invention and artisanship. Positioned in highly visible places – the chancel of Santa Maria Novella, the high altar of the church of the Innocenti, the Sala dei Gigli in the Palazzo Vecchio – they brought honour to their patrons and *buona fama* to the artist. For a loyal clientele, foremost Giovanni Tornabuoni, Ghirlandaio also supplied portraits and devotional works for domestic interiors. His sophisticated technique, distinctive look and prestigious patrons affirmed his reputation as, in Vasari's words, 'one of the most important and most excellent masters of his age'. How Ghirlandaio planned and executed his paintings is the subject of the next chapter.

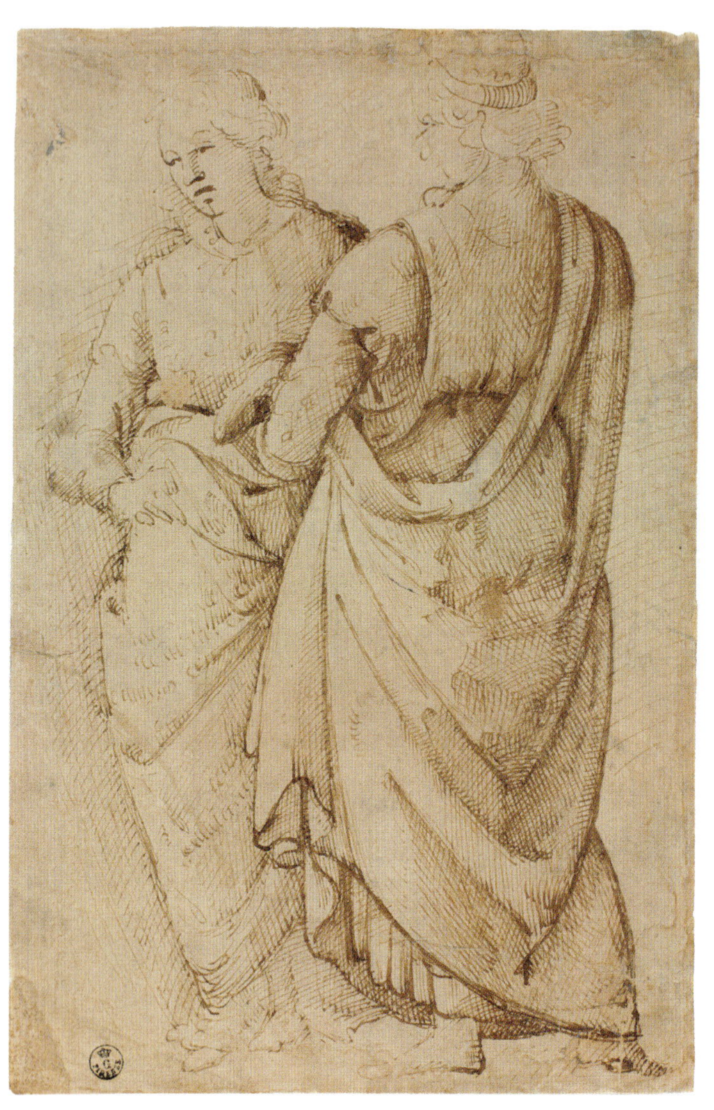

FIVE

The 'Expeditious' Artist: Ghirlandaio's Drawings and Workshop Production

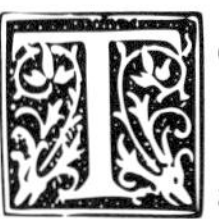Tommaso Bigordi's tax declaration in 1480 said his son Domenico 'is a painter here and there; he doesn't keep a workshop'. As we have seen, Domenico was an itinerant artist in the 1470s, working in Rome, San Gimignano, Pisa and other Tuscan towns. Works on panel painted in Florence, such as the San Giusto altarpiece, could have been painted in temporary quarters in the monastery or in another artist's workshop. Most likely he frequented Andrea del Verrocchio's *bottega* in the mid-1470s, where, as a painter of some experience, he would have been a collaborator or associate taking on independent projects. By the time he returned to Florence following the completion of the Sistine murals in the spring of 1482, however, beginning the Palazzo Vecchio murals and the Sassetti Chapel decoration, he needed a workspace of his own.[1] Although murals had to be executed on-site, large decorative projects required extensive preparation, consisting of drawings in a range of materials and varying scale. He required space to store materials and produce designs and panels. As in the Sistine Chapel, for the murals in the Palazzo Vecchio and Santa Trinita, whose execution overlapped in 1482 and 1483, Ghirlandaio needed assistants in addition to his brothers Davide and Benedetto. Their participation required a larger shared space than had been needed before. Where this workshop was located is unknown. As we

61 Domenico Ghirlandaio, *Two Standing Figures*, 1486–90, pen and brown ink on paper.

have seen, Domenico and Davide rented a house in the Via Cocomero (Via Ricasoli) shortly after their emancipation in October 1484, where Davide was still living in 1495. The rent, slightly more than 17 sealed florins (*fiorini di suggello* were chipped or damaged coins sealed in a bag marked with the value, about 20 per cent less than the gold florin) in 1495, suggests a large space that could accommodate Domenico's growing family. Only in 1490 is it documented that the brothers rented a workshop in the Piazza San Michele Berteldi, the current-day Piazza Antinori, at the corner of the Via dei Rondinelli and Via del Trebbio, a lease that Davide renewed in 1495 and 1500. The yearly rent, 10 sealed florins, suggests the workshop was probably not very large. It consisted of an internal courtyard and two storage areas, and it probably included a workspace on the street, which let in light and air and allowed customer access. The San Michele Berteldi workshop was well located for the ongoing work in the Tornabuoni Chapel in Santa Maria Novella and was adjacent to the large workshop of Baccio d'Agnolo, the woodworker who supplied choir stalls and the grandiose frame for Ghirlandaio's altarpiece. Whether the house on the Via Cocomero was also used as a workshop in the years between 1484 and 1490 is, however, unknown.

The names of Domenico's assistants are difficult to establish with precision. As we have seen, Davide was working with Domenico by at least the autumn of 1474, and he is documented in a subordinate position to him for the works in the Vatican and at Passignano. In subsequent projects, his presence is not documented but can be assumed; in the same 1480 tax record, Tommaso says Davide is Domenico's helper. The Sistine contract does not name Davide but refers to the painters and 'their familiars', that is, their helpers. Moreover, the attendance records of the Company of St Paul note Domenico's, Davide's and Benedetto's absence for the four-month period beginning September 1481, adding 5 May 1482 that the older brothers were in Rome. Works such as the Santa Fina murals of 1477–8 and the second of the altarpieces for San Girolomo dei Gesuati in Pisa from 1478 to 1479 betray the intervention of a weaker hand than Domenico's, which is reasonably inferred to be Davide's, although the altarpieces for Lucca and San Giusto in Florence are entirely by Domenico. It appears that Domenico sought Davide's help for large-scale projects or when he had multiple tasks in hand.

Domenico's episodic employment of helpers, which seems to characterize his production in the 1470s and early 1480s, changed after his emancipation and establishment of an independent household in 1484. Just before, he and Davide established a partnership for the practice of painting and mosaic work, including work already begun and any new commissions they would take up. The agreement, for three years, was written up by Bartolomeo di Stefano, the goldsmith who trained both brothers, and specified that two-thirds of the proceeds were allotted to Domenico and one-third to Davide, signalling Domenico's continuing primary role. As head of the workshop, his role entailed dealing with patrons, inventing designs and exercising control over production. On the date of the agreement, 1 October 1484, these projects included the murals and altarpiece for the Sassetti Chapel; it would eventually encompass the Tornabuoni Chapel decoration and the Innocenti altarpiece. Such partnerships allowed artisans to share the capital costs of doing business, such as paying rent or purchasing tools and materials, as well as the labour of production. In formalizing what previously had been a flexible family collaboration, the brothers signalled separate professional identities just as their independent legal status was established by emancipation. Davide's work in fresco and mosaic is recorded in the 1480s and '90s, and we can assume that he produced panel paintings as well.

Benedetto Ghirlandaio, ten years younger than Domenico, was likely part of the team that painted the Sistine murals, though his role must have been subordinated to those of his brothers. Tommaso's 1480 tax return suggests the 22-year-old had trained as a miniaturist and goldsmith but that eye problems had confined his activity to supplying designs for others to execute. We have no evidence of any work that he might have produced after returning from Rome in 1482.[2] By 1486, as we know from the St Paul attendance lists and recounted by Vasari, he was in France, and he only returned around the time of Domenico's death in January 1494. In France he worked for Gilbert of Bourbon, who was both Count of Montpensier and Dauphin of the Auvergne in central France, for whom his only securely attributed panel painting – a *Nativity* for the palace chapel at Aigueperse – was painted about 1490. While the work bears the imprint of Netherlandish technique and motifs, other aspects, such as the draperies of the Virgin and kneeling angels, show that Benedetto brought with him to France drawings from Domenico's workshop. When Benedetto returned to Florence, he likely helped Davide with Domenico's unfinished commissions, including the altarpiece for the Tornabuoni Chapel, in which his hand can be discerned. In the spring of 1494, Davide and Benedetto were paid for a design for a lost stained-glass window for Pisa Cathedral, confirming their collaboration. It is likely that Benedetto continued to work with Davide until his own death three years later in 1497.

Other than Davide and Benedetto, we have only sporadic documentation of collaborators, assistants and apprentices in Ghirlandaio's workshop. Bartolomeo di Giovanni, a painter specializing in small-scale works, painted the predella to Ghirlandaio's Innocenti altarpiece, as attested to by payments.[3] He also painted the *Massacre of the Innocents* in the background of the main panel. This contribution was not noted in the payments, but it is recognizable by its distinctive style. Although Domenico had been commissioned for the panel, he must have been pressed for time, given the rush of works that he took on in the mid-1480s. Bartolomeo had worked with Ghirlandaio before; his hand can also be recognized in the predella to Ghirlandaio's Lucca altarpiece from 1479 and the predella to another altarpiece for the church of San Marco, commissioned before 1483, as well as background figures in the Sistine *Calling of Peter and Andrew*. While working in a subordinate position to the master, he was not a workshop assistant but an occasional collaborator who maintained his own workshop and worked with a range of other artists, including Botticelli. Later in his career, he produced independent works on a large scale.

From the welter of documents for surviving and lost works, the names of Domenico's helpers emerge – called variously his *garzone*, *fattore* or *lavoratore* – although few can be identified with historical personages and even fewer became recognized artists. The exception is Michelangelo, who as a twelve-year-old on 28 June 1487 collected the master's monthly payment for work on the Innocenti altarpiece.[4] This record, which put to rest the facts about Michelangelo's training that the artist had purposely obscured, has led to a search for his hand among this and contemporaneous works. Except for Davide and Bartolomeo di Giovanni, however, they cannot be isolated.

Ghirlandaio's sixteenth-century biographer Vasari asserted that at his death Ghirlandaio directed a very large workshop, including Sebastiano Mainardi, Michelangelo, Francesco Granacci, Niccolò Cieco, Jacopo del Tedesco, Jacopo dell'Indaco and Baldino Baldini (or Baldinelli) in addition to his brothers Davide and Benedetto. Besides Michelangelo, Mainardi, who married Ghirlandaio's sister in 1494, and Francesco Granacci had independent careers, but the others' later activities are elusive. Jacopo del Tedesco, the son of a painter and agent for King Matthias Corvinus of Hungary, was godparent to Domenico's daughter Francesca, born in 1493, but his later work is unknown; similarly, Baldino Baldini can perhaps be identified as an artist later working in Rome, while Jacopo dell'Indaco worked in Spain.[5]

The records of Ghirlandaio's work in the 1490s in Pisa Cathedral provide a clue as to how he organized large projects. In 1490, Domenico painted organ shutters (moveable panels that covered the organ when not in use) for the cathedral, now sadly lost. He painted them in Florence and shipped them to Pisa, where the cathedral works board coordinated the various artisans involved in the installation and housing of the organ. Davide received several payments in Pisa. By contrast, when Ghirlandaio was commissioned to paint an *Annunciation* and paired angels on the inner arch of the main chapel in the cathedral, and to repair mosaics in the apse, he set up a workshop in Pisa. The payments from September 1492 to August 1493 bring to life the large numbers of workers of all kinds required to complete the project: the labourers who carried, sawed and nailed wooden beams for the scaffolding; workers who slaked lime, sieved sand, carried water and spread mortar; and others who pulverized bricks, ground pigments, brushed on lime and built a trestle. These workers were organized and paid for by the cathedral works board. The payments detail the materials that were used for painting (further discussed below): paper and charcoal, linen, pigments such as blue from the Gesuati and gold leaf. Most of these materials were secured by Ghirlandaio from his suppliers in Florence and debited to his account. We can also tell how Ghirlandaio organized his workforce. He was on-site for most of the project and, when he returned to Florence in February 1493, he left Mainardi in charge until he returned in May. His assistants on the project were brought from Florence and paid in his name, and included Domenico de' Rosso, Poggio, Ambrogio, Baldino, Sebastiano and a certain Barto-lome Ciocio whose task was to grind colours. Of these, only Baldino was mentioned by Vasari and was involved in a subsequent job in Pistoia in the autumn of 1493; the others do not appear in the records for other projects, and it is likely that they were taken on just for this commission. Mainardi assumed the position of second-in-command, his senior status, in the absence of Davide, confirmed in the accounts. By this time, Davide had assumed independent commissions, including mosaics for the facades of the Orvieto and Siena cathedrals.

Although documents like the Pisa records do not survive for Ghirlandaio's Florentine projects in Santa Trinita and Santa Maria Novella, we can make some general statements about his workshop. First, it evolved over the course of his career, from his early partnership with Davide to the extensive *équipe* he employed in his late projects. However, the persistent myth that he employed scores of apprentices, assistants and collaborators over extended periods of time should be set aside. The evidence from written and visual examination suggests that, from the mid-1480s when he established a workshop in Florence, he took in assistants as needed for work he had. For panel paintings, such as the Innocenti altarpiece, there were only three named assistants in the accounts: Bartolomeo di Giovanni, Michelangelo and a certain Ricardo di Simone. For the larger mural projects that had to be painted on-site, such as in Pisa Cathedral, he employed only five, and it is likely that in Santa Maria Novella – the largest project of his career – he would have had very few more. In general, apprentices were contracted for a few years and, like Michelangelo, they often did not complete their term. Other collaborators, like Bartolomeo di Giovanni, were employed for specific, short-term tasks. Associates such as Davide Ghirlandaio and Sebastiano Mainardi, whether part of formalized partnerships or not, eventually pursued independent careers. So we can say that, over the course of his career, Ghirlandaio did train or employ many artists, known and unknown; but they were not there all at once and they did not stay for long periods of time.

Furthermore, the evidence we have suggests Ghirlandaio participated fully in works large and small that emanated from his *bottega*. In design and execution, he maintained control, even if more routine tasks were delegated to assistants. In Renaissance workshops, collaboration was expected, but the master's control was necessary if the works were to meet the quality and stylistic expectations of his patrons. In order to see how Ghirlandaio maintained control over the production process and imprinted his style on the members of the workshop, an account of his procedures for inventing designs and managing their execution will be offered below.

As master of his workshop, Ghirlandaio was in sole charge of creating the designs for panel paintings, murals, mosaics and stained glass produced by him and his assistants.[6] Indeed, the style of his work was the basis for his artistic identity and reputation in the competitive milieu of fifteenth-century Florence.[7] The inventive phase of design creation can be closely followed in Ghirlandaio's drawings, and they reveal aspects of his distinctive way of representing things in his art. They also attest to his creativity or, as Cennino Cennini called it, his *fantasia* – his imagination – which, coupled with skill of hand (*l'operazione di mano*), was key to success in the demanding art market of Renaissance Florence.[8] Both contributed to the artist's *buona fama* (reputation), which was essential for building his client base and securing future commissions. While Ghirlandaio's graphic oeuvre is not large, numbering some forty or so drawings, they vary considerably in scale, materials, technique, function and style. We have no complete sequence of drawings for a finished work that can reveal Ghirlandaio's procedure in detail; but enough examples survive for related works, especially for the Santa Maria Novella murals, that we can gain a general idea of his working method.

For Ghirlandaio's multi-figured narratives, he quickly sketched a first idea of the entire scene, including the main figures and setting. We see this in a drawing in the British Museum for the *Birth of the Virgin* in the Tornabuoni Chapel (illus. 62). The artist

first drew in long pen lines the rectilinear space, the horizontals
of the cornice and diagonals of the walls and ceiling. To the right
of centre in the foreground, he sketched the main figural group
of the servants preparing to bathe the newborn Virgin. He drew
in the heads, torsos and limbs of the figures with a few strokes
of the pen to indicate their poses and positions in space. He then
added slight indications of drapery to the two left figures; the
right figure is shown without drapery. Quick parallel diagonal
strokes from lower left to upper right indicate shading. Other
figures, the reclining St Anne in the background and the advancing
figures at the left, were drawn in the same way without shading.
A sketch for the *Presentation of Christ in the Temple*, part of the original
programme but not of the final decoration, was done in a similar

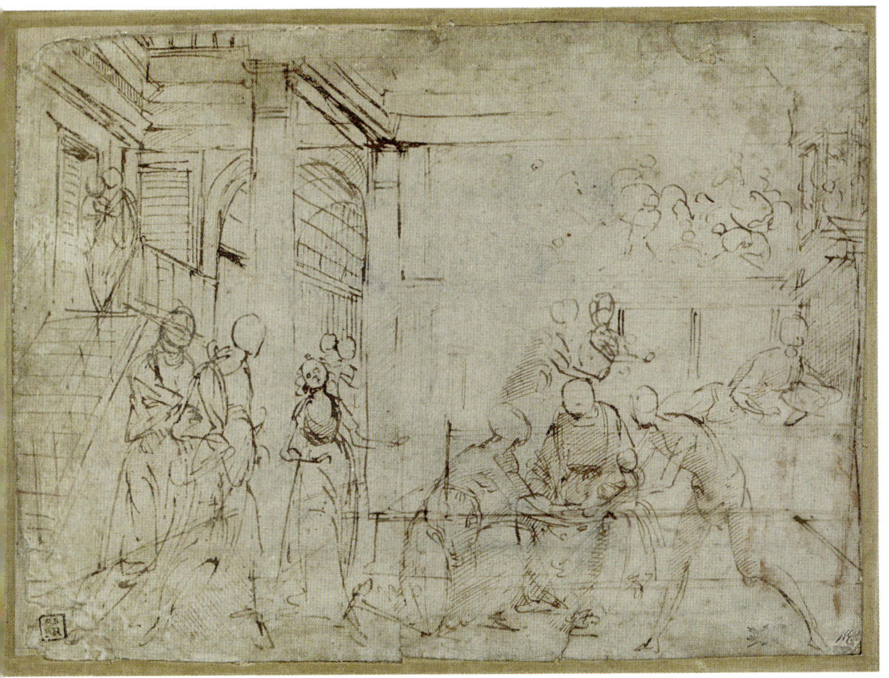

62 Domenico Ghirlandaio, *Birth of the Virgin*, 1486–90, pen and brown ink on
paper.

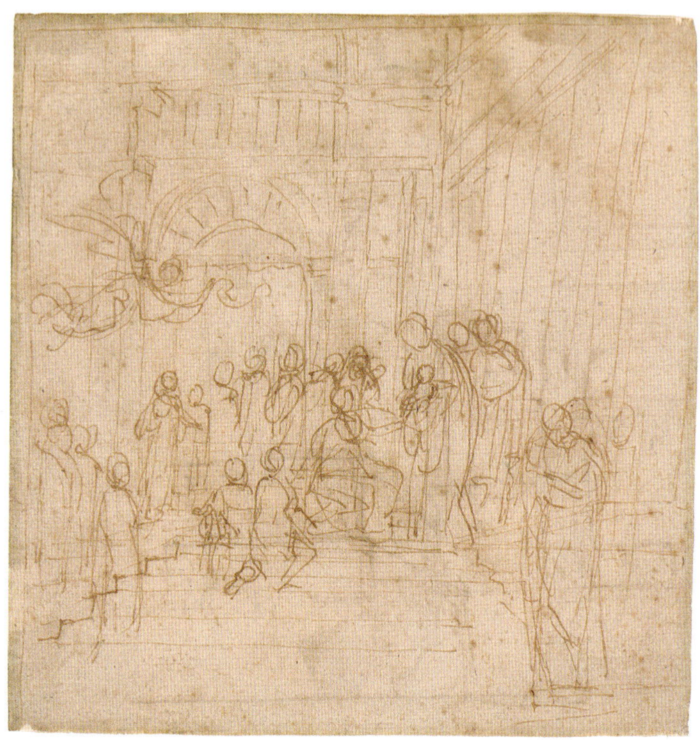

way, with the figures drawn in his characteristic shorthand over the basic lines of the architectural space (illus. 63).

Another drawing for the *Visitation* in the same chapel is done in a different way (illus. 64). Ghirlandaio drew the Virgin and St Elizabeth in shorthand to indicate the figures' poses and principal volumes. He then sketched the drapery over the bodies with long pen strokes, before drawing the cityscape in the background around the figures. He adjusted the Virgin's pose, redrawing it to make a more upright, dignified posture. The angle of the wall to her left was sharpened to create a more emphatic focus on the main figures. Subsidiary figures at the left and right were, however, drawn with only circles for heads and long loops for bodies, with

63 Domenico Ghirlandaio, *Presentation of Christ in the Temple*, 1486, pen and brown ink on paper.

no indication of limbs; they seem only to mark position. Compared to the *Birth of the Virgin* drawing, which establishes the basic formal and dramatic elements of the design and was probably a first sketch, the *Visitation* drawing was done slightly later in the composing process. Here the artist was focused on the positioning of the two main figures and their relationship to the background. The side figures were indicated only summarily, probably with reference to an earlier drawing. Their lack of detail does not indicate what the artist has not resolved, but they are instead summations of what an earlier drawing had already worked out. In this way Ghirlandaio's shorthand notation rapidly transferred basic design elements from one sheet of paper to the next, so that he could build on his previous design to a new idea. We can imagine the artist working from one drawing to the next, elaborating some parts, summarizing others, and interpolating elements from different drawings at various stages in the composing process. The progression from sketchy first thought to a more finished draft was probably repeated many times in the composing process. His graphic style varied depending on the function of the drawing

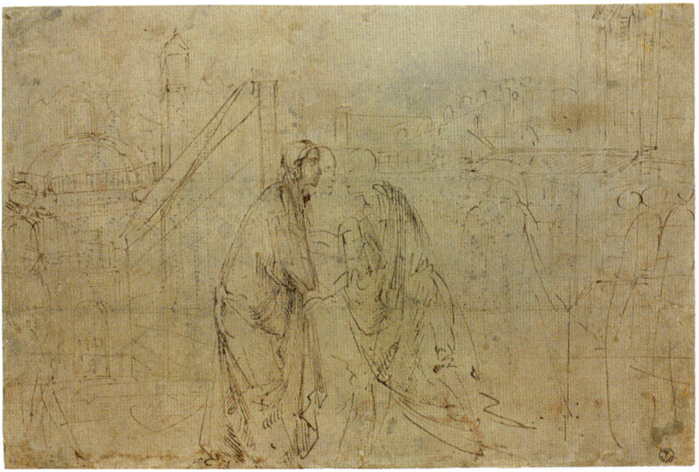

64 Domenico Ghirlandaio, *Visitation*, 1486–90, pen and brown ink on paper.

in the composing sequence. A highly differentiated graphic language, from cryptic shorthand to painterly effects, using a wide range of materials and techniques, emerged in mid-fifteenth-century drawings by artists such as Fra Filippo Lippi, Francesco Pesellino and Maso Finiguerra.[9] Ghirlandaio's drawing oeuvre is one of the first in which the new role of drawings as tools of exploration and creation is visible.

Many drawings of figures relate to the Santa Maria Novella murals and were the logical next step in the composing process. Some show groups of figures, such as for the *Marriage of the Virgin*, in which the poses of the Virgin and St Joseph were studied (illus. 65). The Virgin stands upright and grasps her drapery as St Joseph extends his arm, but at the left the Virgin is drawn again, leaning forward and extending her hand to meet Joseph's as in the finished mural. One of the disappointed suitors at the right raises his arm up straight, while in three quick sketches above, it

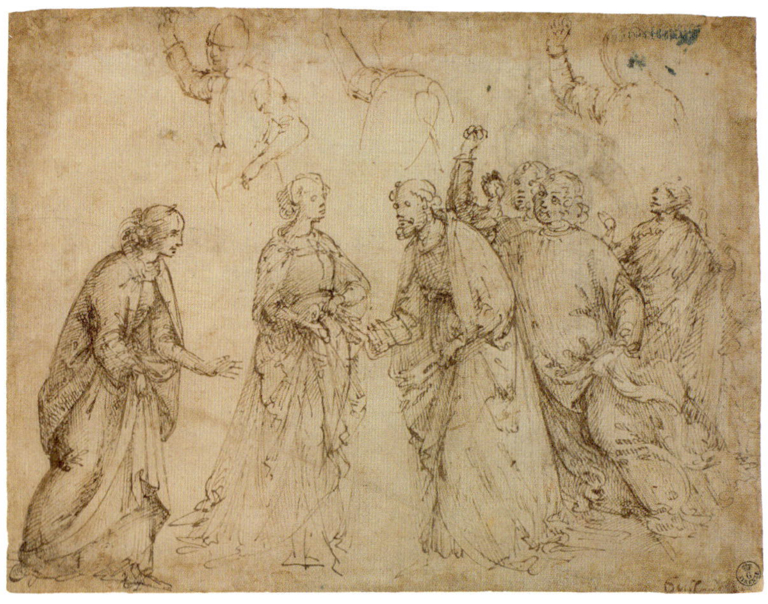

65 Domenico Ghirlandaio, *Marriage of the Virgin*, 1486–90, pen and brown ink on paper.

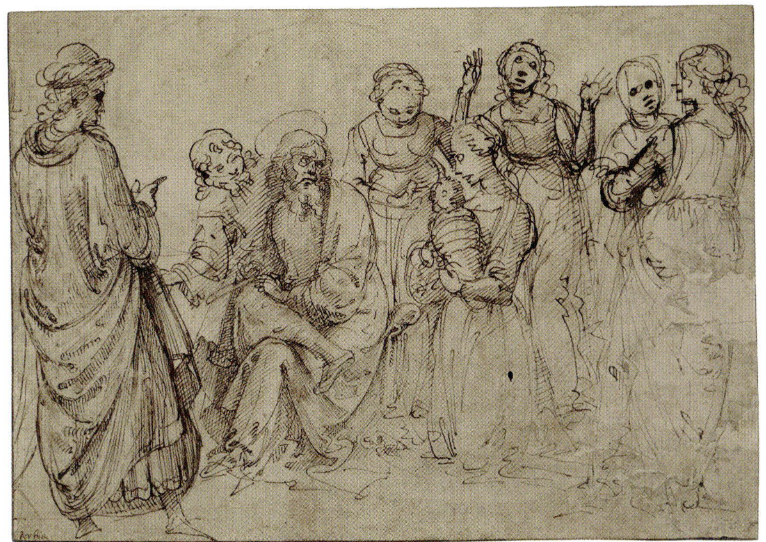

is changed to a diagonal position. On the back of this drawing
is a standing youth playing the flute, a figure that appears in the
mural but not in the recto, indicating that it – like the recto – was
drawn in reference to an earlier compositional sketch. Two drawings on separate sheets for the figures in the *Naming of the Baptist*
mural show a similar relationship. One shows the main group of
figures, centred on the seated Zacharias (illus. 66). A more detailed
drawing presents the conversing figures at the right, which are
close to how they appear in the finished mural (illus. 61). With
firm contours and a delicate mesh of strokes defining the voluminous drapery, the figure drawing refines the poses and spatial
relationship of the pair.

   More detailed studies of figures were drawn from live models
or from posed and draped mannequins. The drawing for the two
figures in the *Naming* might have been done from posed models.
Drawn from a lower viewpoint than the figures in the mural,
they wear labourers' caps, transformed into elaborate headdresses

66 Domenico Ghirlandaio, *Naming of the Baptist*, 1486–90, pen and brown
ink on paper.

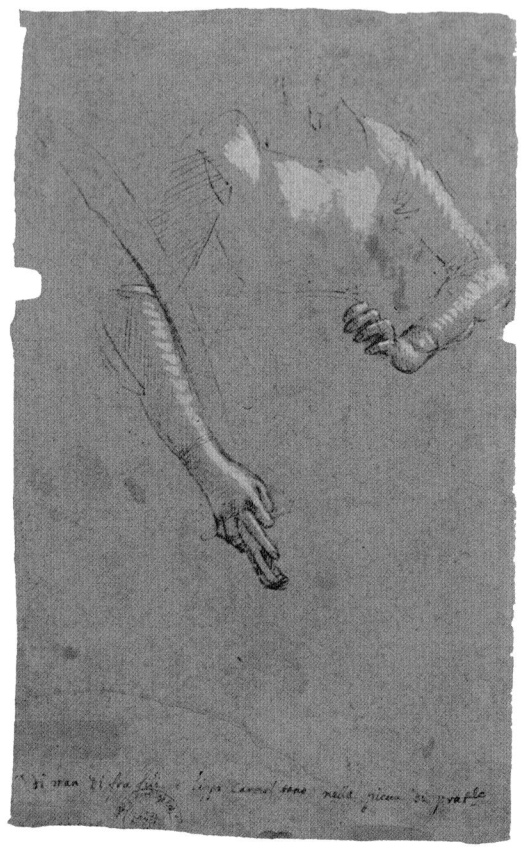

in the painted version. Specialized studies of single figures show increased fragmentation of the model; there are figures without heads and close-up head studies without bodies. An extreme example is the study on blue paper of a posed figure for the panel painting of *Judith and Her Maid* (illus. 67–8). This drawing concentrates on the position of Judith's hands and the modelling of the torso, only barely indicating the arms and omitting the head. The blue paper and the white highlighting vividly convey the sense of the figure occupying a light-filled space.

67 Domenico Ghirlandaio, *Torso and Arms of a Standing Figure*, 1489, pen and brown ink with white highlighting on blue paper.

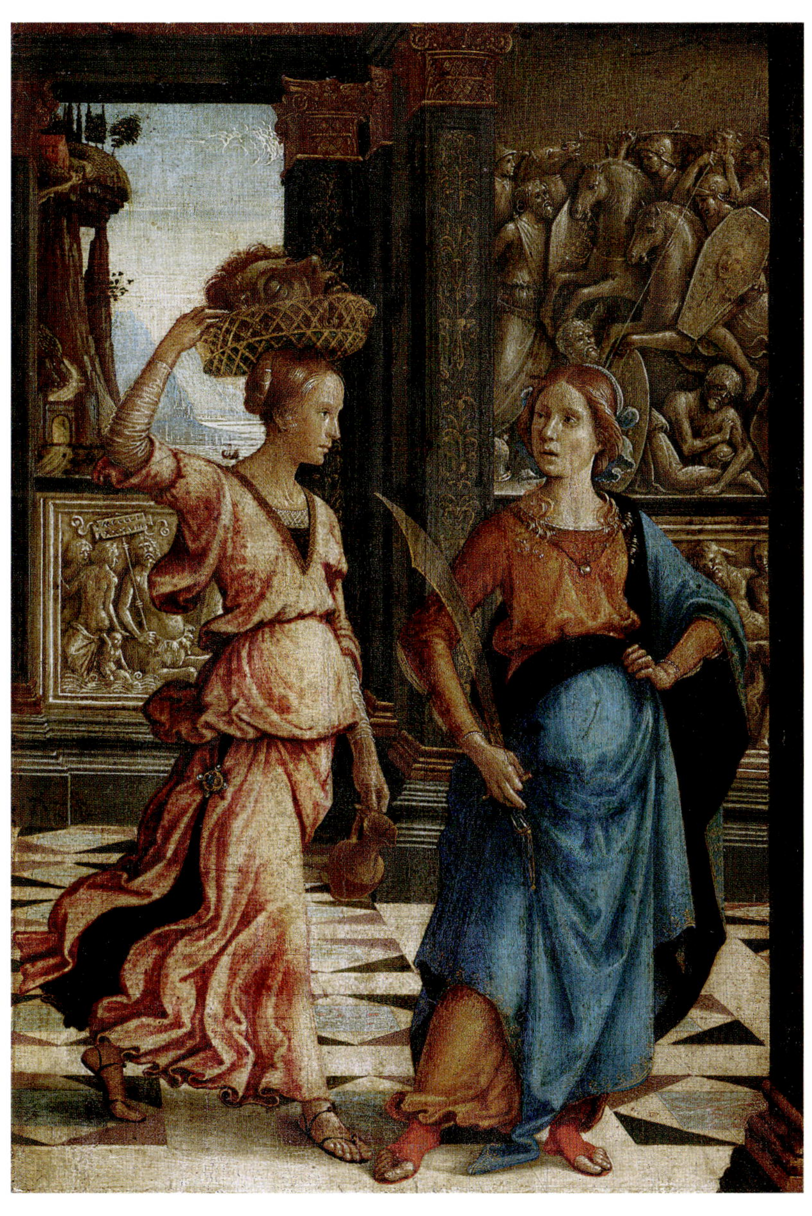

68 Domenico Ghirlandaio, *Judith and Her Maid*, 1489, tempera on panel.

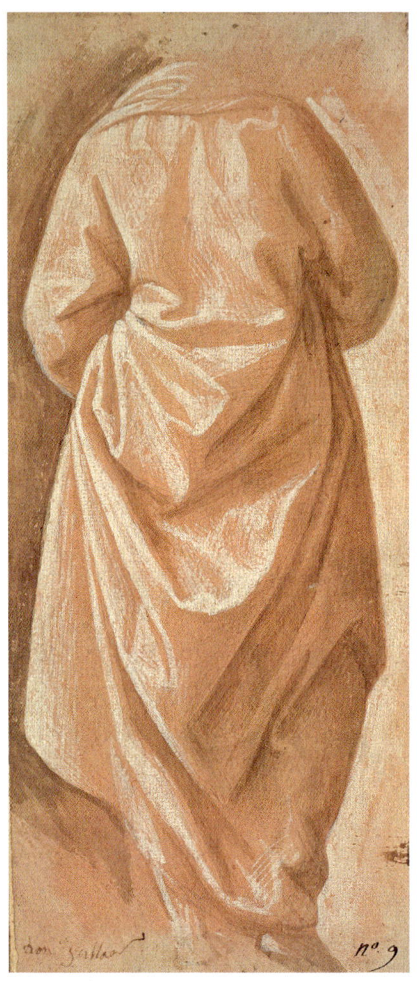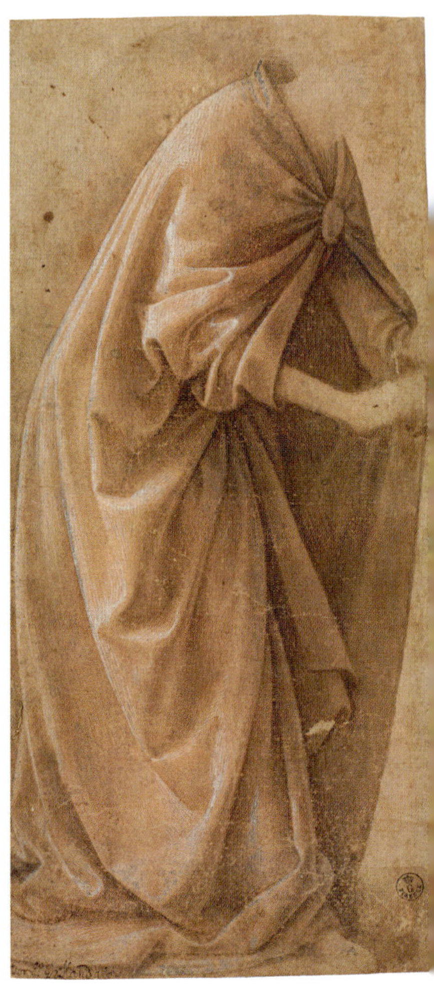

Ghirlandaio made studies of drapery throughout his career
that survive in relative abundance. For Florentine painters since
Giotto, drapery was a major tool of expression, enhancing figural
pose and action, so they made careful studies. Ghirlandaio made
drawings of drapery in various media in the 1470s, some of which

69 Domenico Ghirlandaio, *Standing Figure Seen from Behind*, c. 1481–2, brown
wash and white highlighting over metalpoint on pink prepared paper.
70 Domenico Ghirlandaio, *Drapery Study for a Standing Figure*, 1486–90, brown
wash on pink prepared paper, heightened with white.

relate to his finished works. One is a drawing of a figure seen from the back that is at the left foreground of the *Calling of Peter and Andrew* in the Sistine Chapel (illus. 69). It was done with a brush in brown wash over metalpoint on paper lightly brushed with a red wash. The free application of the wash and highlights suggests it was done from a draped model in the workshop. Some years later, he used the same materials to draw the drapery for the Virgin in the panel of the *Visitation*, done in 1491 for Lorenzo Tornabuoni's chapel in the Florentine church of Cestello (now called Santa Maria Maddalena dei Pazzi; illus. 70). In this drawing, the folds show the rounder, slightly inflated character of his later draperies, and the highlights were done with precise touches of a fine brush. The paper was left blank in the areas of the neck, head and arms, indicating that the drawing was probably done from a draped mannequin.

Drapery studies done with a brush on fine linen cloth instead of paper also survive from the later 1470s.[10] It is likely that Verrocchio's shop was the origin of such studies, inspired by painted cloths imported from Northern Europe, and that several artists who were associated with Verrocchio in the mid-1470s – including Ghirlandaio, Leonardo, Lorenzo di Credi and the master himself – made them. The fine texture of the linen is apparent in these thinly brushed studies, and the monochrome tones, ranging from velvety brownish blacks to opaque whites, create a vivid image of heavy cloth falling over solid form. Ghirlandaio drew the *St Matthew and an Angel* for the vault of the Chapel of Santa Fina in San Gimignano probably around 1476–7 (illus. 71). The linen was prepared with a greyish brown wash. He marked the general lines of the figure with a brush in dark brown wash, then he applied the highlights in lead white and the shadows in a lighter brown with tiny strokes of the tip of the brush. The whites cling to the ridges of the folds, intensifying where the fold breaks and turns a corner, and the blacks invade the deepest troughs of drapery. Both lights and darks are applied in tiny parallel hatches that follow the direction of the fold rather than the direction in which the light falls. Done with a slightly dry brush, the hatches do not form areas of opaque tone, and the hatching pattern avoids defining flat areas of colour. The artist made no attempt to chart every movement of surface into shade or light, so the middle tone of the prepared cloth dominates the tone of the whole. This schematic handling of light and dark precludes descriptive effects of texture. Only after the drapery was finished did the artist sketch in the figure's torso, arms and head in long, wavy lines using an almost dry brush. The bright highlights and the shadow cast outside the right contour create a sense of vigorous plastic form in a brightly lit ambience, some-thing made explicit in the finished roundel by golden rays that emanate from the figure.

The other drapery by Ghirlandaio in this medium is a study for a seated figure, now in the Louvre (illus. 72). He used it for the Madonna's drapery in the altarpiece for San Giusto painted around 1480. This very beautiful drawing has often been judged too refined to have been made by Ghirlandaio and has thus been attributed incorrectly to Leonardo da Vinci. While the materials – brown wash and white highlighting over a grey-brown prepa-ration – are the same as the St Matthew drawing, they are applied somewhat differently. In the Louvre drawing, the highlights are broader and more freely handled, and the transitions of tone from highlight to shadow are smooth and fully described, resulting in a sculpturesque precision of surface. The highlights have been applied with tiny touches of a slightly dry brush, and, as in the Berlin St Matthew drawing, they generally follow the direction of the folds rather than the direction of falling light. In the half-shadows, the highlights are broader and fall into curvilinear patterns that tend to divorce themselves from the illusion of form and emphasize surface. The cloth pleats in rhythmic, looping

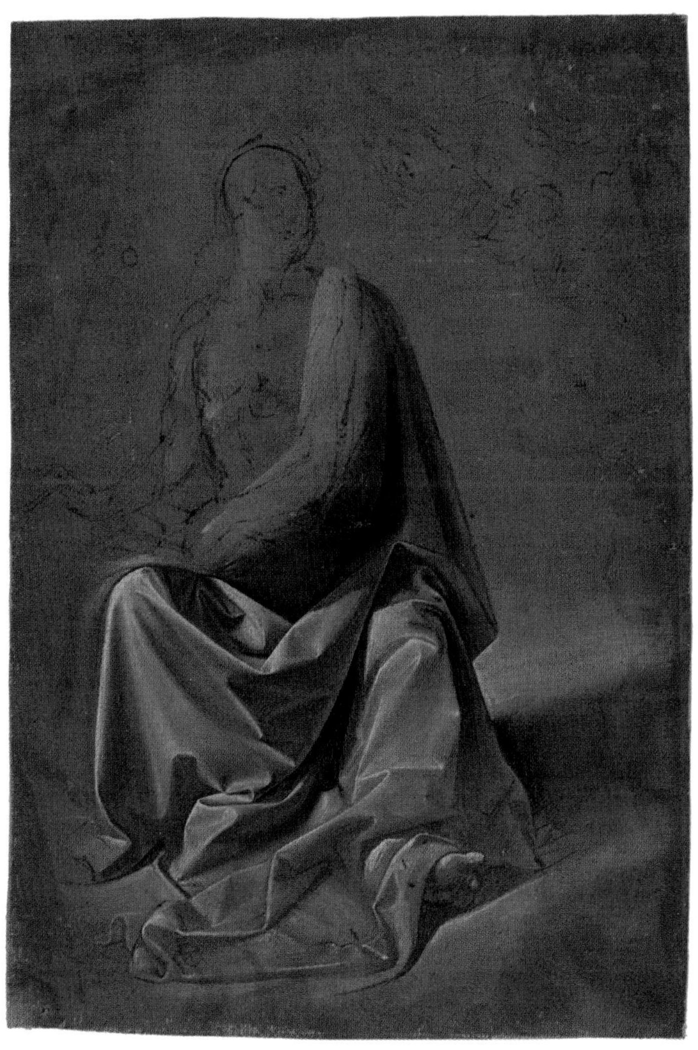

71 Domenico Ghirlandaio, *Drapery Study for a Seated Figure*, c. 1477–8, brown
and black washes heightened with white on brown prepared linen.

patterns instead of the jagged shapes of the earlier drawing, and it appears almost inflated. The figure is monumental, its limbs easily discernible beneath the cloth. If we compare the under-drawing of the San Giusto panel to the study in the Louvre, there are considerable differences in the arrangement of the folds, particularly over the Virgin's right foot, which is naked in the underdrawing, covered in the drawing and clothed with a slipper in the painting. The highlights, shown with subtle gradations in the drawing, were also simplified when enlarged and transposed into paint. These changes were likely made in a series of drawings that the artist created after the Louvre study, incorporating indi-vidual studies of figure parts into a design of the whole composition and preparing full-scale cartoons.

The differences between Ghirlandaio's two drawings on linen are mirrored in the change in style from Ghirlandaio's Pisa altarpiece of 1478–9 to the San Giusto altar from a year or two later. As we have seen, both altarpieces were painted at the time Ghirlandaio was likely associated with Verrocchio's workshop, and hence their closeness to works produced by the master and his associates is not surprising. The stately figures, softer forms and suffused light of the San Giusto picture are also found in the Louvre drawing. Additionally, both the St Matthew drawing and the Louvre study depict a cascade of light behind the figure at the right. This highlighting outside of contour establishes a back-ground plane and accentuates the solidity of the form as it projects forward in space, akin to high relief; and it is seen in other drapery studies that he drew on paper, such as the model studies discussed above. Leonardo's drapery studies on linen, by contrast, focus on minute actions of light falling on textured forms without reference to spatial context. They are close studies of surface effects of sheen and texture rather than volumes, and often the contours are undefined or engulfed in shadow – prefiguring the sfumato in his paintings. Leonardo's pictorial approach to representing form

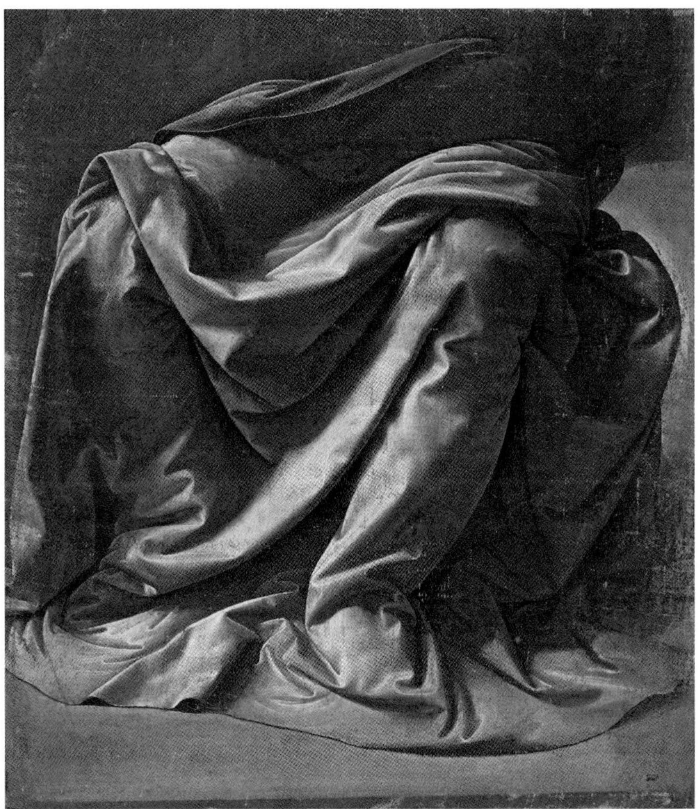

is different from Ghirlandaio's sculpturesque conception of form. It is also noteworthy that none of Leonardo's drapery studies is directly related to his paintings. Ghirlandaio's pragmatic approach distinguishes his procedure from Leonardo's habit of pure exploration.

Ghirlandaio's next step integrated the many figure studies he had made into a detailed compositional study. The drawings that survive from this stage in the design process show slightly different styles and may have been made for different purposes. An especially detailed drawing, for the *Annunciation to Zacharias*

72 Domenico Ghirlandaio, *Drapery Study for a Seated Figure*, c. 1480, grey and black washes on linen, heightened with white.

mural in Santa Maria Novella, shows narrative figures and bystanders against a classical facade (illus. 73). In the contract, Giovanni Tornabuoni required the artist to submit his designs for approval before painting, and this drawing may have been made for that purpose. Names of several bystanders, kin and associates of the patron, are written across four of the figures. In the finished mural, even more portraits were added, undoubtedly at Giovanni's request.

With a draft of his composition in hand, the artist now turned to the surface to be painted, either a panel or wall. In either case, the design had to be enlarged to the scale of the final surface. A large drawing for the woman at the left in the *Birth of the Virgin* in Santa Maria Novella suggests that Ghirlandaio made full-scale figure designs for this purpose (illus. 74). It is drawn in black chalk and is identical in details and scale to the figure in the mural. The drawing has been pricked with a needle along the major contours, signalling it is a cartoon. Even so, it was probably not used directly on the wet plaster *intonaco*, for it is too well preserved. Very likely

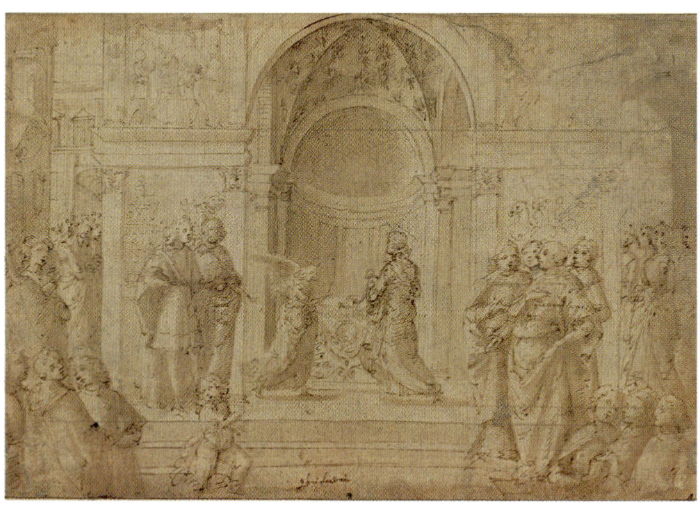

73 Domenico Ghirlandaio, *Annunciation to Zacharias*, 1486–90, pen and brown ink and brown wash, over metalpoint and stylus and black chalk.

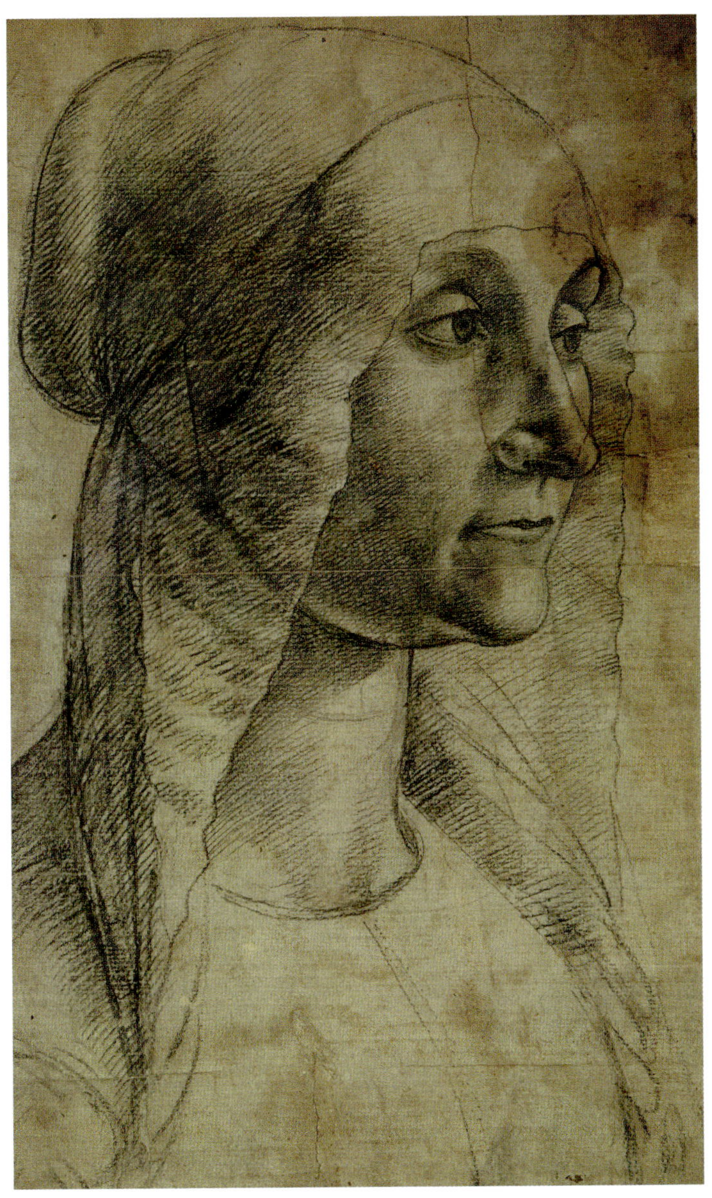

74 Domenico Ghirlandaio, *Head of a Woman*, 1486–90, black and white chalk on paper.

it was used to transfer the design to another sheet that was laid on the intonaco. We can imagine the wet plaster would ruin the paper, the reason so few cartoons survive.

Whether Ghirlandaio made full-scale drawings of the whole composition – figures and setting in one large cartoon – for his wall paintings, as Vasari described artists doing in the sixteenth century, is doubtful. The difficulty of handling such large drawings, assembled from many sheets of paper glued together, and the labour required to produce them, suggest he followed another procedure. At Brozzi and Ognissanti, I propose that he assembled figure cartoons on the wall. For the complex designs in Santa Maria Novella, he likely made large-scale cartoons only of the figure groups, and then cut them up to use in painting the *giornate* that comprise the *intonaco*. Some figures were transferred with the *spolvero* method and others with the incising method. The architectural settings were not part of the cartoon but were done with markings guided by plumb lines and straight edges in the fresh plaster.

We have no surviving cartoons for Ghirlandaio's panel paintings. The underdrawing made for the portrait of Giovanna Tornabuoni of about 1490 is an economical design made freehand with a brush over a charcoal or black chalk sketch, perhaps with reference to a cartoon on paper. Several changes, notably where the contour of her torso was altered in the painted version to render it less curvaceous or where her beaded necklace was changed to a thin cord, are notable, in addition to changes in her curls at the nape of her neck or the elaborate brocaded designs on her overdress. Ghirlandaio paid special attention to this painting – undoubtedly because of its patron, Lorenzo Tornabuoni, and its subject, his much-lamented bride. These changes suggest that it might have been based on life drawings but that it was completed after the sitter's death, rendering her unmoving and remote, a fixed icon instead of a remembered encounter.

Apart from the earliest stages of his creative processes, Ghirlandaio's procedure allowed the participation of assistants. In the later stages of design, assistants could have performed the labour-intensive tasks of pricking cartoons and transferring the designs to another surface of paper, panel or wall. The two carefully stroked cartoons by Ghirlandaio that survive, in the Uffizi and at Chatsworth, suggest that the master drew the cartoons himself, however, and he likely made the preliminary underdrawings on the panels and walls as well. In wall paintings, the execution of the *intonaco* in *giornate* facilitated participation of many hands. The *giornate* varied in size according to motif; those for heads were small, allowing the painter time for careful execution on the wet plaster. Drapery was done in larger patches, and the landscape and architecture were often done in large areas of a single *giornata*. The most expressive parts of a scene – the faces, hands and principal figures – were painted by the master himself or his most accomplished associates, Davide in the early works and perhaps one or two others in the works from the mid-1480s. Draperies and architecture may have been allocated to other assistants.

In panel paintings, the firm contours separating colour areas facilitated the participation of several hands, but as in the murals the most important areas of figures were executed by the master himself. Since egg tempera dries quickly, the colours once mixed had to be used immediately. In order to avoid waste of expensive pigments such as ultramarine, the painter likely completed all areas of the panel surface in the same colour at the same time, rather than moving from motif to motif. Quick drying meant that successive layers could be applied relatively close in time. Assistants might have been enlisted to paint marginal areas of landscape or drapery.

Not every painting that came from Ghirlandaio's shop shows his active participation. Some paintings were entirely workshop productions, such as the recently restored altarpiece in

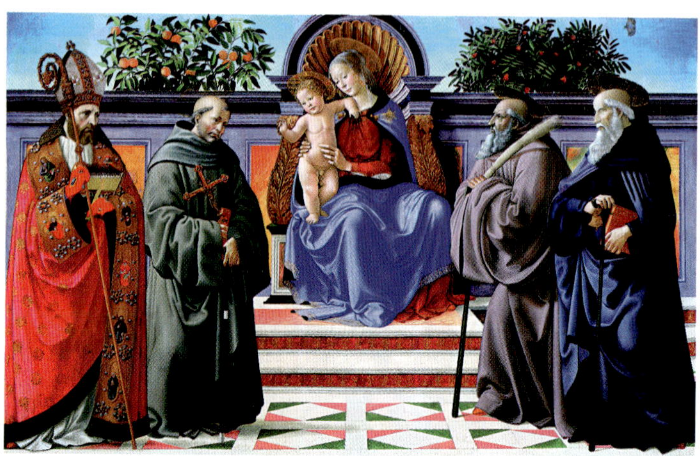

Vallombrosa (illus. 75).[11] This altarpiece shows that Ghirlandaio's drawings guided the execution; the underdrawing for the Virgin's drapery was drawn from a transferred cartoon and perhaps blocked in by the master himself. The tempera paint application, while following the technique of Ghirlandaio's panels, shows none of the exquisite control of stroke and tone of his autograph paintings. Instead of the radiantly smooth surfaces of his figures, those in the altarpiece are turgid and schematic. Rather than heavy, volumetric draperies cladding solid form, the draperies in the altarpiece seem inflated and unresponsive to the figures' limbs underneath.

Other paintings were probably made for the open market. The group of panels centred around the tondo of the *Madonna and Child with Angels* in the Louvre, while based on a drawing by the master, reveal assistants' work (illus. 76).[12] The variations in the composition – sometimes with three angels, sometimes with one or none – suggest that individual cartoons of the figures could be used in different combinations to produce different versions. From the beginning of his career, Ghirlandaio kept drawings in the workshop for reuse and reference, as attested to by recurring

75 Workshop of Domenico Ghirlandaio, *Virgin and Child with Sts Biagio, Giovanni Gualberto, Benedict and Anthony Abbot*, c. 1490, tempera and oil on panel.

motifs in paintings done at different times. The drawing for the figure in the Sistine mural, studied in the drawing in Rennes (illus. 69), was repeated in the Santa Maria Novella murals. The cartoon for the Child in the London National Gallery *Virgin and Child* (illus. 29) was reused, likely by Davide, for the altarpiece the *Madonna and Child with Sts Jerome, Raphael and Two Unidentified Sts* in Pisa. Both children assume the same pose, with their left arms resting on the Virgin's torso, but it is more logical and organic in the London version. Similarly, the design for the archangel Raphael in the San Giusto picture (illus. 28) is repeated, with minor variations, in the same altarpiece in Pisa. It is noteworthy that the colour scheme, yellow for the angel's tunic and red lined

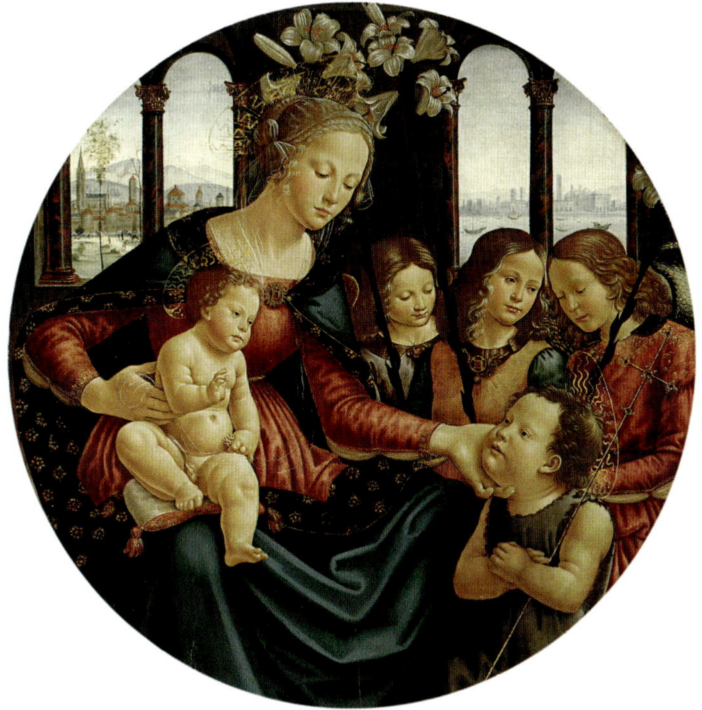

76 Workshop of Domenico Ghirlandaio, *Madonna and Child with Angels*, *c.* 1485–90, tempera on panel.

with green for her mantle, is used in both pictures, so the drawing likely had colour notes. The drapery designs of the Virgin and angels in Benedetto's *Nativity* in Aigueperse were clearly based on drapery studies, perhaps on linen, that he had carried to France with him several years before. Many more instances of recurring motifs could be cited. Few of these numerous drawings survive. One, however, in Dresden, has been identified for the mantle of the Virgin in the *Adoration of the Magi* in Santa Maria Novella.[13] It shows none of the searching lines of an initial creation but was likely a stock drawing kept for reference and reuse (illus. 77).

Ghirlandaio controlled the style and quality of paintings from his workshop primarily through drawings as tools of design invention and execution. His distinctive compositions and meticulous technique were responsive to the demands of every kind of task, from his early provincial murals to the exquisite portrait of Lorenzo Tornabuoni's departed wife. While his style changed over the course of his career and his technique responded to changing tastes, especially to demands for convincing representation and authentic emotional expression, he never abandoned the traditional palette and tempera technique of Florentine painting. Coupled with the echoes of Giotto and Masaccio in his mural paintings, especially in Santa Trinita and Santa Maria Novella, his hewing to tradition was not mere conservatism but was rather essential to his distinctive look, his 'brand'. How insistently Ghirlandaio pursued this essence of his output is evident from the works his shop produced after his sudden death in January 1494. One of these, the multi-panel altarpiece for the Tornabuoni Chapel, as we know from documents, was finished and installed in the spring of 1494 (illus. 55).[14] While no drawings for the panels exist, infrared examination revealed that the figures were thoroughly prepared by Domenico and drawn freehand, probably over traced cartoons, on the *gesso* ground. The side saints of the main panel, St Dominic on the left and St Thomas (sometimes

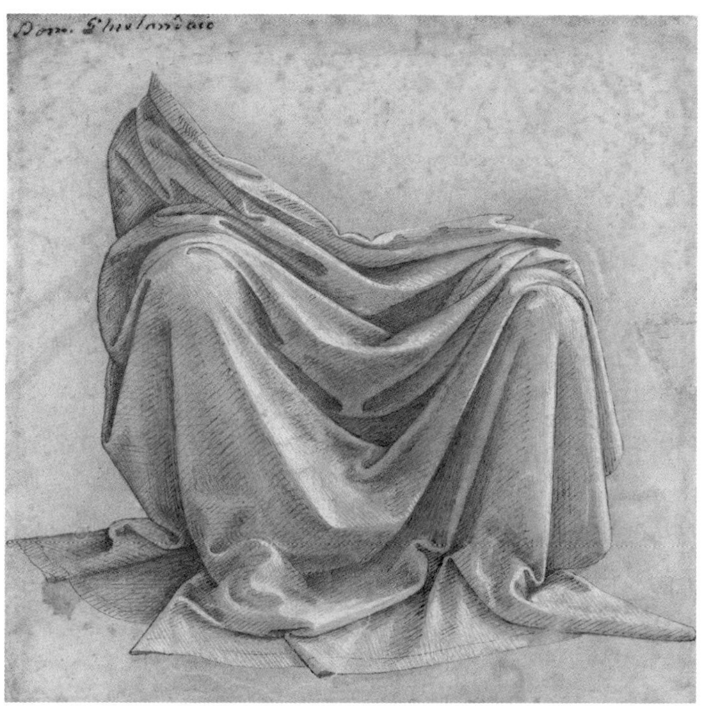

identified as John the Evangelist) on the right, were originally
standing instead of kneeling. The main panel of the *Madonna of the
Apocalypse with Sts* was painted in a tempera and mixed technique.[15]
The faces were done in Ghirlandaio's typical process with a green
earth underlayer. Strokes of lead white and vermilion form the
highlights, while a darker layer of brown tone, in *verdaccio* (a mixture
of yellow ochre, black, white and pink) form the shadows. Mixed
tempera and walnut oil were used for the blue sky. (In a side
panel, St Lawrence's green drapery also used walnut oil as the
medium, as in Ghirlandaio's early *Madonna* in London.) The greens
in the landscape were applied in a mixture of tempera and linseed
oil over a layer of blue, green and yellow pigments in egg tempera.
Ghirlandaio painted the Virgin's dress in pure red lake pigment,

77 Domenico Ghirlandaio, *Drapery Study for a Seated Figure, c.* 1485–90, pen and
brown ink, brow wash heightened with white on pink prepared paper.

without the admixture of white lead in the shadows, imitating the rich colours of Flemish painting while maintaining his point-of-the-brush tempera technique. The dark blue of her mantle was painted over a dark grey underlayer, unusual in Florentine painting, mimicking the sombre, rich tones of Netherlandish models. St Thomas, the hands of St Dominic and the feet of St John the Baptist were painted entirely in oil paint with wet-in-wet blended brushwork, perhaps by Benedetto, newly returned from France. The stark differences between the figures are visible when the panel is seen up close, but in general the oil paint is handled in controlled strokes that are like those in tempera, and they are not noticeable from a distance. However, it is clear that Ghirlandaio's enforcement of a consistent workshop technique had lapsed. Davide, as head of the *bottega*, may have been unable or unwilling to control assistants' personal variations of Ghirlandaio's style, and he moved towards the blended brushwork and opticality of Flemish-inspired facture that rapidly became the norm by 1500. The sudden turn towards oil confirms that Ghirlandaio's signature egg tempera, point of the brush style was consciously cultivated and hard won. His meticulous technique and lively recreations of historical and biblical narratives form the basis of his reputation even today.

Conclusion: 'A Man to be Reckoned With'

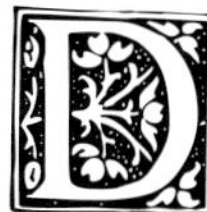omenico Ghirlandaio died on 11 January 1494, as noted by the scribe of the confraternity of St Paul who recorded his death:

Domenico di Tommaso di Churrado Bighordi, painter, called del Grillandaio, died Saturday morning the 11 of January 1493 [1494] of plague . . . He was buried Saturday evening in Santa Maria Novella between the twenty-fourth and first hour: and may God forgive his sins. It is the greatest shame, because he was everywhere a man to be reckoned with for his quality; and he is widely mourned.[1]

The scribe's description of Domenico as 'a man to be reckoned with' conforms to the portrayal of Domenico by Vasari, writing fifty years later, whose colourful anecdotes emphasized his diligence and technical excellence.[2] Ghirlandaio's relationship with his patrons, to the degree we can understand it, suggests a certain social ease as well as honest dealings. In the spring of 1489, he negotiated a yearlong extension to the deadline for the Tornabuoni Chapel murals, not all of which he needed.[3] His relationship with patrons such as Tornabuoni was more than just professional, as again suggested by Vasari: 'As he lay ill, the Tornabuoni sent him a hundred ducats of gold as a gift, proving their regard and particular friendship for Domenico in return for his unceasing labours in the service of Giovanni and his house.'[4] Ghirlandaio's self-portrait in the *Expulsion of Joachim* mural is unusually prominent, a visual counterpart to that of the patron's son opposite (illus. 2). Giovanni Tornabuoni must have approved its inclusion in the mural, as he seems to have done for all the portraits. Indeed, as this book has shown, Ghirlandaio's web of social connections underlay his ability to negotiate complex personal and professional relationships in early Renaissance Florence.

Contemporary observations of the Florentine art scene offer insight that can, however, be difficult for us to interpret. About 1490, when Ludovico Sforza, the duke of Milan, was seeking painters to decorate the Certosa di Pavia, he looked to Florence, well known for its competitive artistic market. An unknown agent sent back to Milan his assessment of four painters then active in Florence. Ghirlandaio, he says, is 'a good master on panel and even more so on walls. His things have a good air, and he is an expeditious man who executes a lot of work.' This statement follows assessments of Botticelli, who is 'most excellent' and whose works 'have a virile air and are done with the best method and perfect proportion'; Filippino Lippi, who is 'excellent' and whose works have a 'sweet air' but less skill; and Perugino, who is 'outstanding', adding 'his things have an angelic and very sweet air.' 'All these masters have given proof of themselves in the chapel of Pope Sixtus, except Filippino, but all of them afterwards at the Spedaletto for the Magnificent Lorenzo, and it is hard to say who bears off the palm.'[5]

The memo, much discussed in art-historical literature, is one of the earliest texts that puts into words the distinctive characteristics of an artist's works.[6] Art criticism was a new kind of writing at the time, inspired by models from Roman authors such as Pliny. The author of the memo was someone familiar with the writings of Florentine humanists, who modelled their prose on ancient examples and assimilated their ideas. He seems also to have had direct experience of the contemporary artistic scene. The artists on his list appear to be ranked in order from the best to the least. His conclusion, 'it is hard to say who bears off the palm,' alludes to winners of ancient Greek games who were awarded the palm of victory, as recounted by Latin authors. This remark acknowledges that the ultimate choice of artists resides with the duke. What's more, his note that all the painters worked for prestigious patrons, such as Sixtus IV and Lorenzo de' Medici, suggests that the duke would join this illustrious group by employing one of them.

The agent attributes to each artist a distinctive 'air'. As we have seen, Cennini advised students to develop a personal style. The term *aria* was used by Petrarch (whose ideas influenced Cennini) to describe the distinctive look of individuals. In a letter to Boccaccio, Petrarch discussed a student's attempt to imitate Virgil's poems. Petrarch distinguished literary imitation from the goals of a portraitist, who sought to represent a live model in his art, and he urged writers to strive for resemblance not replication in his work:

> While often very different in their individual features, they [painted portraits] have a certain something our painters call an 'air,' especially noticeable about the face and eyes, that produces a resemblance; seeing the son's face, we are reminded of the father's, although if it came to measurement, the features would all be different, but there is something subtle that creates this effect.[7]

The link between the artist and his work is implicit in *aria*, a term Petrarch says comes from the world of painters. Alberti related in his treatise that painting began when Narcissus, the mythological youth, fell in love with his own image reflected in a pool, reinforcing this idea.[8] We might conclude that, for the agent, the word *aria* means a distinctive style belonging to each master, to his character as well as his works.

What does Ghirlandaio's 'good air' refer to? The French term *débonnaire* was used in the fourteenth century to refer to a generally pleasing quality.[9] In Italian, *di buon aere* perhaps meant 'gracious'. The phrase 'Debonario' was defined by John Florio's 1611 Italian–English dictionary as 'honest' and 'upright'. This last definition conforms to the contemporary characterization of Ghirlandaio as 'a man to be reckoned with'. His 'good air' perhaps alludes to his sociability and worldliness.

As applied to Ghirlandaio's style, his 'good air' is hard to pin down. We have described in his drawings his search for just the right figure poses and groupings, and their position in a clearly defined space generated by linear perspective. The figures and spaces are geared to their architectural settings and to the position and viewing distance of spectators. We have seen in drawings and paintings, both on the wall and on panel, how his meticulous, point-of-the-brush strokes controlled shading, surface texture and detail. He imitated the precise transcription of surfaces in Flemish painting, but he achieved it with traditional Florentine technique and with very different effects. In clinging to traditional techniques, he perhaps asserted his distinctive look, his brand. But he may have also wished to call attention to his skill of hand (*arte*) and his talent (*ingenio*), equally intrinsic to his reputation, in conjuring these images. When seen up close, they are unmistakably composed of minute, precisely placed touches. Flemish artists fused brush strokes into a continuous, luminous surface that effaced the artist's touch and transformed paint into perceived stuffs such as cloth. Ghirlandaio's facture calls attention to the materiality of paint and to the work's artifice, its craft. That they were painted representations, and not real, asserts the artist's role as mediator between life and art. By the end of the century, the artist would be likened by Leonardo da Vinci to the ultimate Creator, to God himself.[10]

The realism of an artist like Giotto was celebrated in his own time as a direct transcription of nature, without the filter of an artist's personal style.[11] Giovanni Villani, writing in the fourteenth century, said that Giotto 'traced all figures and acts from nature'. Boccacio said that Giotto so closely imitated nature that his paintings often fooled spectators, who 'mistook for real that which was but painted'. Ghiberti, writing in the mid-fifteenth century, said that Giotto replaced the 'Greek manner' (*maniera greca*), the highly conventionalized style of the twelfth- and thirteenth-century panels imported from Byzantium, with 'the natural art' (*l'arte naturale*). In classical literature, 'nature' had several meanings.[12] 'Created nature' (*natura naturata*) referred to the appearance of things in the real world that the artist experienced. Leon Battista Alberti in his treatise *On Painting*, written around 1435, described how the artist should use contour and shading to depict three-dimensional objects in space. The active concept of nature, *natura naturans*, captured the idea of nature as a creative force. An artist imitated the creative acts of nature in the invention of his compositions, which Alberti described in his directions for painting a narrative. In composing figures, he recommended the painter select the best parts of several observed models and combine them in one invented one. In this sense, the direct transcription of nature is opposed to artistic invention or style.

We might begin to understand Ghirlandaio's 'good air' if we compare it to the critic Cristoforo Landino's characterizations of earlier artists.[13] In his commentary to Dante in 1481, Landino wrote of several mid-century artists. Masaccio, he wrote, 'was a very good imitator of nature, with great and comprehensive relief, a good composer, and pure, without ornament, because he devoted himself only to imitation of the truth and to the relief of his figures'. Fra Filippo Lippi, on the other hand, 'was gracious and ornate and exceedingly skilful; he was very good at compositions and at variety, at colouring, relief, and very much at ornaments of every kind, whether imitated after the real or invented'. Masaccio, it seems, painted reality, while Lippi added something extra to his transcriptions of nature. This idea of ornament derived from the writings of the Roman rhetorician Quintilian (*fl.* 35–100) in his treatise on oration.[14] He advocated adjusting the style of an address to its audience to be more persuasive. In this context, ornateness described what the orator added to a straightforward recitation of fact. Ghirlandaio consciously imitated Masaccio and Giotto in his work, as we saw most directly in the Sassetti Chapel murals, and it was documented by Vasari, who numbered him among those artists who had flocked to Masaccio's Brancacci Chapel to draw. Ghirlandaio's art, which employed firm contours, precise transcription of surfaces and clear disposition of volumes in space, might have been seen by contemporaries as without ornament. In this aspect, it would have been very different from the poetic sensibilities of Botticelli or Filippino Lippi, who created in the linear style of Fra Filippo, called by the Milanese agent 'the most singular master of his time', and which he, and art historians since Bernard Berenson, evidently preferred. These aspects of Ghirlandaio's style are perhaps owing to his work as a goldsmith, crafting objects in three dimensions and attending to surface detail, colour, sheen and texture. Filippo Lippi and his son were exclusively painters, and they approached representation in an entirely different way, as did Botticelli, who briefly trained as a goldsmith before entering Filippo Lippi's workshop. These artists were especially known for their interpretations of Greek and Roman literary themes, such as Botticelli's *Birth of Venus* or Filippino's *Death of Laocoön*, both painted for Medici patrons in villa settings, which it is likely the Milanese agent had seen or heard discussed. Vasari described Ghirlandaio's only known mythology, a story of Vulcan for Lorenzo de' Medici's villa at Spedaletto, 'in which many nude figures are at work with hammers making thunderbolts for Jove'.[15] The mural is sadly lost, so we cannot know how Ghirlandaio might have adapted his style to a novel subject in a villa setting. Ghirlandaio's *debonario*, assured, honest style was preferred by Giovanni Tornabuoni and others, especially for religious narratives and portraiture. It is noteworthy that, in the early 1490s when Giovanni employed a painter for the allegorical subjects at his villa at Chiasso Macieregli, he hired Botticelli, who was well known for such works.[16]

Ghirlandaio's preference for crisp contours, tactile surfaces and sculpturesque treatment of form recalls his interest in ancient and modern sculpture.[17] His acquaintance with Roman antiquities is evident in objects and motifs derived from them in many works, especially the Palazzo Vecchio murals and the Tornabuoni and Sassetti chapels (illus. 40, 41, 47). These depictions of classical statuary appealed to patrons' humanist interests and signalled their inclusion in an educated elite. Ancient sculpture had had a central role in the development of naturalistic style throughout the fifteenth century. Relief – that is, the illusion of volumes – resulting from the painter's manipulation of shadows was referred to by Landino as something that both Masaccio and Lippi had mastered. To achieve relief, Alberti and Leonardo da Vinci urged artists to draw from sculpture as they sought to 'follow nature'. Ancient sculpture was a model of nature; it offered a repertoire of figure proportion and gesture that artists could copy. Earlier artists such as Pisanello compiled notebooks of drawings after ancient sculpture, although none of these motifs found their way into Pisanello's surviving works. That Ghirlandaio drew from sculpture is evident in a book of drawings called the *Codex Escurialensis*, after its home in the Royal Library at the Escorial outside Madrid.[18] Leaves of the book are filled with copies from reliefs, statuary and buildings that he would have had occasion to study on his several trips to Rome. He noted their location in his distinctive script. Several sheets record panoramas of the city, early examples of a tradition that endured for centuries. Vasari perhaps referred to these drawings when he noted that Ghirlandaio

> is said to have been so accurate in draughtsmanship, that, when making drawings of the antiquities of Rome, such as arches, baths, columns colossea, obelisks, amphi-theaters, and aqueducts, he would work with the eye alone, without rule, compass or measurements, and after he had made them, on being measured, they were found absolutely correct, as if he had used measurements.[19]

The *Codex* has been much discussed by historians, but I believe many of the leaves were copied by Ghirlandaio himself from drawings he made on-site as a guide or memoir of the Eternal City for an elite patron such as Giovanni Tornabuoni. Designs related to those from the *Codex* found their way into Ghirlandaio's compositions, notably in the architectural details and sculpted reliefs in the Tornabuoni Chapel, perhaps solidifying their link to the patron (illus. 51). In these instances, the Roman fragments are treated as figural relief or architectural details. In other cases, as in the *Presentation of the Virgin*, ancient models inspired the design of the narrative actors (illus. 49). The seated nude at the lower right that Vasari praised was likely modelled on an ancient statue, as were the nudes in the *Baptism of Christ*.

In the panel *Judith and Her Maid*, Ghirlandaio pursued several strategies for incorporating ancient sculpture into his design, ranging from replication to a more general imitation of classical forms (illus. 68).[20] Sculptural reliefs adorn the architectural background; the one to the left of the maid is recorded in the *Codex*. Judith's pose, her left arm resting on her hip, her right cradling a sword, is based on an ancient statue formerly in the

Roman church of Santissimi Apostoli, also recorded in the *Codex*. Ghirlandaio refined the pose in a drawing from a live model in which the position of her hands and the light falling on her arms and torso were carefully denoted (illus. 67). In this way, the ancient sculpture provided an armature onto which details of surface and lighting studied from life were interpolated (Michelangelo followed a similar procedure as seen in some of his early drawings).[21] Notably, however, Judith's and her maid's drapery in the painting do not replicate that of the ancient sculpture. Nor do the looping folds and fluttering pleats of their clothing bear any relation to Ghirlandaio's studies from draped models, which record heavy drapery cascading over volumes and falling in angular folds. Instead, Judith's and her maid's garments are invented; indeed, they come from the same imaginative world as the famous nymph striding into the birth chamber of St John the Baptist in Santa Maria Novella that so fascinated earlier scholars (illus. 54).[22] These fanciful garments show how ancient sculpture inspired creativity as much as it modelled naturalism.

On occasion, Ghirlandaio imitated the general compositional form of the ancient model rather than a particular motif. In the *Massacre of the Innocents* in Santa Maria Novella, the chaotic scene mimics the crowded fields and dramatic action of ancient battle sarcophagi, amply represented in the *Codex* (illus. 50). Individual figures were drawn from Roman examples, such as the soldier attacking the woman in the centre middle ground and the falling warrior grasping his horse to their left, both taken from a relief on the Arch of Constantine. The shocking incident on the right – the frantic mother pulling the hair of a soldier bearing away her child – is drawn from a relief that was, in the sixteenth century, in the Villa Medici's garden in Rome. Vasari praised the range of emotions expressed by this group's athletic poses, concluding that 'the whole is truly more the work of a philosopher admirable in judgment than a painter.' In these instances, ancient art led the artist to an imitation of nature beyond surface detail and relief to a vivid recreation of the event. Alberti's vision for a new painting not only embraced naturalism of appearances but cited the ability of images to delight, to hold the viewer's attention and to live in memory. In this vivacious scene, and in other works, Ghirlandaio synthesized nature and antique sculpture into his signature style, in which naturalism and ornament are not opposed but mutually reinforced.

Ghirlandaio's contract with Giovanni Tornabuoni can perhaps help us understand how not only the patron but the artist himself saw his style.[23] The contract specifies the materials, subjects, techniques and even the style to be painted. It calls for 'figures, buildings, castles, cities, villas, mountains, hills, plains, water, rocks, garments, animals, birds and beasts'. Giovanni, who had employed Ghirlandaio for earlier projects, certainly knew his style and seems to call for even richer detail. Perhaps this passage reflects ideas or promises made by the artist in conversation with his patron, as a kind of self-characterization of his style. Indeed, recent accounts of Renaissance patronage envision it as a collaboration between the patron and his client.[24] The sequence of nouns also recalls descriptions of paintings in ancient literature, called in Greek *ekphrases*, known to Renaissance humanists, and it may have appealed to Giovanni's acquaintance with classical texts. The murals include many of these details, among them a depiction of the Medici villa at Fiesole, a pointed reference to Giovanni's family ties to the Medici and to classical ideals underlying life in country estates. Ghirlandaio, while not schooled in humanist studies, surely shared values derived from them, among them that skill brought honour and that creativity secured fame and reputation. His *buon aria* thus encapsulates his social and artistic persona, one that embodied and visualized the cultural aspirations of late quattrocento Florence.

REFERENCES

Introduction

1 Francesco Albertini, *Memorial of Many Statues and Paintings in the Illustrious City of Florence*, ed. Waldemar H. de Boer and Michael Kwakkelstein (Florence, 2010).
2 The first quotation is from the entry recording his death in the record book of the Confraternity of St Paul, in the Archivio di Stato, Florence (hereafter ASF), Compagnie religiose soppresse da Pietro Leopoldo, 1594 (Compagnia di San Paolo), no. 42 (*Fratelli Morti della Compagnia di San Paolo*), p. 42 verso, no. 140. The second is from the report of an anonymous agent for the Duke of Milan transcribed in Jonathan K. Nelson, 'Botticelli's "Virile Air": Reconsidering the Milan Memo of 1493', in *Sandro Botticelli (1445–1510): Artist and Entrepreneur in Renaissance Florence*, ed. Gert Jan van der Sman and Irene Mariani (Florence, 2015), p. 168. The third is quoted from Heinrich Wölfflin, *Classic Art: An Introduction to the Italian Renaissance*, trans. P. and L. Murray (London, 1952), p. 15.
3 Giorgio Vasari, *Lives of the Painters, Sculptors and Architects*, trans. G. De Vere, ed. D. Ekserdjian (New York, 1996), vol. I, pp. 515–16.
4 Bernard Berenson, *The Italian Painters of the Renaissance*, vol. II: *The Florentine and Central Italian Schools* (London and New York, 1952), pp. 27–8.
5 The works referred to are Gerald S. Davies, *Ghirlandaio* (London, 1908); Jan Lauts, *Domenico Ghirlandaio* (Vienna, 1943); Ronald Kecks, *Domenico Ghirlandaio*, trans. F. Signorini et al. (Florence, 1998). See also Ronald Kecks, *Domenico Ghirlandaio und die Malerei der Florentiner Renaissance* (Munich, 2000) and Jean K. Cadogan, *Domenico Ghirlandaio: Artist and Artisan* (New Haven, CT, and London, 2000).
6 Kecks, *Domenico Ghirlandaio und die Malerei der Florentiner Renaissance*; Cadogan, *Domenico Ghirlandaio*.

7 Lisa Venturini and Nicoletta Baldini, ed., *Ghirlandaria: Un manoscritto di ricordi della famiglia Ghirlandaio* (Florence, 2017).

1 *Casa* Ghirlandaio: Family, Wealth and Social Status

1 The sources most useful for this biographical account are the following: Jean K. Cadogan, *Domenico Ghirlandaio: Artist and Artisan* (New Haven, CT, and London, 2000); Annamaria Bernacchioni, 'Familia et civitas; I Ghirlandaio e Scandicci', in *Ghirlandaio: Una famiglia di pittori del Rinascimento tra Firenze e Scandicci*, ed. Annamaria Bernacchioni (Florence, 2010), pp. 17–51; Lisa Venturini and Nicoletta Baldini, ed., *Ghirlandaria: Un manoscritto di ricordi della famiglia Ghirlandaio* (Florence, 2017); Nicoletta Baldini, *I Ghirlandaio a Colle Ramole: Storia di una dimora della famiglia nel contado fiorentino* (Florence, 2019). See also, more generally, Christiane Klapisch-Zuber, 'Kin, Friends, and Neighbors: The Urban Territory of a Merchant Family in 1400', in *Women, Family, and Ritual in Renaissance Italy*, trans. Lydia G. Cochrane (Chicago, IL, 1985), pp. 68–9. The best account of contemporary clothing is Carole Collier Frick, *Dressing Renaissance Florence: Families, Fortunes, and Fine Clothing* (Baltimore, MD, 2002).

2 Matteo Gianeselli, 'Dans l'intimité de Ridolfo del Ghirlandaio: les collections d'un "uomo da bene"', in *Le collezioni degli artisti in Italia*, ed. Francesca Parrilla and Matteo Borchia (Rome, 2019), pp. 209–21.

3 Samuel Cohn Jr, *The Laboring Classes in Renaissance Florence* (New York, 1980), table 2.2; Anthony Molho, *Marriage Alliance in Late Medieval Florence* (Cambridge, MA, 1994), table 7.3.

4 For a description of the currency in Renaissance Florence, see Richard Goldthwaite, *The Economy of Renaissance Florence* (Baltimore, MD, 2009), pp. 609–14.

5 David Herlihy and Christiane Klapisch-Zuber, *Tuscans and Their Families: A Study of the Florentine Catasto of 1427* (New Haven, CT, 1985), p. 103.

6 In 1410, on the death of Doffo di Currado, the house was returned to Currado's mother as restitution of her dowry, although she resided with the family there. At some point the house was rented out, as declared in the 1430 *catasto*, and the family resided in rented quarters nearby, in a place called la Ciella di Ciardo, which by 1442 Currado had purchased for 55 florins. By the 1458 *catasto*, the smaller house had been sold and the house on the Via dell'Ariento was again the family residence, Currado having inherited it from his mother

and enlarged it by purchase of a small house behind; see Venturini and Baldini, ed., *Ghirlandaria*, pp. 41–3.

7 Christiane Klapisch-Zuber, 'The "Cruel Mother": Maternity, Widowhood, and Dowry in Florence in the Fourteenth and Fifteenth Centuries', in *Women, Family, and Ritual*, trans. Cochrane, pp. 117–31.

8 For a general account, see John Najemy, *A History of Florence, 1200–1575* (Oxford, 2008), pp. 6–7; see also Herlihy and Klapisch-Zuber, *Tuscans and Their Families*, pp. 280–336.

9 Herlihy and Klapisch-Zuber, *Tuscans and Their Families*, p. 129, table 4.8; Molho, *Marriage Alliance*, p. 165.

10 The essential study for emancipation is Thomas Kuehn, *Emancipation in Late Medieval Florence* (New Brunswick, NJ, 1982).

11 For a detailed account of the ownership history of Colle Ramole between 1482 and 1491, see Baldini, *I Ghirlandaio*, pp. 36–40.

12 Christiane Klapisch-Zuber, 'The Griselda Complex: Dowry and Marriage Gifts in the Quattrocento', in *Women, Family, and Ritual*, pp. 213–46; and Jacqueline Marie Musacchio, *Art, Marriage and Family in the Florentine Renaissance Palace* (New Haven, CT, and London, 2008), pp. 2–61.

13 This dowry was greater than the sums invested in the dowry fund for Domenico's half-sister Alessandra (450 florins) in 1479 or for his own daughters Antonia (born 1484; 500 florins) and Costanza (born 1487; 500 florins), and indeed, more than the 500 florins Domenico received when he married his second wife in 1486.

14 Giovanni Ciappelli, *Memory, Family, and Self: Tuscan Family Books and other European Egodocuments (14th–18th Century)* (Leiden, 2014), esp. pp. 12–29.

15 Giorgio Vasari, *Le vite de' più eccellenti pittori, scultori e architettori* [1568], ed. G. Milanesi (Florence, 1906, repr. 1973), vol. III, pp. 253–83; Giorgio Vasari, *Lives of the Painters, Sculptors and Architects*, trans. G. De Vere, ed. D. Ekserdjian (New York, 1996), vol. I, pp. 515–29. The goals and methods of history were different when Vasari was writing from what they are today. Vasari would make up stories and invent dialogue so that his biographies were entertaining; see Patricia Lee Rubin, *Giorgio Vasari: Art and History* (New Haven, CT, and London, 1995). Nonetheless, Vasari was acquainted with Ghirlandaio family members and had access to the family memoirs. His biography of Ghirlandaio is more accurate than those of other artists.

16 Jean K. Cadogan, 'Michelangelo in the Workshop of Domenico Ghirlandaio', *Burlington Magazine*, CXXXV (1993), pp. 30–31.

17 Author's translation. The original text reads: 'Per memoria
    et intelligenzia di chi appresso verrà mi son resolute ridurre e
    ristrignere appresso quello che mi parrà più bisognare della memoria
    e seguito delli mia antinati e predecessori cavandolo dalli libri e
    scritture loro datemi alle mani vechie e maltratte e consumate dalla
    lungheza del tempo, e serva per quello che occhorressi'; Venturini
    and Baldini, ed., *Ghirlandaria*, p. 185.

18 Author's translation. 'E io Alessandro di Ridolfo fui allevato più in
    casa di detta Madonna Gostanza [his aunt, Ridolfo's sister] che in
    casa di mio padre con molta amorevolezza'; ibid., p. 295.

19 Samuel Cohn Jr, *The Cult of Remembrance and the Black Death: Six
    Renaissance Cities in Central Italy* (Baltimore, MD, 1992).

20 Silvia Maddalo, 'Di un autografo inedito di Domenico Ghirlandaio',
    Arte documento (1988), vol. 11, pp. 72–5, publishes the document in
    Archivio Apostolico Vaticano, Arciconfraternita del Gonfalone,
    1276, Notizie Diverse, parte 1, Protocollo D, no. 3, cc. 94–7.
    It is also recorded in Venturini and Baldini, ed., *Ghirlandaria*,
    pp. 216–17.

21 There may have been a personal connection, too. Party to the
    agreement between Domenico and the prior of the church were
    'all the masters and fathers of the council'. One of them, the
    sixteenth-century memorialist notes, Fra Martino di Pacino de'
    Bigordi, was called *parente nostro* – 'our family member'.

22 For the history of Santa Maria Novella, see most recently Andrea
    de Marchi, ed., *Santa Maria Novella: La basilica e il convento*, vol. 1: *Dalla
    fondazione al tardogotico* (Florence, 2015).

23 Andrew Butterfield, 'Monument and Memory in Early Renaissance
    Florence', in *Art, Memory, and Family in Renaissance Florence*, ed.
    Giovanni Ciappelli and Patricia Lee Rubin (Cambridge, 2000),
    pp. 143–4.

24 Author's translation. 'Il giostrantino o' voglia in dire il bigordo che
    cosi e il nome del giostrante a cavallo'; Venturini and Baldini, ed.,
    Ghirlandaria, p. 217.

25 Domenico Maria Manni, 'Vita di Domenico Ghirlandaio', *Raccolta
    d'opuscoli scientifici e filologici* (Venice, 1751), vol. XIV, p. 166; Vincenzio
    Fineschi, *Memorie sopra il cimitero antico della Chiesa di S. Maria Novella di
    Firenze* (Florence, 1787), p. 65.

26 Christiane Klapisch-Zuber, 'The Name "Remade": The
    Transmission of Given Names in Florence in the Fourteenth and
    Fifteenth Centuries', in *Women, Family, and Ritual*, pp. 283–309.

27 A nephew of Tommaso di Currado, son of his brother Giovanni
    (born *c.* 1419), was named Bigordo, but he was born in 1456, after
    the name had already become widely used in reference to the family.

28 The record books of the Compagnia di San Paolo are in the ASF
    Compagnie religiose soppresse da Pietro Leopoldo, 1579, c. 23
    verso [1448]; and ibid., 1582, no. 6: *Libri di ricordi e partiti*, cc. 34
    verso [1453], 37 verso, no. 45 [1455], 86 verso, no. 104 [1456/7 and
    1472]). For Tommaso's matriculation see ASF, Arte dei Galigai, I
    (Matricole 1320–1532), c. 95 recto, as cited in Venturini and Baldini,
    ed., *Ghirlandaria*, p. 196, note 54. Domenico's inscription into the
    Compagnia di San Luca is in ASF, Accademia del disegno, I (*Matricole
    1340–1550*), c. 7, in Cadogan, *Domenico Ghirlandaio*, p. 340, doc. no. 8.

29 For a description of the Florentine government structure and
    functioning, see Nicolai Rubinstein, *The Government of Florence under the
    Medici (1434–1494)* (Oxford, 1966).

30 See, in general, Najemy, *History of Florence*.

31 For these, see ASF, Mercanzia, 88 (Libro delle Tratte di tutti i
    Consoli delle Arti dal 1488 al 1498), no pagination; 15 April 1495
    (Domenico); 12 January 1490/91 and 18 August 1494 (Davide).
    Davide also served as consul for the guild of the Galigai in 1506 and
    1513, according to the sixteenth-century memoirs; Venturini and
    Baldini, ed., *Ghirlandaria*, p. 228.

32 ASF Tratte, 81 (Libro di età, 3), c. 249; see also Paolo Viti and
    Raffaella Maria Zaccaria, *Archivio delle Tratte: Archivio di Stato di Firenze*
    (Rome, 1989), pp. 157–9. On Ridolfo's nominations for office, see
    Venturini and Baldini, ed., *Ghirlandaria*, pp. 128–9 and 250–51; these
    nominations are not traceable in the ASF.

33 On the Gaddi, see Daniele Giusti, *I Gaddi da pittori a uomini di governo:
    Ascesa di una famiglia nella Firenze dei Medici* (Florence, 2019) and Jean
    K. Cadogan, 'The Social Identity of Agnolo Gaddi and His Family:
    A Florentine "Success Story"', *Zeitschrift für Kunstgeschichte*, LXXIV
    (2011), pp. 153–76.

2 Building Networks: Guilds and Confraternities

1 Among the rich bibliography on the subject, see notably, Ronald
   Weissman, *Ritual Brotherhood in Renaissance Florence* (New York, 1982),
   pp. 1–41; Lauro Martines, *Power and Imagination: City-States in Renaissance
   Italy* (Baltimore, MD, 1988), pp. 72–9; Paul McLean, *The Art of the
   Network: Strategic Interaction and Patronage in Renaissance Florence* (Durham,

NC, 2007), pp. 1–34; D. V. Kent, *Friendship, Love, and Trust in Renaissance Florence* (Cambridge, MA, 2009); and Francis W. Kent, 'Patron-Client Networks in Renaissance Florence and the Emergence of Lorenzo as "Maestro della Bottega"', in *Princely Citizen: Lorenzo de' Medici and Renaissance Florence*, ed. Carolyn James (Turnhout, 2013), pp. 199–225.

2 Lorenzo de' Medici, *Lettere*, ed. Nicolai Rubinstein et al. (Florence, 1977–2021), vols I–XVII; Lapo Mazzei, *Lettere di un notaro a un mercante del XIV secolo*, ed. Cesare Guasti, 2 vols (Florence, 1880).

3 See Lisa Venturini and Nicoletta Baldini, ed., *Ghirlandaria: Un manoscritto di ricordi della famiglia Ghirlandaio* (Florence, 2017), pp. 48–58 and 206–7.

4 Maria Luisa Bianchi and Maria Letizia Grossi, 'Botteghe, economia, e spazio urbano', in *Arti fiorentine: La grande storia dell'Artigianato*, ed. Franco Franceschi and Gloria Fossi (Florence, 1999), vol. II, pp. 27–63.

5 General sources for the history of guilds are Alfred Doren, *Le arti fiorentine*, trans. G. B. Klein, 2 vols (Florence, 1940); Donata Degrassi, *L'economia artigiana nell'Italia medievale* (Rome, 1996); John Najemy, *A History of Florence, 1200–1575* (Oxford, 2008); and Richard Goldthwaite, *The Economy of Renaissance Florence* (Baltimore, MD, 2009).

6 For the Medici e Speziali, see Doren, *Le arti fiorentine*, trans. Klein, vol. I, pp. 85–9; and Raffaele Ciasca, *L'arte dei medici e speziali nella storia e nel commercio fiorentino dal sec. XII al XV* (Florence, 1927), pp. 1–64.

7 Donata Degrassi, 'Tra vincoli corporative e libertà d'azione: le corporazioni e l'organizzazione della bottega artigiana', in *Tra economia e politica: le corporazioni nell'Europa medievale* (Pistoia, 2007), pp. 359–84.

8 Degrassi, *L'economia artigiana*, pp. 48–63; Maria Morello, 'L'organizzazione del lavoro nelle botteghe artigiane tra XIII e XV secolo. Il contratto di apprendistato', *Historia et ius*, X (2016), pp. 1–32; Franco Franceschi, 'Il mondo della produzione urbana: artigiani, salariati, corporazioni', in *Storia del lavoro in Italia. Il Medioevo. Dalla dipendenza personale al lavoro contrattato*, ed. Franco Franceschi (Rome, 2017), pp. 374–421.

9 Raffaele Ciasca, *Statuti dell'Arte dei medici e speziali* (Florence, 1922), pp. 81–2.

10 Cennino Cennini, *Il libro dell'arte*, ed. and trans. Lara Broecke (London, 2015), pp. 20–21, ch. 1.

11 For this information and what follows, see Jean K. Cadogan, *Domenico Ghirlandaio: Artist and Artisan* (New Haven, CT, and London, 2000), pp. 14–15, 27–9; Jean K. Cadogan, 'An "Huomo di Chonto":

Reconsidering the Social Status of Domenico Ghirlandaio and His Family', *Zeitschrift für Kunstgeschichte*, LXXVII/I (2014), pp. 27–46; Venturini and Baldini, ed., *Ghirlandaria*, pp. 32–4.

12 Degrassi, *L'economia artigiana*, p. 96.

13 The materials included small brass discs (*bisantini*); thin fragments of foil of an alloy of copper and zinc (the colour of gold) used to mount precious stones or to decorate clothing (*tremolanti*); enamelled rays (such as from a star or sun; *razi smaltati*); enamelled jasmine flowers (*fiori gelsomini smaltati*); other assorted enamelled flowers (*fiorellini di diverse sorte smaltati*); and peacock and white feathers (*penne di pagone e penne bianche*). The prices paid for these materials ranged from 5 to 22 soldi (a soldo was equivalent to 12 denari and was one-twentieth of a lira; the ratio of soldi to gold florins fluctuated throughout the period) for a thousand pieces, so they were not very expensive. The memoirs also list some of the clients who bought these garlands, among them Giovanni di Cosimo de' Medici, the son of Cosimo and brother of Piero, who on 20 December 1451 spent 16 florins, presumably for his bride, whom he married in 1452. Giovanni di Cosimo spent far less than Marco Parenti, who in 1447 had spent nearly 60 florins on his bride's headdress, which included pearls, peacock feathers and enamelled and gilded metalwork. For more information on these hair ornaments, see Carole Collier Frick, *Dressing Renaissance Florence: Families, Fortunes, and Fine Clothing* (Baltimore, MD, 2002), pp. 123–8; for the materials and clients, see Venturini and Baldini, ed., *Ghirlandaria*, pp. 196–9; for accessories related to male dress, see Timothy McCall, *Brilliant Bodies: Fashioning Courtly Men in Early Renaissance Italy* (University Park, PA, 2022), pp. 56–74.

14 Luca Landucci, *A Florentine Diary from 1450 to 1516*, ed. Iodoco del Badia, trans. Alice de Rosen Jervis (New York, 1969), pp. 6–7.

15 Degrassi, *L'economia artigiana*, pp. 100–106; Marco Tangheroni, 'Le arti del cuoio', in *Arti fiorentine: La grande storia dell'Artigianato*, 3 vols (Florence, 1998–2000), vol. I, pp. 215–34.

16 See Maria Grazia Ciardi Duprè Dal Poggetto, ed., *L'oreficeria nella Firenze del quattrocento* (Florence, 1977); John Cherry, *Goldsmiths* (Toronto, 1992); Antonella Capitanio, 'Scultura preziosa. Il quattrocento orafo a Firenze', in *Arti Fiorentine: La grande storia dell'Artigianato*, vol. II, pp. 251–75.

17 In general, on goldsmith's techniques, see Angelo Lipinsky, *Oro, argento, gemme e smalti: Tecnologia delle arti dalle origini alla fine del medioevo* (Florence, 1975); Dal Poggetto, *L'oreficeria*, pp. 203–9.

18 Benvenuto Cellini, *The Treatises of Benvenuto Cellini on Goldsmithing and Sculpture*, trans. C. R. Ashbee (New York, 1967).

19 Neri di Bicci's *ricordanze* note that the painter Cosimo Rosselli received 18 florins in salary when he was an apprentice in 1457; Bruno Santi, ed., *Le ricordanze* (Pisa, 1977), pp. 51–2; Michelangelo's salary when apprenticed for three years to Ghirlandaio in about 1488 was 6 florins the first year, 8 the second and 10 in the third year; Jean K. Cadogan, 'Michelangelo in the Workshop of Domenico Ghirlandaio', *Burlington Magazine*, CXXXV/I (1993), pp. 30–31.

20 Venturini and Baldini, ed., *Ghirlandaria*, pp. 58–61 and 206–7.

21 Cadogan, *Domenico Ghirlandaio*, pp. 28–9.

22 Venturini and Baldini, ed., *Ghirlandaria*, pp. 206–7.

23 Giorgio Vasari, *Lives of the Painters, Sculptors and Architects*, trans. G. De Vere, ed. D. Ekserdjian (New York, 1996), vol. I, p. 516.

24 Goldthwaite, *The Economy of Renaissance Florence*, pp. 349–51.

25 On apprenticeships, see especially Degrassi, *L'economia artigiana*, pp. 48–57.

26 Cadogan, 'An "Huomo di Chonto"', p. 38.

27 Doren, *Le arti fiorentine*, pp. 130–32.

28 For example, Cosimo de' Medici joined the Arte di Por Santa Maria by 1433; his son Piero joined in 1436; and his grandson Lorenzo in 1469, although there is no evidence that they practised any of the crafts in the guild; Raymond de Roover, *The Rise and Decline of the Medici Bank, 1397–1494* (Washington, DC, 1999), p. 20.

29 As noted by Amy R. Bloch in 'Sculpture, Donatello, and the Goldsmith's Art in Fifteenth-Century Florence', *Art Bulletin*, CIV/I (2022), pp. 61–8. The guild of Por Santa Maria created a new category of *orafo d'ottone* (goldsmith in bronze) in its amended statutes of 1404 to accommodate the creators of this new type of monumental metal sculpture.

30 Katalin Prajda, 'Goldsmiths, Goldbeaters and other Gold Workers in Early Renaissance Florence, 1378–1433', in *Craftsmen and Guilds in the Medieval and Early Modern Periods*, ed. Eva Jullien and Michel Pauly (Stuttgart, 2016), pp. 195–220.

31 Dario Covi, *Andrea del Verrocchio: Life and Work* (Florence, 2005), pp. 267–8, doc. no. 3.

32 Alison Wright, *The Pollaiuolo Brothers: The Arts of Florence and Rome* (New Haven, CT, and London, 2005), pp. 35–46.

33 Marco Tangheroni, 'Firenze centro culturale ed economico nel tardo Medioevo', in *Arti fiorentine: La grande storia dell'Artigianato*, vol. I,

pp. 29–36; Diletta Corsini, 'Botteghe "drento la città" e laboratori in Galleria: Gli orafi a Firenze nel Cinquecento', in *Arti fiorentine: La grande storia dell'Artigianato*, vol. III, pp. 107–16; Irma Passeri, 'Gold Coins and Gold Leaf in Early Italian Paintings', in *The Matter of Art: Materials, Practices, Cultural Logics, c. 1250–1750*, ed. Christy Anderson, Anne Dunlop and Pamela H. Smith (Manchester, 2015), pp. 97–115.

34 Lorenzo Ghiberti, *I Commentari*, ed. Ottavio Morisani (Naples, 1947), pp. 40–41; Creighton Gilbert, 'Ghiberti on the Destruction of Art', *I Tatti Studies*, VI (1995), pp. 141–2.

35 Venturini and Baldini, ed., *Ghirlandaria*, pp. 58 and 196, note 54.

36 Tangheroni, 'Le arti del cuoio', p. 229.

37 Essential works on confraternities include Weissman, *Ritual Brotherhood*, pp. 64–8; David Franklin, 'Towards a New Chronology for Ridolfo Ghirlandaio and Michele Tosini', *Burlington Magazine*, CXL (1998), pp. 445–55; Dennis Geronimus and Louis Waldman, 'Children of Mercury: New Light on the Members of the Florentine Company of St Luke (*c.* 1475–*c.* 1525)', *Mitteilungen des Kunsthistorischen Institutes in Florenz*, XLVII/I (2003), pp. 118–58.

38 Weissman, *Ritual Brotherhood*, is the essential source for the Confraternity of St Paul. See also, Cadogan, *Domenico Ghirlandaio*, pp. 18–20.

39 Franklin, 'Towards a New Chronology for Ridolfo Ghirlandaio and Michele Tosini', p. 446.

40 Ronald Weissman, 'Lorenzo de' Medici and the Confraternity of San Paolo', in *Lorenzo de' Medici: New Perspectives*, ed. Bernard Toscani (New York, 1993), pp. 315–29.

41 Weissman, *Ritual Brotherhood*, pp. 16–19; Christiane Klapisch-Zuber, 'Compérage et clientélisme, à Florence (1360–1520)', *Ricerche storiche*, XV/I (1985), pp. 61–76; Louis Haas, 'Il Mio Buono Compare: Choosing Godparents and the Uses of Baptismal Kinship in Renaissance Florence', *Journal of Social History*, XXIX/2 (1995), pp. 341–56; Dale Kent, *Friendship, Love, and Trust in Renaissance Florence* (Cambridge, MA, 2009), pp. 149–54.

42 For this and the following, see the rich documentation in Venturini and Baldini, ed., *Ghirlandaria*, pp. 65–9, 189–96, 211–14, 243–8.

43 The designation 'da Milano' is probably a transcription error. Giuliano's father Lionardo (Nardo) d'Antonio's tax returns of 1460 and 1469 list the house on the Via dell'Ariento as bordered on one side by 'Currado di . . .'; see Doris Carl, *Benedetto da Maiano:*

A Florentine Sculptor at the Threshold of the High Renaissance, 2 vols (Turnhout, 2006), vol. II, pp. 25 and 443, doc. 2. Ghirlandaio's grandfather Currado di Doffo in his return of 1458 lists the house on the Via dell'Ariento bordered by 'Nardo d'Antonio legniaiuolo'; see Cadogan, *Domenico Ghirlandaio*, p. 336, doc. 5.

44 Alessandra Civai, *Dipinti e sculture in casa Martelli* (Florence, 1990), pp. 17–36.

45 For an account of Ridolfo's career and social standing, see David Franklin, *Painting in Renaissance Florence, 1500–1550* (New Haven, CT, and London, 2001), pp. 103–25.

3 Making a Career: The Itinerant Artist

1 Sources for Baldovinetti include the still-useful monograph by Ruth Wedgwood Kennedy, *Alesso Baldovinetti: A Critical and Historical Study* (New Haven, CT, 1938) and Arne Jörgen Huebscher, *Alesso Baldovinetti und die Florentiner Malerei der Frührenaissance* (Münster, 2020). Indispensable for the Chapel of the Cardinal of Portugal, including all documentation, is Frederick Hartt, Gino Corti and Clarence Kennedy, *The Chapel of the Cardinal of Portugal, 1434–1459, at San Miniato in Florence* (Philadelphia, PA, 1964).

2 The essential study is Margaret Haines, *La Sacrestia delle Messe del Duomo di Firenze* (Florence, 1983).

3 Kennedy, *Baldovinetti*, pp. 236–8, reprints these transcriptions.

4 For Finiguerra, see Lorenza Melli, *Maso Finiguerra: I disegni* (Florence, 1995).

5 For discussion of intarsia techniques and history, see Antoine M. Wilmering, *The Gubbio Studiolo and Its Conservation*, 2 vols (New York, 1999), vol. II.

6 Haines, *La Sacrestia delle Messe*, pp. 220–23.

7 Jean K. Cadogan, *Domenico Ghirlandaio: Artist and Artisan* (New Haven, CT, and London, 2000), pp. 191–2, cat. no. 1. To keep the notes brief, I will refer to this work for previous bibliography.

8 Alison Wright, *The Pollaiuolo Brothers: The Arts of Florence and Rome* (New Haven, CT, and London, 2005), pp. 192–208.

9 Dario Covi, *Andrea del Verrocchio: Life and Work* (Florence, 2005), pp. 181–8; see also, more recently, the exhibition catalogues Francesco Caglioti and Andrea de Marchi, ed., *Verrocchio: Master of Leonardo*, Palazzo Strozzi, Florence (2019), pp. 58–61; and Andrew Butterfield et al., *Verrocchio: Sculptor and Painter of Renaissance Florence*,

National Gallery of Art, Washington, DC (Princeton, NJ, 2019), pp. 71–7.

10 For Verrocchio's sculpture, see Andrew Butterfield, *The Sculptures of Andrea del Verrocchio* (New Haven, CT, and London, 1997), pp. 192–8.

11 These include Baldovinetti's panel from the silver cupboard at Santissima Annunziata, or Pollaiuolo's relief from the base of the silver cross in the Baptistery. For these works, see Kennedy, *Baldovinetti*, pp. 45–51; Huebscher, *Alesso Baldovinetti*, pp. 211–20, cat. no. 1; and Wright, *The Pollaiuolo Brothers*, pp. 35–46.

12 Cennino Cennini, *Il libro dell'arte*, ed. and trans. Lara Broecke (London, 2015), p. 47. The concept of imitation in artistic creation, pedagogy and history are examined in Thomas Greene, *The Light in Troy: Imitation and Discovery in Renaissance Poetry* (New Haven, CT, and London, 1982).

13 Francesco Petrarch, *Letters on Familiar Matters*, trans. Aldo Bernardo (New York, 2005), vol. I, pp. 41–2. The analogy of the creative process with a bee making honey was inspired by Seneca, as Petrarch states; see Ronald Witt, *'In the Footsteps of the Ancients': The Origins of Humanism from Lovato to Bruni* (Leiden, 2000), pp. 261–2.

14 Richard Goldthwaite, 'Economic Parameters of the Italian Art Market (15th to 17th Centuries)', in *The Art Market in Italy*, ed. Marcello Fantoni et al. (Ferrara, 2003), pp. 423–44; Federico Etro, 'The Economics of Renaissance Art', *Journal of Economic History*, LXXVIII/2 (2018), pp. 500–538.

15 See Cennini, *Il libro dell'arte*, pp. 97–125, chs 67–88.

16 I have discussed the process for mural painting in Jean K. Cadogan, 'Drawings for Frescoes: Ghirlandaio's Techniques', in *Drawings Defined*, ed. W. Strauss and T. Felker (New York, 1987), pp. 63–75, and Jean K. Cadogan, 'Domenico Ghirlandaio in Santa Maria Novella: Invention and Execution', in *Florentine Drawing at the Time of Lorenzo the Magnificent*, ed. Elizabeth Cropper (Bologna, 1994), pp. 63–72. For a general account, see Cecilia Frosinini, 'Design, Planning and Drawing in the Legend of the True Cross', in *Agnolo Gaddi and the Cappella Maggiore in Santa Croce in Florence: Studies after Its Restoration*, ed. Cecilia Frosinini (Milan, 2014), pp. 217–33.

17 Cennini, *Il libro dell'arte*, pp. 101–3, ch. 67, describes *verdaccio* for fresco painting as a mixture of black, yellow ochre, St John's white and sinoper. Cennini recommends its use in panel painting, using lead white and vermillion, pp. 190–91, ch. 93. St John's white (*bianco di San Giovanni*) is a mixture of calcium hydroxide and calcium

carbonate that is used on walls, p. 84, ch. 58. Green earth (*terra verde*) is primarily clay and was widely available in Florence and used on walls and panels, pp. 77–8, ch. 51.

18 Cadogan, *Domenico Ghirlandaio*, pp. 195–6, cat. no. 3.

19 Michelle O'Malley, *Painting under Pressure: Fame, Reputation and Demand in Renaissance Florence* (New Haven, CT, and London, 2013), pp. 34–42.

20 Maria Matilde Simari, *Il museo di arte sacra di San Donnino a Campi Bisenzio* (Florence, 2006), pp. 36–7.

21 Cadogan, *Domenico Ghirlandaio*, pp. 192–4, cat. no. 2; for an updated bibliography of these murals, see Julia Miller and Laurie Taylor-Mitchell, *From Giotto to Botticelli: The Artistic Patronage of the Humiliati in Florence* (University Park, PA, 2015), pp. 97–105; Nicoletta Pons, 'La pittura del quattrocento in Ognissanti', in *San Salvatore in Ognissanti: La chiesa e il convento*, ed. Riccardo Spinelli (Florence, 2018), pp. 87–93. For the documents associated with the murals, see Karl Schlebusch, 'Neue Dokumente zu Vespucci-Kapelle in Ognissanti und zur Familie Domenico Ghirlandaios', *Mitteilungen des Kunsthistorischen Institutes in Florenz*, LIII (2009), pp. 364–74. Further information on the Vespucci family is in Karl Schlebusch, *Giorgio Antonio Vespucci (1434–1514): Maestro canonico domenicano* (Florence, 2017) and Claudia Tripodi, *Prima di Amerigo: I Vespucci da Peretola a Firenze alle Americhe* (Rome, 2018).

22 Paula Nuttall, *From Flanders to Florence: The Impact of Netherlandish Painting, 1400–1500* (New Haven, CT, and London, 2004), pp. 26, 113–14, 146.

23 Michael Baxandall, *Giotto and the Orators: Humanist Observers of Painting in Italy and the Discovery of Pictorial Composition, 1350–1450* (Oxford, 1971), pp. 15–17; O'Malley, *Painting under Pressure*, pp. 9–10; Cennini, *Il libro dell'arte*, p. 20, ch. 1.

24 These records are printed in Cadogan, *Domenico Ghirlandaio*, pp. 337–40, doc. no. 7.

25 Cadogan, *Domenico Ghirlandaio*, pp. 195–202, cat. no. 6; and, generally, Fabio Benzi, ed., *Sisto IV: Le arti a Roma nel primo Rinascimento* (Rome, 2000).

26 O'Malley, *Painting under Pressure*, pp. 38–40.

27 Schlebusch, *Giorgio Antonio Vespucci*, pp. 27–46.

28 Cadogan, *Domenico Ghirlandaio*, pp. 202–3, cat. no. 7; Nicoletta Pons, 'L'Ultima cena di Domenico e David Ghirlandaio nella Badia di Passignano', *Correspondenza*, XXXVI/2 (2016), pp. i–viii; O'Malley, *Painting under Pressure*, p. 40.

29 Cadogan, *Domenico Ghirlandaio*, pp. 203–7, cat. no. 8; Francesco Quinterio, *Giuliano da Maiano: 'grandissimo domestico'* (Rome, 1996),

pp. 186–206; Deborah Krohn, 'Between Legend, History and Power Politics: The Santa Fina Chapel in San Gimignano', in *Artistic Exchange and Cultural Translation in the Italian Renaissance City*, ed. Stephen Campbell and Stephen Milner (Cambridge, 2004), pp. 246–69; Doris Carl, *Benedetto da Maiano: A Florentine Sculptor at the Threshold of the High Renaissance*, 2 vols (Turnhout, 2006), vol. I, pp. 151–88.

30 Deborah Krohn, 'Onofrio di Pietro and the "Opera della Pieve" in San Gimignano', in *Opera: Carattere e ruolo delle fabbriche cittadine fino all'inizio dell'età moderna*, ed. Margaret Haines and Lucio Riccetti (Florence, 1996), pp. 345–70.

31 Detailed interpretations of the imagery are presented in Linda Koch, 'The Portrayal of Female Sainthood in Renaissance San Gimignano: Ghirlandaio's Frescoes of Santa Fina's Legend', *Artibus et Historiae*, XIX/38 (1998), pp. 143–70; and Carl, *Benedetto da Maiano*, pp. 175–87.

32 Cadogan, *Domenico Ghirlandaio*, pp. 248–9, cat. nos 25–6.

33 Diane Cole Ahl, 'An Unpublished Frieze in Pisa and the Workshop of Benozzo Gozzoli', in *Benozzo Gozzoli: Viaggio attraverso un secolo*, ed. Enrico Castelnuovo and Alessandra Malquori (Pisa, 2003), pp. 175–81.

34 Marta Battistoni, 'Antonio di Jacopo dalle Mura, orafo e operaio del Duomo di Pisa (1461–1488)', *Bollettino storico pisano*, LXIII (1994), pp. 131–48.

35 Christa Gardner von Teuffel, 'The First Florentine Tavola Quadra? Fra Angelico's High Altar-Piece in San Marco', in *La Pala di San Marco del Beato Angelico: restauro e ricerche*, ed. Cecilia Frosinini (Florence, 2021), pp. 51–88.

36 David Alan Brown, *Leonardo da Vinci: Origins of a Genius* (New Haven, CT, and London, 1998), pp. 127–36.

37 Sarah Cadagin, 'Domenico Ghirlandaio and His Workshop in Pisa: Panel Paintings for the Gesuati', *Predella*, XIII–XIV (2018), pp. 251–66.

38 Paolo Bensi, 'Gli arnesi dell'arte: I gesuati di San Giusto alle mura e la pittura del Rinascimento a Firenze', *Studi di storia delle arte*, III (1980), pp. 33–47.

39 For the Lucca picture, see Cadogan, *Domenico Ghirlandaio*, pp. 245–6, cat. no. 21; Dario Cimorelli, *Matteo Civitali e il suo tempo: pittori, scultori e orafi a Lucca nel tardo quattrocento*, exh. cat., Museo Nazionale di Villa Guinigi, Lucca (Milan, 2004), pp. 426–8, 569; Sarah Cadagin, 'The Interrelation of Curtains, Altarpieces, Relics: Domenico Ghirlandaio's Response to the Cult of the *Volto Santo*

in Lucca Cathedral', in *The Interaction of Art and Relics in Late Medieval and Early Modern Art*, ed. Livia Stoenescu (Turnhout, 2020), pp. 67–85.

40   On these fabrics, see Lisa Monnas, *Merchants, Princes and Painters: Silk Fabrics in Italian and Northern Paintings, 1300–1550* (New Haven, CT, and London, 2008), pp. 5–6, 149–67.

41   Lisa Venturini and Nicoletta Baldini, ed., *Ghirlandaria: Un manoscritto di ricordi della famiglia Ghirlandaio* (Florence, 2017), pp. 71, 208.

42   Giorgio Vasari, *Lives of the Painters, Sculptors and Architects*, trans. G. De Vere and ed. D. Ekserdjian (New York, 1996), vol. I, p. 518.

43   For the history of collecting these carpets in Florence, see Rosamond Mack, *Bazaar to Piazza: Islamic Trade and Italian Art, 1300–1600* (Berkeley, CA, 2002), pp. 73–93; and Alberto Boralevi, 'Collecting Oriental Carpets in Florence', in *Islamic Art and Florence from the Medici to the 20th Century*, ed. Giovanni Curatola, exh. cat., Gallerie degli Uffizi, Florence (2018), pp. 123–35.

44   Covi, *Verrocchio*, pp. 174–81; Caglioti and de Marchi, ed., *Verrocchio: Master of Leonardo*, pp. 252–5, cat. no. 8.10a.

45   Cennini, *Il libro dell'arte*, pp. 147–99, chs 113–66, on panel painting.

46   David Bomford, ed., *Underdrawings in Renaissance Paintings* (London, 2002); see also Jill Dunkerton et al., *Giotto to Dürer: Early Renaissance Painting in the National Gallery* (New Haven, CT, and London, 1991), pp. 164–74.

47   Cecilia Frosinini, 'The Under-Line; Revealing Drawing and Modeling Beneath Botticelli's Paintings', in *Botticelli Drawings*, ed. Furio Rinaldi, exh. cat., Fine Arts Museums of San Francisco (New Haven, CT, and London, 2023), pp. 47–63.

48   On panel painting technique, see Dunkerton et al., *Giotto to Dürer*, pp. 174–9. For the technique of Verrocchio's paintings, see Jill Dunkerton and Luke Syson, 'In Search of Verrocchio the Painter: The Cleaning and Examination of the *Virgin and Child with Two Angels*', *National Gallery Technical Bulletin*, XXXI (2010), pp. 4–41; Jill Dunkerton, 'Leonardo in Verrocchio's Workshop: Re-Examining the Technical Evidence', *National Gallery Technical Bulletin*, XXXII (2011), pp. 4–31; Jill Dunkerton and Luke Syson, 'Andrea del Verrocchio's First Surviving Panel Painting and other Early Works', *Burlington Magazine*, CLIII/1299 (2011), pp. 368–78. On the use of oil in Florentine painters' works, Kristin DeGhetaldi, 'From Egg to Oil: The Early Development of Oil Painting during the Quattrocento', PhD diss., University of Delaware, 2016.

49 For the Washington picture, see Alessandro Angelini in *Verrocchio: Master of Leonardo*, pp. 166–7, cat. no. 5.5; Gretchen Hirschauer and Elizabeth Walmsley, 'Verrocchio's Spring: Collaboration in the Painting Workshop', in *Verrocchio: Sculptor and Painter of Renaissance Florence*, ed. Butterfield, pp. 69–84, 220–22, cat. no. 29. The National Gallery, London picture is discussed in Michael Hirst and Jill Dunkerton, *Making and Meaning: The Young Michelangelo*, exh. cat., The National Gallery, London (1994), pp. 93–4. The San Giusto underdrawing is illustrated in Carmen Bambach, 'Leonardo and Drapery Studies on "tela sottilissima di lino"', *Apollo*, CLIX/503 (2004), pp. 46–7, figs 4–5; for the portrait of Giovanna Tornabuoni, see Ubaldo Sedano Espin, 'Infrared Reflectography', in *Ghirlandaio y el Renacimiento en Florencia*, ed. Gert Jan van der Sman, exh.cat., Museo Thyssen-Bornemisza, Madrid (2010) pp. 322–4. Maria Clelia Galassi, *Il disegno svelato: progetto e immagine nella pittura italiana del primo Rinascimento* (Nuoro, 1998), pp. 114–15, no. 17, illustrates details of the underdrawing for the Pisa altarpiece that are comparable to those of the London picture of similar date.
50 Cennini, *Il libro dell'arte*, pp. 205–6, ch. 173.
51 Dunkerton and Syson, 'In Search of Verrocchio the Painter', pp. 15–19.
52 Cadogan, *Domenico Ghirlandaio*, pp. 216–18, cat. no. 12; Miller and Taylor-Mitchell, *From Giotto to Botticelli*, pp. 105–15; Schlebusch, *Giorgio Antonio Vespucci*, pp. 57–8; Pons, 'La pittura del quattrocento in Ognissanti', pp. 93–6. Giorgio Antonio Vespucci invested in a mill owned by the monks at Ognissanti in 1480 and, after his brothers' deaths in 1479 and 1482, he seems to have become the sole steward of the chapel, as implied by his testament; Schlebusch, *Giorgio Antonio Vespucci*, docs. 72, 235.
53 Venturini and Baldini, ed., *Ghirlandaria*, p. 211.
54 Maria Rosa Lanfranchi et al., 'Il restauro e lo studio del "San Girolamo" di Domenico Ghirlandaio per la chiesa di Ognissanti a Firenze', *OPD Restauro*, XXXI (2019), pp. 94–108.
55 Cadogan, *Domenico Ghirlandaio*, pp. 218–20, cat. no. 13; Miller and Taylor-Mitchell, *From Giotto to Botticelli*, pp. 115–23; Pons, 'La pittura del quattrocento in Ognissanti', pp. 96–103.
56 Vasari, *Lives of the Painters, Sculptors and Architects*, trans. De Vere and ed. D. Ekserdjian, vol. I, p. 585.
57 Cadogan, *Domenico Ghirlandaio*, pp. 343–4, doc. no. 13.

4 'A Good Master on Panel and Even More So on Walls': Paintings for the Pope, the City and the Merchant Elite

1 The most relevant sources for the Sistine Chapel include Eugène Müntz, *Les Arts à la cour des papes pendant le XVe et le XVIe siècle: Recueil de documents inédits* (Paris, 1882), vol. III, pp. 89–91; Ernst Steinmann, *Die Sixtinische Kapelle: Bau und Schmuck der Kapelle unter Sixtus IV* (Munich, 1901), pp. 208–15, 369–91; Leopold D. Ettlinger, *The Sistine Chapel before Michelangelo* (Oxford, 1965); John Monfasani, 'A Description of the Sistine Chapel under Pope Sixtus IV', *Artibus et Historiae*, IV/7 (1983), pp. 9–18; Sylvia Ferino Pagden, 'Perugino al servizio dei della Rovere: Sisto IV e il cardinale Giuliano', in *Sisto IV e Giulio II: mecenati e promotori di cultura*, ed. S. Bottaro, A. Dagnino and G. Rotondi Terminiello (Savona, 1989), pp. 53–72; John Shearman, 'La storia della Cappella Sistina', in *Michelangelo e la Sistina: La tecnica, il restauro, il mito*, ed. F. Mancinelli et al. (Rome, 1990), pp. 19–28; Starleen Kay Meyer, 'The Papal Series in the Sistine Chapel: The Embodiment, Vesting and Framing of Papal Power', PhD thesis, University of Southern California, 1998; Jorge María Cardinal Mejía et al., *The Fifteenth Century Frescoes in the Sistine Chapel* (Vatican City, 2003); Ulrich Pfisterer, *La Cappella Sistina* (Rome, 2014).

2 The contract and appraisal have been published many times, including Steinmann, *Die Sixtinische Kapelle*, pp. 633–5; Ettlinger, *The Sistine Chapel before Michelangelo*, pp. 120–23; Jean K. Cadogan, *Domenico Ghirlandaio: Artist and Artisan* (New Haven, CT, and London, 2000), pp. 345–6, doc. no. 18.

3 Monfasani, 'A Description of the Sistine Chapel under Pope Sixtus IV', pp. 9–18.

4 Herbert Kessler, *Experiencing Medieval Art* (Toronto, 2019), pp. 99–109.

5 Cadogan, *Domenico Ghirlandaio*, pp. 91–3, 221–6, cat. no. 14, with previous bibliography; Arnold Nesselrath, 'The Painters of Lorenzo the Magnificent in the Chapel of Pope Sixtus IV in Rome', in Mejía et al., *The Fifteenth Century Frescoes in the Sistine Chapel*, pp. 39–75.

6 The history of Giovanni Tornabuoni and his family is related by Maria DePrano in *Art Patronage, Family, and Gender in Renaissance Florence: The Tornabuoni* (Cambridge, 2018), pp. 9–21. Giovanni Tornabuoni's role in the Medici bank is described by Raymond de Roover in *The Rise and Decline of the Medici Bank, 1397–1494* (New York, 1966), pp. 211–24.

7   On the assassination attempt (the Pazzi conspiracy) and subsequent
    war, see Lauro Martines, *April Blood: Florence and the Plot against the Medici*
    (Oxford, 2003).

8   Michelle O'Malley, *Painting under Pressure: Fame, Reputation and Demand in
    Renaissance Florence* (New Haven, CT, and London, 2013), pp. 55–8,
    has questioned Lorenzo's role in the commission, pointing instead
    to Platina or Giovannino de' Dolci. For Lorenzo's cultural diplomacy,
    see Caroline Elam, 'Art and Diplomacy in Renaissance Florence',
    Journal of the Royal Society of Arts, CXXXVI/5387 (1988), pp. 813–26.

9   The function of portraits in narrative murals has been discussed in
    Charles Hope, 'Religious Narrative in Renaissance Art', *Journal of the
    Royal Society of Arts*, CXXXIV/5364 (1986), pp. 806–18; Charles
    Rosenberg, 'Virtue, Piety and Affection: Some Portraits by Domenico
    Ghirlandaio', in *Il ritratto e la memoria: Materiali*, ed. A. Gentili, P. Morel
    and C. Cieri Via, 3 vols (Rome, 1993), vol. II, pp. 173–97; Eckart
    Marchand, 'The Representation of Citizens in Religious Fresco
    Cycles in Tuscany', in *With and Without the Medici: Studies in Tuscan Art
    and Patronage 1434–1530*, ed. Eckart Marchand and Alison Wright
    (Aldershot, 1998), pp. 107–28; Matteo Gianeselli, 'Domenico
    Ghirlandaio et les marges de l'historia: du figurant profane à l'acteur
    sacré', in *Regardeurs, flâneurs et voyageurs dans la peinture*, ed. Anne-Laure
    Imbert (Paris, 2015), pp. 91–110.

10 John O'Malley, *Praise and Blame in Renaissance Rome* (Durham, NC,
    1979); Jorge María Cardinal Mejía, 'Biblical Reading of the Frescoes
    on the Walls of the Sistine Chapel', in Mejía et al., *The Fifteenth
    Century Frescoes in the Sistine Chapel*, pp. 9–37.

11 Leon Battista Alberti, *On Painting and On Sculpture*, ed. and trans. Cecil
    Grayson (London, 1972), p. 61.

12 Primary references for the Sala dei Gigli decoration are Cadogan,
    Domenico Ghirlandaio, pp. 226–30, cat. no. 15, with previous
    bibliography; Ugo Muccini, ed., *La Sala dei Gigli in Palazzo Vecchio*
    (Florence, 2001); Philine Helas, 'Ghirlandaios Fresken in der Sala
    dei Gigli – "ewiges" Abbild einer ephemeren Inszenierung?', in
    *Domenico Ghirlandaio: Künstlerische Konstruktion von Identität im Florenz
    der Renaissance*, ed. Michael Rohlmann (Weimar, 2003), pp. 63–88;
    Doris Carl, *Benedetto da Maiano: A Florentine Sculptor at the Threshold of the
    High Renaissance*, 2 vols (Turnhout, 2006), vol. I, pp. 219–60.

13 Classical sources for the roundels are identified by J. Albert
    Dobrick, 'Ghirlandaio and Roman Coins', *Burlington Magazine*,
    CXXIII/939 (1981), pp. 358–9.

14 On the Sassetti Chapel, see Cadogan, *Domenico Ghirlandaio*,
pp. 230–36, cat. no. 16, and pp. 253–5, cat no. 30, with previous
bibliography; Jonathan Katz Nelson, 'Memorial Chapels in
Churches: The Privatization and Transformation of Sacred Spaces',
in *Renaissance Florence: A Social History*, ed. Roger Crum and John
Paoletti (Cambridge, 2006), pp. 353–75; Ulrich Pfisterer, 'Florenz
1485; Stiloptionen und Wahrnehmungskriterien in der Sassetti-
Kapelle', in *Florenz und seine Maler*, ed. Andreas Schumacher,
exh. cat., Alte Pinakothek, Munich (2018), pp. 85–95.

15 Guillelmus Durandus, *Rationale Divinorum Officiorum* [1284], vol. VI:
A Modern Translation of Books Seven and Eight, trans. Janet Gentles
(Bedford, 2019), pp. 108–9, 113.

16 The full text of Sassetti's charge is in 'Francesco Sassetti's Last
Injunctions to His Sons', in Aby Warburg, *The Renewal of Pagan
Antiquity*, ed. Kurt Forster, trans. David Britt (Los Angeles, CA,
1999), pp. 233–9.

17 Ghirlandaio's family memoir states that Domenico began painting
the Sassetti Chapel on 17 June 1483, just two months after he
finished the mural in the Sala dei Gigli, and it was finished by
25 December 1485; Lisa Venturini and Nicoletta Baldini, ed.,
Ghirlandaria: Un manoscritto di ricordi della famiglia Ghirlandaio (Florence,
2017), p. 215.

18 On altarpieces, see Christa Gardner von Teuffel, 'Clerics and
Contracts: Fra Angelico, Neroccio, Ghirlandaio and Others: Legal
Procedures and the Renaissance High Altarpiece in Central Italy',
Zeitschrift für Kunstgeschichte, LXII/2 (1999), pp. 190–208; Beth
Williamson, 'Altarpieces, Liturgy, and Devotion', *Speculum*, LXXIX/2
(2004), pp. 341–406; David Ekserdjian, *The Italian Renaissance Altarpiece:
Between Icon and Narrative* (New Haven, CT, and London, 2021).

19 On the Tornabuoni Chapel in Santa Maria Novella, see
Cadogan, *Domenico Ghirlandaio*, pp. 236–43, cat. no. 17, and
pp. 264–8, cat. no. 38, with previous bibliography; and documents
no. 25, 28, 36, 39; Takuma Ito, 'Domenico Ghirlandaio's Santa Maria
Novella Altarpiece: A Reconstruction', *Mitteilungen des Kunsthistorischen
Institutes in Florenz*, LVI/2 (2014), pp. 170–91; Cecilia Martelli, 'Uno
spettacolo per i Tornabuoni, regista Domenico Ghirlandaio', in
Santa Maria Novella: La basilica e il convento, vol. II: *Dalla Trinità di Masaccio
alla metà del Cinquecento*, ed. Andrea De Marchi (Florence, 2016),
pp. 155–205; Andreas Schumacher, ed., *Florentiner Malerei: Alte
Pinakothek: die Gemälde des 14. bis 16. Jahrhunderts* (Munich, 2017),

pp. 384–417, cat. no. 26; DePrano, *Art Patronage, Family, and Gender in Renaissance Florence*, pp. 111–40.

20 The most complete account is Nicole Dacos, 'Ghirlandaio et l'antique', *Bulletin de l'Institut historique belge de Rome*, XXXIV (1962), pp. 419–55.

21 Laurie Fusco and Gino Corti, *Lorenzo de'Medici: Collector and Antiquarian* (Cambridge, 2006), pp. 13–15.

22 For this altarpiece, see Cadogan, *Domenico Ghirlandaio*, pp. 259–61, cat. no. 34, and pp. 351–7, doc. no. 26; Diana Bullen Presciutti, *Visual Cultures of Foundling Care in Renaissance Italy* (Farnham, 2015), pp. 151–86.

23 Cadogan, *Domenico Ghirlandaio*, pp. 256–8, cat. no. 32; Gert Jan van der Sman, ed., *Ghirlandaio y el Renacimiento en Florencia*, exh.cat., Museo Thyssen-Bornemisza, Madrid (2010), pp. 296–7, cat. no. 27; Brenda Preyer, 'Palazzo Tornabuoni in 1498: A Palace "in Progress" and Its Interior Arrangement', *Mitteilungen des Kunsthistorischen Institutes in Florenz*, LVII/1 (2015), pp. 43–63.

24 Patricia Rubin, 'Understanding Renaissance Portraiture', and Stefan Weppelmann, 'Some Thoughts on Likeness in Italian Early Renaissance Portraits', in *The Renaissance Portrait from Donatello to Bellini*, ed. Keith Christiansen and Stefan Weppelmann exh. cat., Metropolitan Museum of Art, New York (New Haven, CT, and London, 2011), pp. 2–25, 64–76.

25 Cadogan, *Domenico Ghirlandaio*, pp. 276–7, cat. no. 45; Christiansen and Weppelmann, ed., *The Renaissance Portrait*, pp. 159–62, cat. no. 43.

26 Carole Collier Frick, *Dressing Renaissance Florence: Families, Fortunes, and Fine Clothing* (Baltimore, MD, 2002), pp. 214–19.

27 Cadogan, *Domenico Ghirlandaio*, pp. 277–8, cat. no. 46; van der Sman, ed., *Ghirlandaio y el Renacimiento en Florencia*, p. 289, cat. no. 20; Patricia Simons, 'Giovanna and Ginevra: Portraits for the Tornabuoni Family by Ghirlandaio and Botticelli', *I Tatti Studies*, XIV–XV (2011–12), pp. 103–35; DePrano, *Art Patronage, Family, and Gender in Renaissance Florence*, pp. 142–52.

28 For Giovanna's medals, see DePrano, *Art Patronage, Family, and Gender in Renaissance Florence*, pp. 61–81.

29 Cadogan, *Domenico Ghirlandaio*, pp. 174–6, 270–73, cat. no. 41, and pp. 377–8, doc. no. 45; Jonathan Nelson, 'Breaking Conventions: Donor Portraits in Ghirlandaio's Malatesta Altarpiece', in *The Art and Language of Power in Renaissance Florence: Essays for Alison Brown*, ed. Amy Bloch, Carolyn James and Camilla Russell (Toronto, 2019), pp. 221–46.

30 For the painting technique of the portrait of Giovanna Tornabuoni,
see Andrés Sánchez Ledesma, 'Material Analysis', and Alejandra
Martos Figueroa and Juan Alberto Soler Miret, 'Painting Technique,
UV Photography and State of Preservation of the Work', in *Ghirlandaio
y el Renacimiento en Florencia*, ed. van der Sman, pp. 331–2, 336–7.

31 On Italians' response to Netherlandish technique, see Paula Nuttall,
From Flanders to Florence: The Impact of Netherlandish Painting, 1400–1500
(New Haven, CT, and London, 2004), pp. 170–87.

5 The 'Expeditious' Artist: Ghirlandaio's Drawings and Workshop Production

1 On workshops in general, see Jill Dunkerton et al., *Giotto to Dürer:
Early Renaissance Painting in the National Gallery* (New Haven, CT, and
London, 1991), pp. 137–51; Anabel Thomas, *The Painter's Practice
in Renaissance Tuscany* (Cambridge, 1995), pp. 55–62; Maria Luisa
Bianchi and Maria Letizia Grossi, 'Botteghe, economia e spazio
urbano', and Franco Franceschi, 'La bottega come spazio di
sociabilità', in *Arti fiorentine: La grande storia dell'Artigianato*, ed. Franco
Franceschi and Gloria Fossi (Florence, 1999), vol. II, pp. 27–63,
65–83; Nicoletta Pons, 'Maler in Florentiner Werkstätten des 15.
Jahrhunderts', in *Florenz und seine Maler*, ed. Andreas Schumacher,
exh. cat., Alte Pinakothek, Munich (2018), pp. 49–57; Cecilia
Frosinini, 'Artists' Workshops in Fifteenth-Century Florence', in
Botticelli and Renaissance Florence: Masterworks from the Uffizi, ed. Cecilia
Frosinini and Rachel McGarry, exh. cat., Minneapolis Institute of
Art (2022), pp. 24–33. On Ghirlandaio's workshop, see Jean K.
Cadogan, *Domenico Ghirlandaio: Artist and Artisan* (New Haven, CT, and
London, 2000), pp. 153–71; Lucia Aquino, 'I Ghirlandaio, Baccio
d'Agnolo e le loro botteghe "in sulla piazza di San Michele Berteldi"',
in *Invisibile agli occhi: Atti della Giornata di studio in ricordo di Lisa Venturini*,
ed. Nicoletta Baldini (Florence, 2007), pp. 64–76; Matteo
Gianeselli, 'De Domenico à Ridolfo del Ghirlandaio: Pratiques et
fortune d'un atelier familial à Florence entre le XVe et le XVIe
siècles', *ArtItalies*, XVIIII (2013), pp. 39–46; Lisa Venturini and
Nicoletta Baldini, ed., *Ghirlandaria: Un manoscritto di ricordi della famiglia
Ghirlandaio* (Florence, 2017), pp. 82–3, 216; Takuma Ito, 'In the
Shadow of Domenico: The Workshop Practice of the Ghirlandaio
Brothers', *Proceedings of the 34th World Congress of Art History*, I (2019),
pp. 584–92.

2 For a reconsideration of Benedetto's oeuvre, see Takuma Ito,
   'Ghirlandaio Brothers Reconsidered: The Master of the Saint Louis
   Madonna as the Young Benedetto Ghirlandaio', *Journal of the Warburg
   and Courtauld Institutes*, LXXXIII/1 (2020), pp. 81–130.

3 On Bartolomeo, see Nicoletta Pons, *Bartolomeo di Giovanni: Collaboratore
   di Ghirlandaio e Botticelli*, exh. cat., Museo di San Marco, Florence
   (2004); and Nicoletta Pons, 'Problemi di collaborazione e compagnie
   di artisti: Cassoni e spalliere di Jacopo del Sellaio, Biagio d'Antonio e
   Bartolomeo di Giovanni', in *Virtù d'amore: Pittura nuziale nel Quattrocento
   fiorentino*, ed. Claudio Paolini et al., exh. cat., Galleria dell'Accademia,
   Florence (2010), pp. 127–42.

4 Jean K. Cadogan, 'Michelangelo in the Workshop of Domenico
   Ghirlandaio', *Burlington Magazine*, CXXXV (1993), pp. 30–31.

5 Lisa Venturini's essential studies of Mainardi include 'Tre tabernacoli
   di Sebastiano Mainardi', *Kermes*, V/15 (1992), pp. 41–8. For Granacci,
   see Christian von Holst, *Francesco Granacci* (Munich, 1974). On Jacopo
   del Tedesco, see Louis Waldman, 'Commissioning Art in Florence
   for Matthias Corvinus: The Painter and Agent Alexander Formoser
   and His Sons, Jacopo and Raffaello del Tedesco', in *Italy and Hungary:
   Humanism and Art in the Early Renaissance*, ed. Péter Farbaky and Louis
   Waldman (Florence, 2011), pp. 427–501. On Baldino Baldini
   (Baldinelli), see Tom Henry, 'Cesare da Sesto and Baldino Baldini in
   the Vatican Apartments of Julius II', *Burlington Magazine*, CXLII/1162
   (2000), pp. 29–35. For Jacopo dell'Indaco, see Michela Zurla,
   'Jacopo Torni detto l'Indaco, pittore e scultore tra Italia e Spagna',
   Proporzioni, XI–XII (2010–11), pp. 39–68.

6 For Ghirlandaio's drawings, see Cadogan, *Domenico Ghirlandaio*,
   pp. 103–51, 288–309, cat. nos 74–114; Jean K. Cadogan, 'From
   Relief to Mimesis: Drawing the Human Figure from Life and
   from Antique Sculpture in the Renaissance', in *From Pattern to
   Nature in Italian Renaissance Drawing: Pisanello to Leonardo*, ed. Michael
   Kwakkelstein and Lorenza Melli (Florence, 2012), pp. 195–213;
   Jean K. Cadogan, 'Piero and Ghirlandaio: Drawing the Figure', in
   Piero di Cosimo: Painter of Faith and Fable, ed. Michael Kwakkelstein and
   Dennis Geronimus (Leiden and Boston, MA, 2018), pp. 236–58.

7 See Michelle O'Malley, *Painting under Pressure: Fame, Reputation and
   Demand in Renaissance Florence* (New Haven, CT, and London, 2013),
   pp. 63–93.

8 Cennino Cennini, *Il libro dell'arte*, ed. and trans. Lara Broecke
   (London, 2015), pp. 19–21, ch. 1.

9   Recent contributions include Jean K. Cadogan, 'Notes on a Drawing
    by Pesellino', *Burlington Magazine*, CXLIX/1256 (2007), pp. 767–71;
    Hugo Chapman and Marzia Faietti, *Fra Angelico to Leonardo: Italian
    Renaissance Drawings* (London, 2010), pp. 15–75; Lorenza Melli,
    'Verrocchio the Draftsman: Model and Maestro', in *Verrocchio:
    Sculptor and Painter of Renaissance Florence*, ed. Andrew Butterfield, exh.
    cat., National Gallery of Art, Washington, DC (Princeton, NJ, 2019),
    pp. 87–100; Lorenza Melli, *I Disegni di Antonio e Piero del Pollaiolo*
    (Petersberg, 2023).

10 The drawings on linen have been much studied; see Jean K. Cadogan,
    'Linen Drapery Studies by Verrocchio, Leonardo and Ghirlandaio',
    Zeitschrift für Kunstgeschichte, XLVI/1 (1983), pp. 27–62; Françoise
    Viatte et al., *Léonard de Vinci: Les études de draperie*, exh. cat., Musée du
    Louvre, Paris (1989); Francesco Caglioti and Andrea de Marchi,
    ed., *Verrocchio: Master of Leonardo*, exh. cat., Palazzo Strozzi, Florence
    (Venice, 2019), pp. 272–9, 284–9, cat. nos 9.5–9.8, 9.10–9.11.

11 Caterina Caneva, ed., *Il Ghirlandaio di Vallombrosa* (Florence, 2006).

12 Lisa Venturini, 'Modelli fortunati e produzione di serie', in *Maestri e
    botteghe: Pittura a Firenze alla fine del Quattrocento*, ed. Mina Gregori
    et al., exh. cat., Palazzo Strozzi, Florence (Milan, 1992), pp. 147–63;
    Matteo Gianeselli, 'L'Atelier du peintre: L'original multiple', in
    Primitifs italiens: le vrai, le faux, la fortune critique, ed. Esther Moench,
    exh. cat., Palais Fesch, Musée des Beaux-Arts, Ajaccio (Milan, 2012),
    pp. 83–109.

13 Lorenza Melli, *I disegni italiani del Quattrocento nel Kupferstich-Kabinett di
    Dresda* (Florence, 2006), pp. 160–63, cat. no. 31.

14 For this altarpiece, see Cadogan, *Domenico Ghirlandaio*, pp. 264–8,
    cat. no. 38; Takuma Ito, 'Domenico Ghirlandaio's Santa Maria
    Novella Altarpiece: A Reconstruction', *Mitteilungen des Kunsthistorischen
    Institutes in Florenz*, LVI/2 (2014), pp. 171–91; Cecilia Martelli,
    'Uno spettacolo per i Tornabuoni, regista Domenico Ghirlandaio',
    in *Santa Maria Novella: La basilica e il convento*, vol. II: *Dalla Trinità di
    Masaccio alla metà del Cinquecento*, ed. Andrea De Marchi (Florence,
    2016), pp. 155–205; Andreas Schumacher, ed., *Florentiner Malerei:
    Alte Pinakothek: die Gemälde des 14. Bis 16. Jahrhunderts* (Munich, 2017),
    pp. 384–417, cat. no. 26.

15 See the detailed technical analysis by Daniela Karl in *Florentiner
    Malerei: Alte Pinakothek*, ed. Schumacher, pp. 404–17, cat. no. 26.

Conclusion: 'A Man to Be Reckoned With'

1 'Domenico di Tommaso di Churrado Bighordi dipintore detto del
  Grillandaio morì sabato mattina a dì xi di gennaio 1493 [1494] di
  febre pestilenziale . . . sotterrassi sabato sera in Santa Maria Novella
  tra le 24 e l'unna: e Dio gli perdoni. Funne grandissimo danno perchè
  era huomo di chonto per ogni parte di suo qualità e dolse molto
  gieneralmente'. ASF, Compagnie religiose soppresse da Pietro
  Leopoldo, 1594 Compagnia di San Paolo, no. 42, *Fratelli morti della
  Compagnia di San Paolo*, c. 42v, no. 130. The Florentine new year began
  on 24 March, the feast of the Annunciation, so Domenico died in
  1494 according to modern dating. The confraternity's burial service
  for Domenico was recorded with simple emotion in idem, 1582,
  Compagnia di San Paolo, no. 8, *Ricordi e partiti 1488–1502*, c. 277:
  'Ricordo come adì 25 di gennaio 1493 [1494] si fece l'uficio de morti
  della chompagnia per l'anima di domenicho di tomaso di churado
  nostro charo fratello al quale iddio abbia fatto verace perdono.'
  On 11 January 1493 [1494] Davide purchased 15 pounds and
  8 ounces of wax for Domenico's funeral, as recorded in the sacristy
  book; ASF Corporazioni religiose soppresse dal governo francese,
  102, Appendix 86, c. 31r. Again, on 1 November 1495 (the All Souls'
  Day vigil), Davide purchased 1 pound of wax to commemorate
  Domenico; ASF Corporazioni religiose soppresse dal governo francese,
  102, Appendix 86, c. 43v. Florentines counted the hours of the day
  from sunset, so Domenico was buried in the late afternoon on
  11 January 1493 [1494].
2 Giorgio Vasari, *Le vite de' più eccellenti pittori, scultori e architettori italiani*
  [1568], ed. G. Milanesi (Florence, 1878, repr. Florence, 1906), vol.
  III, pp. 253–83; *Lives of the Painters, Sculptors and Architects*, trans. G. De
  Vere, ed. D. Ekserdjian (New York, 1996), vol. I, pp. 515–29.
3 Jean K. Cadogan, *Domenico Ghirlandaio: Artist and Artisan* (New Haven,
  CT, and London, 2000), pp. 359–60, doc. no. 33.
4 Vasari, *Lives of the Painters, Sculptors and Architects*, trans. De Vere,
  ed. D. Ekserdjian, vol. I, p. 528.
5 Michael Baxandall, *Painting and Experience in Fifteenth Century Italy*,
  2nd edn (Oxford, 1988), pp. 26–7; this translation is taken
  from Jonathan K. Nelson, 'Botticelli's "virile air": Reconsidering
  the Milan Memo of 1493', in *Sandro Botticelli (1445–1510): Artist and
  Entrepreneur in Renaissance Florence*, ed. Gert Jan van der Sman and
  Irene Mariani (Florence, 2015), pp. 167–81.

6 Recent discussions include Joost Keizer, 'Style and Authorship in Early Italian Renaissance Art', *Zeitschrift für Kunstgeschichte*, LXXVIII/3–4 (2015), pp. 370–85.

7 Francesco Petrarch, *Letters on Familiar Matters*, trans. Aldo Bernardo (New York, 2005), vol. III, pp. 301–2; Ronald Witt, *'In the Footsteps of the Ancients': The Origins of Humanism from Lovato to Bruni* (Leiden, 2000), pp. 263–4.

8 Leon Battista Alberti, *On Painting and On Sculpture*, ed. and trans. Cecil Grayson (London, 1972), p. 63.

9 Nelson, 'Botticelli's "virile air"', p. 177.

10 Pamela H. Smith, *The Body of the Artisan: Art and Experience in the Scientific Revolution* (Chicago, IL, 2004), pp. 31–55; Caroline Walker Bynum, *Christian Materiality* (New York, 2011); Herbert Kessler, *Experiencing Medieval Art* (Toronto, 2019), pp. 31–58.

11 For what follows, Keizer, 'Style and Authorship', pp. 371–3.

12 Jan Białostocki, 'The Renaissance Concept of Nature and Antiquity', in *The Message of Images: Studies in the History of Art* (Vienna, 1988), pp. 64–8.

13 Baxandall, *Painting and Experience in Fifteenth Century Italy*, pp. 114–51.

14 Caroline van Eck, *Classical Rhetoric and the Visual Arts in Early Modern Europe* (Cambridge, 2007), pp. 17–29; Keizer, 'Style and Authorship', pp. 380–81.

15 Vasari, *Lives of the Painters, Sculptors and Architects*, trans. De Vere, ed. Ekserdjian, vol. I, p. 519.

16 Maria DePrano, *Art Patronage, Family, and Gender in Renaissance Florence: The Tornabuoni* (Cambridge, 2018), pp. 167–89.

17 Nicole Dacos, 'Ghirlandaio et l'antique', *Bulletin de l'Institut historique belge de Rome*, XXXIV (1962), pp. 419–55; Nicole Dacos, 'Graffiti de la Domus Aurea', *Bulletin de l'Institut historique belge de Rome*, XXXVIII (1967), pp. 145–75; Jean K. Cadogan, 'From Relief to Mimesis: Drawing the Human Figure from Life and from Antique Sculpture in the Renaissance', in *From Pattern to Nature in Italian Renaissance Drawing: Pisanello to Leonardo*, ed. Michael Kwakkelstein and Lorenza Melli (Florence, 2012), pp. 180–98.

18 On the *Codex*, see Cadogan, *Domenico Ghirlandaio*, pp. 306–9, cat. no. 114; F. Marias, 'Il Codice Escurialense', in *La Roma di Leon Battista Alberti, umanisti, architetti e artisti alla scoperta dell'antico nella città del Quattrocento*, ed. F. P. Fiore, exh cat., Musei Capitolini, Rome (Milan, 2005), pp. 234–5, cat. no. II.7.2.

19 Vasari, *Lives of the Painters, Sculptors and Architects*, trans. De Vere
    and ed. Ekserdjian, vol. I, p. 526.
20 The classic essay treating sixteenth-century art is Ernst Gombrich,
    'The Style "all'antica": Imitation and Assimilation', in *Norm and Form:
    Studies in the Art of the Renaissance* (London, 1966), pp. 122–8.
21 Johannes Wilde, 'Eine Studie Michelangelos nach der Antike',
    Mitteilungen des Kunsthistorischen Institutes in Florenz, IV/I (1932),
    pp. 41–64; Cammy Brothers, *Michelangelo, Drawing, and the Invention
    of Architecture* (New Haven, CT, and London, 2008), pp. 76–80;
    Carmen C. Bambach, *Michelangelo: Divine Draftsman and Designer*, exh.
    cat., Metropolitan Museum of Art, New York (2017), p. 52.
22 Ernst Gombrich, *Aby Warburg: An Intellectual Biography* (London, 1970),
    pp. 105–15; Aby Warburg, *The Renewal of Pagan Antiquity*, trans. David
    Britt and ed. Kurt Forster (Los Angeles, CA, 1999), pp. 15–19.
23 Cadogan, *Domenico Ghirlandaio*, pp. 350–51, cat. no. 25.
24 Jonathan Nelson and Richard Zeckhauser, 'Main Players: Patrons,
    Artists, and Audiences', in *The Patron's Payoff: Conspicuous Commissions in
    Italian Renaissance Art*, ed. Jonathan Nelson and Richard Zeckhauser
    (Princeton, NJ, 2008), pp. 17–35.

BIBLIOGRAPHY

Alberti, Leon Battista, *On Painting and On Sculpture*, ed. and trans. Cecil
    Grayson (London, 1972)
Albertini, Francesco, *Memorial of Many Statues and Paintings in the Illustrious
    City of Florence*, ed. Waldemar H. de Boer and Michael Kwakkelstein
    (Florence, 2010)
Bambach, Carmen C., *Michelangelo: Divine Draftsman and Designer*,
    exh. cat., Metropolitan Museum of Art, New York (2017)
Baxandall, Michael, *Giotto and the Orators: Humanist Observers of Painting
    in Italy and the Discovery of Pictorial Composition, 1350–1450* (Oxford, 1971)
—, *Painting and Experience in Fifteenth Century Italy*, 2nd edn (Oxford, 1988)
Bomford, David, ed., *Underdrawings in Renaissance Paintings* (London, 2002)
Brothers, Cammy, *Michelangelo, Drawing, and the Invention of Architecture*
    (New Haven, CT, and London, 2008)
Brown, David Alan, *Leonardo da Vinci: Origins of a Genius* (New Haven, CT,
    and London, 1998)
Butterfield, Andrew, *The Sculptures of Andrea del Verrocchio* (New Haven, CT,
    and London, 1997)
—, et al., *Verrocchio: Sculptor and Painter of Renaissance Florence*, exh.
    cat., National Gallery of Art, Washington, DC (Princeton,
    NJ, 2019)
Cadogan, Jean K., *Domenico Ghirlandaio: Artist and Artisan* (New Haven, CT,
    and London, 2000)
Caglioti, Francesco, and Andrea de Marchi, eds, *Verrocchio: Master of
    Leonardo*, exh. cat., Palazzo Strozzi, Florence (Venice, 2019)
Carl, Doris, *Benedetto da Maiano: A Florentine Sculptor at the Threshold of the High
    Renaissance*, 2 vols (Turnhout, 2006)
Cellini, Benvenuto, *The Treatises of Benvenuto Cellini on Goldsmithing and
    Sculpture*, trans. C. R. Ashbee (New York, 1967)

Christiansen, Keith, and Stefan Weppelmann, eds, *The Renaissance Portrait from Donatello to Bellini*, exh. cat., Metropolitan Museum of Art, New York (New Haven, CT, and London, 2011)

Ciappelli, Giovanni, *Memory, Family, and Self: Tuscan Family Books and other European Egodocuments (14th–18th Century)* (Leiden, 2014)

Cimorelli, Dario, *Matteo Civitali e il suo tempo: pittori, scultori e orafi a Lucca nel tardo quattrocento*, exh. cat., Museo Nazionale di Villa Guinigi, Lucca (Milan, 2004)

Cohn, Samuel Jr, *The Cult of Remembrance and the Black Death: Six Renaissance Cities in Central Italy* (Baltimore, MD, 1992)

Covi, Dario, *Andrea del Verrocchio: Life and Work* (Florence, 2005)

Dal Poggetto, Maria Grazia Ciardi Duprè, *L'oreficeria nella Firenze del quattrocento* (Florence, 1977)

De Marchi, Andrea, ed., *Santa Maria Novella: La basilica e il convento*, vol. I: *Dalla fondazione al tardogotico* (Florence, 2015); vol. II: *Dalla trinità di Masaccio alla metà del Cinquecento* (Florence, 2016)

Degrassi, Donata, *L'economia artigiana nell'Italia medievale* (Rome, 1996)

DePrano, Maria, *Art Patronage, Family, and Gender in Renaissance Florence: The Tornabuoni* (Cambridge, 2018)

Doren, Alfred, *Le arti fiorentine*, trans. G. B. Klein, 2 vols (Florence, 1940)

Dunkerton, Jill, et al., *Giotto to Dürer: Early Renaissance Painting in the National Gallery* (New Haven, CT, and London, 1991)

Ekserdjian, David, *The Italian Renaissance Altarpiece: Between Icon and Narrative* (New Haven, CT, and London, 2021)

Fantoni, Marcello, et al., eds, *The Art Market in Italy* (Ferrara, 2003)

Franceschi, Franco, and Gloria Fossi, eds, *Arti fiorentine: La grande storia dell'Artigianato*, vols I–III (Florence, 1998–2000)

Frick, Carole Collier, *Dressing Renaissance Florence: Families, Fortunes, and Fine Clothing* (Baltimore, MD, 2002)

Frosinini, Cecilia, and Rachel McGarry, eds, *Botticelli and Renaissance Florence: Masterworks from the Uffizi*, exh. cat., Minneapolis Institute of Art (2022)

Fusco, Laurie, and Gino Corti, *Lorenzo de'Medici: Collector and Antiquarian* (Cambridge, 2006)

Gardner von Teuffel, Christa, 'The First Florentine Tavola Quadra? Fra Angelico's High Altar-Piece in San Marco', in *La Pala di San Marco del Beato Angelico: restauro e ricerche*, ed. Cecilia Frosinini (Florence, 2021), pp. 51–88

Goldthwaite, Richard, *The Economy of Renaissance Florence* (Baltimore, MD, 2009)

Gregori, Mina, et al., eds, *Maestri e botteghe: Pittura a Firenze alla fine del Quattrocento*, exh. cat., Palazzo Strozzi, Florence (Milan, 1992)

Haines, Margaret, *La Sacrestia delle messe del Duomo di Firenze* (Florence, 1983)

Hartt, Frederick, Gino Corti and Clarence Kennedy, *The Chapel of the Cardinal of Portugal, 1434–1459, at San Miniato in Florence* (Philadelphia, PA, 1964)

Herlihy, David, and Christiane Klapisch-Zuber, *Tuscans and Their Families: A Study of the Florentine Catasto of 1427* (New Haven, CT, 1985)

Hirst, Michael, and Jill Dunkerton, *Making and Meaning: The Young Michelangelo*, exh. cat., The National Gallery, London (1994)

Huebscher, Arne Jörgen, *Alesso Baldovinetti und die Florentiner Malerei der Frührenaissance* (Münster, 2020)

Kecks, Ronald, *Domenico Ghirlandaio und die Malerei der Florentiner Renaissance* (Munich, 2000)

Kennedy, Ruth Wedgwood, *Alesso Baldovinetti: A Critical and Historical Study* (New Haven, CT, 1938)

Kessler, Herbert, *Experiencing Medieval Art* (Toronto, 2019)

Kuehn, Thomas, *Emancipation in Late Medieval Florence* (New Brunswick, NJ, 1982)

Landucci, Luca, *A Florentine Diary from 1450 to 1516*, ed. Iodoco del Badia, trans. Alice de Rosen Jervis (New York, 1969)

Martines, Lauro, *April Blood: Florence and the Plot against the Medici* (Oxford, 2003)

Mejía, Jorge María Cardinal, et al., *The Fifteenth Century Frescoes in the Sistine Chapel* (Vatican City, 2003)

Melli, Lorenza, *Maso Finiguerra: I disegni* (Florence, 1995)

Miller, Julia, and Laurie Taylor-Mitchell, *From Giotto to Botticelli: The Artistic Patronage of the Humiliati in Florence* (University Park, PA, 2015)

Molho, Anthony, *Marriage Alliance in Late Medieval Florence* (Cambridge, MA, 1994)

Monnas, Lisa, *Merchants, Princes and Painters: Silk Fabrics in Italian and Northern Paintings, 1300–1550* (New Haven, CT, and London, 2008)

Musacchio, Jacqueline Marie, *Art, Marriage and Family in the Florentine Renaissance Palace* (New Haven, CT, and London, 2008)

Najemy, John, *A History of Florence, 1200–1575* (Oxford, 2008)

Nelson, Jonathan, and Richard Zeckhauser, eds, *The Patron's Payoff: Conspicuous Commissions in Italian Renaissance Art* (Princeton, NJ, 2008)

Nuttall, Paula, *From Flanders to Florence: The Impact of Netherlandish Painting, 1400–1500* (New Haven, CT, and London, 2004)

O'Malley, Michelle, *Painting under Pressure: Fame, Reputation and Demand in Renaissance Florence* (New Haven, CT, and London, 2013)

Pfisterer, Ulrich, *La Cappella Sistina* (Rome, 2014)

Pons, Nicoletta, *Bartolomeo di Giovanni: Collaboratore di Ghirlandaio e Botticelli*, exh. cat., Museo di San Marco, Florence (2004)

Presciutti, Diana Bullen, *Visual Cultures of Foundling Care in Renaissance Italy* (Farnham, 2015)

Rubinstein, Nicolai, *The Government of Florence under the Medici (1434–1494)* (Oxford, 1966)

Schumacher, Andreas, ed., *Florentiner Malerei: Alte Pinakothek, die Gemälde des 14. bis 16. Jahrhunderts* (Munich and Berlin, 2017)

—, ed., *Florenz und seine Maler von Giotto bis Leonardo da Vinci*, exh. cat., Alte Pinakothek, Munich (2018)

Sman, Gert Jan van der, ed., *Ghirlandaio y el Renacimiento en Florencia*, exh. cat., Museo Thyssen-Bornemisza, Madrid (2010)

Sman, Gert Jan van der, and Irene Mariani, eds, *Sandro Botticelli (1445–1510): Artist and Entrepreneur in Renaissance Florence* (Florence, 2015)

Spinelli, Riccardo, ed., *San Salvatore in Ognissanti: La chiesa e il convento* (Florence, 2018)

Vasari, Giorgio, *Le vite de' più eccellenti pittori, scultori e architettori*, 2nd edn [1568], ed. G. Milanesi, 6 vols (Florence, 1878, repr. Florence, 1906)

Vasari, Giorgio, *Lives of the Painters, Sculptors and Architects*, trans G. De Vere, ed. D. Ekserdjian, 2 vols (New York, 1996)

Venturini, Lisa, and Nicoletta Baldini, eds, *Ghirlandaria: Un manoscritto di ricordi della famiglia Ghirlandaio* (Florence, 2017)

Viatte, Françoise et al., *Léonard de Vinci: Les études de draperie*, exh. cat., Musée du Louvre, Paris (1989)

Warburg, Aby, *The Renewal of Pagan Antiquity*, trans. David Britt and ed. Kurt Forster (Los Angeles, CA, 1999)

Weissman, Ronald, *Ritual Brotherhood in Renaissance Florence* (New York, 1982)

Wilmering, Antoine M., *The Gubbio Studiolo and Its Conservation*, 2 vols (New York, 1999)

Wright, Alison, *The Pollaiuolo Brothers: The Arts of Florence and Rome* (New Haven, CT, and London, 2005)

ACKNOWLEDGEMENTS

This book could not have been written without the help of countless scholars, conservators and curators who, over many years, have taken the time to show and discuss Ghirlandaio's murals, panel paintings and drawings with me. These colleagues are too numerous to list individually, but special thanks go to Roberto Bellucci, Keith Christiansen, Maria DePrano, Jill Dunkerton, Cecilia Frosinini, Matteo Gianeselli, Gretchen Hirschauer, Arnold Nesselrath, Dominique Thiébaut, Elizabeth Walmsley and the late Joanna Woods-Marsden. I am especially grateful to Diane Cole Ahl, who read the manuscript in its early stages and offered incisive comments. At Reaktion Books, Michael Leaman and François Quiviger offered advice and encouragement, Alex Ciobanu aided in securing images and Amy Salter meticulously led the editing of the manuscript. The illustrations were supported by the William Ravenel Peelle, Jr. and Agnes Stroud Peelle Art History Endowment of Trinity College, and the Morris and Donna Stroud Fund for Art History. My sisters, Paula Cadogan and Carol Cadogan, themselves accomplished professionals and art history enthusiasts, read the entire manuscript and saved me from unfounded assumptions and art-historical jargon. This book is dedicated to them.

PHOTO ACKNOWLEDGEMENTS

The author and publishers wish to express their thanks to the sources listed below for illustrative material and/or permission to reproduce it. Some locations of artworks are also given below, in the interest of brevity:

akg-images/Rabatti & Domingie: 2, 48; Albertina, Vienna: 73; Alte Pinakothek, Munich (CC BY-SA 4.0): 55; Archivio Apostolico Vaticano, Vatican City (Archivio dell'Arciconfraternita del Gonfalone, 1276, fol. 87r): 6; © S. Ballard 2025: 5; Basilica di Santa Trinita: 44; photos © Raffaello Bencini/Bridgeman Images: 40, 46; The British Museum, London: 62, 66; photos Jean K. Cadogan: 4, 7; Collegiata di Santa Maria Assunta, San Gimignano: 24, 25; Duke of Devonshire Collection, Chatsworth: 74; Duomo di San Martino, Lucca: 27; Flickr: 3 (photo Dimora Ghirlandaio, CC BY-SA 2.0); Gabinetto dei Disegni e delle Stampe delle Gallerie degli Uffizi, Florence, photos Roberto Palermo, courtesy Ministero Beni e Attività Culturali, all rights reserved: 61 (Inv. 294 E r.), 64 (Inv. 291 E), 65 (Inv. 292 E r.), 70 (Inv. 315 E); Gallerie degli Uffizi, Florence: 1, 17, 28, 58; Gemäldegalerie, Staatliche Museen zu Berlin/Christoph Schmidt: 68; Gemäldegalerie Alte Meister, Staatliche Kunstsammlungen Dresden, photo Scala, Florence/bpk, Bildagentur für Kunst, Kultur und Geschichte, Berlin: 77; Hessisches Landesmuseum, Darmstadt: 67; Kupferstichkabinett, Staatliche Museen zu Berlin/Jörg P. Anders: 71; The Morgan Library & Museum, New York: 63; Musée des beaux-arts de Rennes, photo RMN-Grand Palais/Adélaïde Beaudoin/Dist. Foto Scala, Florence: 69; Musée du Louvre, Paris: 59, 72, 76; Museo d'Arte Sacra dell'Abbazia di Vallombrosa, Reggello: 75; Museo degli Innocenti, Florence: 56 (photo © Raffaello Bencini/Bridgeman Images), 57; Museo Nacional Thyssen-Bornemisza, Madrid: 60; The National Gallery, London: 29, 30, 31; National Gallery of Art, Washington, DC: 32; photos © Antonio Quattrone: 42, 47, 49, 50, 51, 52, 53, 54; photos G. Roli –

C. Vannini per Scripta Maneant 2016, © Governatorato SCV – Direzione dei Musei e dei Beni Culturali: 37, 38, 39; photos Scala, Florence: 41, 43, 45; Wikimedia Commons: 8 (photo Web Gallery of Art, public domain), 9 (photo Mongolo1984, CC BY-SA 3.0), 10 and 11 (photos Sailko, CC BY 3.0), 12 and 13 (photos Sailko, CC BY-SA 3.0), 14 (photo Sailko, CC BY 3.0), 15 (photo Web Gallery of Art, public domain), 16, 18, 19, 21 and 22 (photos Sailko, CC BY 3.0), 23 (public domain), 26 (Museo Nazionale di San Matteo, Pisa; photo Federigo Federighi, CC BY-SA 4.0), 33 and 34 (photos Sailko, CC BY 3.0), 35 (photo Web Gallery of Art, public domain), 36 (photo Sailko, CC BY 3.0); photo P. Zigrossi, © Governatorato SCV – Direzione dei Musei e dei Beni Culturali: 20.